FREEDOM PAPERS

FREEDOM PAPERS

AN ATLANTIC ODYSSEY
IN THE AGE OF EMANCIPATION

Rebecca J. Scott and
Jean M. Hébrard

HARVARD UNIVERSITY PRESS

Cambridge, Massachusetts

London, England

2012

Library of Congress Cataloging-in-Publication Data

Scott, Rebecca J. (Rebecca Jarvis), 1950–
     Freedom papers : an Atlantic odyssey in the age of emancipation / Rebecca J. Scott
and Jean M. Hébrard.
         p.   cm.
     Includes bibliographical references and index.
     ISBN 978-0-674-04774-7 (alk. paper)
     1. Tinchant family.   2. Creoles—Atlantic Ocean Region—Migrations.
3. Creoles—Atlantic Ocean Region—Social conditions.   4. Creoles—Atlantic Ocean
Region—Biography.   5. Blacks—Atlantic Ocean Region—Migrations.   6. Blacks—
Atlantic Ocean Region—Social conditions.   7. Blacks—Atlantic Ocean Region—
Biography.   I. Hébrard, Jean M.   II. Title.
E29.C73S36   2012
305.896'0163—dc23   2011038130

For our spouses,
Peter Railton and Martha Jones

CONTENTS

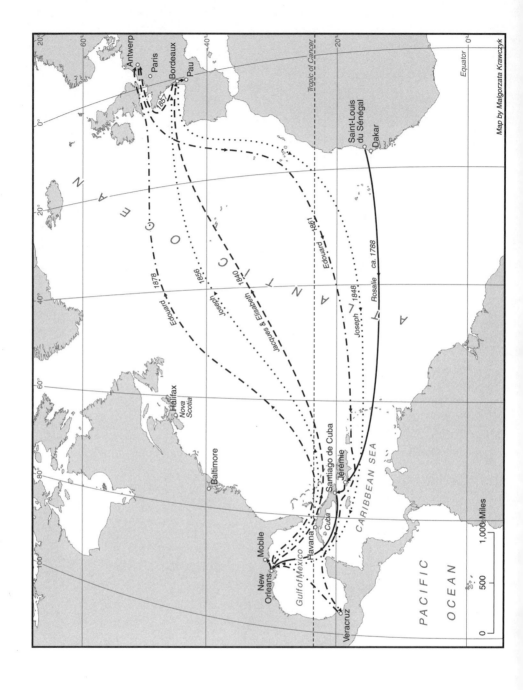

Map by Malgorzata Krawczyk

Three Generations of the Vincent/Tinchant Family

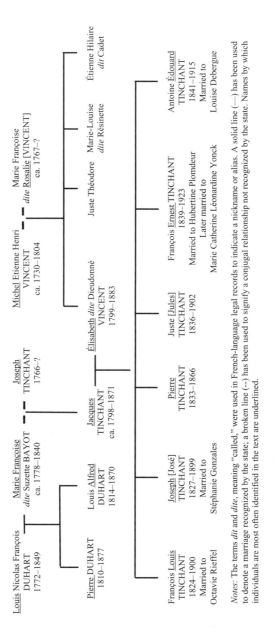

Notes: The terms *dit* and *dite*, meaning "called," were used in French-language legal records to indicate a nickname or alias. A solid line (—) has been used to denote a marriage recognized by the state; a broken line (– –) has been used to signify a conjugal relationship not recognized by the state. Names by which individuals are most often identified in the text are underlined.

FREEDOM PAPERS

Prologue:
The Cigar Maker Writes to the General

By 1899, the decades-long military struggle for the independence of Cuba from the rule of Spain had been completed. The scene, however, was not the one anticipated by Cuban patriots when the war had begun. In the last months of the conflict the United States had intervened, and as Spanish troops withdrew from the island, authority devolved not to the figures who had led the rebellion, but to a U.S. military occupation and accompanying military government.

Throughout the summer and autumn of that year, Cubans from across the island wrote to General Máximo Gómez, the revered surviving leader of the struggle, to tell him of the difficulties they faced in what they had imagined would become a free and independent Cuba. Often landless and without work or resources, ordinary veterans looked to their former commanding officer for advice and assistance. In hundreds of letters, they expressed their aspirations for citizenship in a new nation, aspirations that now seemed thwarted.

One letter, dated September 1899, written in English on business letterhead, came from an unusual source, however, and carried an unusual request. The author was not a Cuban, but instead a cigar merchant from Antwerp named Édouard Tinchant. He addressed General Gómez as follows:

> In early and ardent sympathy with the Cuban cause, I have been always and pride myself in being still one of your most sincere admirers.
>
> I would be highly honored, should you have the kindness to authorize me to use your illustrious name for a brand of my best articles, your portrait adorning the labels whereof a proof is enclosed.[1]

Tinchant suggested that he might not be "altogether unknown to some of the survivors of the last struggle," referring to the thirty years of Cuban challenges to Spanish rule, beginning with the Ten Years' War of 1868–1878. He explained that he had been "a humble but steady contributor to the Cuban fund and many are your countrymen, the Cubans and your followers to whom I have lent a helping hand." Tinchant hoped that some of Gómez's colleagues, presumably those who had been in exile in New Orleans in the 1860s, might still "remember me as a member of Company C 6th Louisiana Volunteers, Banks Division in 1863; as representative of the 6th Ward of the city of New Orleans, at the Constitutional Convention of the State of Louisiana in 1867–68 and as a cigar manufacturer in Mobile Alabama from 1869 till 1877."

Speaking as one veteran to another, Tinchant was giving Gómez a clue to his own politics and identity. The 6th Louisiana Volunteers were a Civil War unit of the Union army recruited among the free and recently freed populations of color in New Orleans. The 1867–1868 Louisiana convention had drafted one of the most radical state constitutions ever seen, beginning with a resounding guarantee that all the state's citizens, independent of color, would have the same "civil, political, and public rights." Yet, how on earth had a man from Belgium ended up as a Union soldier and an elected delegate to such a gathering?

Tinchant probably suspected that Máximo Gómez would wonder the same thing, so he hinted at an answer:

> Born in France in 1841 I am of Haïtian descent as both my father and mother were born at Gonaïves in the beginning of this century. Settled in New Orleans after the Revolution, my father, although in modest circumstances left Louisiana for France with the only object in view of raising his six sons in a country where no infamous laws or stupid prejudices could prevent them from becoming MEN.

Here, then, was the crux of the matter, an evocation of the Haitian Revolution and an implicit appeal to the antiracism that Tinchant knew Gómez endorsed, with a particular emphasis on dignified adulthood and masculinity.

Édouard Tinchant's letter portrayed an Atlantic world in which various struggles over race and rights were intertwined, and in which ideas and concepts were exchanged along with mutual aid, memories, and cigars. For a historian, however, the initial question raised by this letter is blunt:

Might an unknown Belgian cigar merchant, in his person and his family, embody a link between three of the great antiracist struggles of the "long nineteenth century": the Haitian Revolution, Civil War and Reconstruction in the United States, and the Cuban War for Independence? Or was Édouard Tinchant an adroit fabulist, trying to coax the most famous man in Havana into adding luster to what were, in all likelihood, cigars rolled in Belgium, not in Cuba?

To see whether, or how, Édouard's account might hold together, one can follow the trail of his family's itinerary, using the records kept by local priests, notaries, officials, and census takers in Cuba, Louisiana, Haiti, France, Mexico, and Belgium. Astonishingly, these turn out to lead us even further back, to a place that Édouard Tinchant's letter did not name: the middle valley of the Senegal River in West Africa, in the era of the deportation of African captives to the Americas as slaves.

This family emerges as one with a tenacious commitment to claiming dignity and respect. Members of each generation, moreover, showed an awareness of the crucial role of documents in making such claims, as they arranged for papers to be brought into being—sacramental records when taking a child to be baptized, notarial records when registering a contract, letters to the editor when engaging in public debate, private correspondence when conveying news to each other. For many members of the family, individual nationality and formal citizenship were not clearly defined, but a person could still make things happen by putting words on paper. The manumission documents drafted to protect the members of the first generations from slavery or reenslavement, for example, turn out to be highly complex creations, with a power both more fragile and more real than one might imagine.

A family odyssey that had begun with a passage from Senegambia to Saint-Domingue in the late eighteenth century continued on to Santiago de Cuba, New Orleans, Port-au-Prince, Pau, Paris, Antwerp, Veracruz, and Mobile, with several returns to Louisiana and Belgium. At each step of the way these travelers interpreted and conveyed to others the path the family had followed, and framed the journey in terms that could validate the choices they had made and the social standing they hoped to secure. Édouard Tinchant's letter to Máximo Gómez was one such reframing, but there were many others.

A pivot point for the family's story is the city of New Orleans. In 1809 thousands of refugees originally from the French Caribbean colony of Saint-Domingue—recently become the independent nation of Haiti—reached

Louisiana after having been expelled from their exile in Cuba. One of these refugees was Édouard Tinchant's mother, Élisabeth Vincent. So although Édouard Tinchant shaded some of the details of his life history to fit his goals, he was indeed "of Haïtian descent"—though not quite in the way he implied. And it was his mother's years in New Orleans, during which she married the man named Jacques Tinchant, that left the key archival traces that have made the telling of this portion of the family's history possible.

The story that develops is a public as well as a private one, for Édouard Tinchant and his ancestors and descendants repeatedly sought to circumvent or challenge different variants of racial prejudice and exclusion. When he stepped forward in 1867–1868 to participate in the drafting of Louisiana's remarkable Reconstruction-era state constitution, Édouard exhorted his colleagues to secure the civil rights of women, independent of color, and to recognize conjugal unions that had not been formalized by marriage. In that effort, we see a reflection of a family memory of the obstacles that had confronted the generations before him. Although he could never have known it, Édouard Tinchant's insistence on the right to marriage, and his refusal of stigma—describing himself as a man of color and "a son of Africa"—also prefigured the challenges that would face some of those who followed him.

Édouard Tinchant died in exile in England, having left the southern United States for Belgium in 1878, after the collapse of Reconstruction, and then having fled Belgium during the German invasion in World War I. The story that opens with the letter to Máximo Gómez might logically conclude with Édouard's exile and his death in 1915. But in 1937 an article in the British press gave Édouard's Belgian grandniece, Marie-José Tinchant, a sudden moment of public visibility—in England, in the year when the aftermath of Mussolini's invasion of Ethiopia and the formation of the Rome-Berlin Axis filled the headlines. The episode began when the parents of Marie-José's Belgian fiancé intervened with a registrar's office in London to try to block their son from marrying her. Interviewed by a journalist, Marie-José Tinchant boldly explained, "I am not a white girl. . . . I have colour, and André's parents will not hear of our match." But, she insisted, "We shall be married." The fate of Marie-José Tinchant, after her marriage and her subsequent activities in the Belgian resistance to the Nazis, thus became a dramatic epilogue to her family's odyssey.[2]

This book is an experiment that might be characterized as micro-history set in motion. It rests on the conviction that the study of a carefully chosen place or event, viewed from very close to the ground, may reveal dynamics that are not visible through the more familiar lens of region or nation. In this case, we follow an interlinked chain of events defined by one family's itinerary. There is, of course, nothing "micro" about the Atlantic world of the nineteenth century, but even on that wide canvas the deepest analysis may emerge from close attention to the particular.

We make no claim to typicality or representativeness for the Vincent/ Tinchant family. Our inquiry is shaped instead by the vicissitudes of a genealogy and a pattern of activity that we could not have foreseen. We began with a set of quite specific clues and interpretive puzzles that emerged from a chance discovery in the Cuban archives. These, in turn, led us to the heart of the problem of freedom, and of the phenomena of race, racism, and antiracism. The story of this family evolved into a narrative of individual and shared choices constrained by slavery, war, and social hierarchy. Despite those constraints, the members of this family made their way with discernment and ingenuity across the age of emancipation, whose intricacies become more visible as one traces their winding paths. These lives were characterized by a continual movement of people and paper across the Caribbean, the Gulf of Mexico, and the Atlantic itself. The chapters that follow thus generally open with an arrival and close with a departure, reflecting different stages in this odyssey. At each step of the way, moreover, someone usually put pen to paper, or caused others to put pen to paper, building up an archive of movement and memory.

1

"Rosalie, Black Woman
of the Poulard Nation"

When Édouard Tinchant, writing to General Máximo Gómez in 1899, referred to himself as "of Haïtian descent," he linked his own history to the era during which his parents had felt the shock waves of three great revolutions—those that gave rise to the United States of America, the French Republic, and the nation of Haiti. When he spoke of himself as a "son of Africa," he further signaled his ancestors' place among those in the Caribbean whose status was that of slaves, or whose status balanced precariously somewhere between slavery and freedom.[1]

For a number of the African men and women brought as captives to the Caribbean, these had not been the first revolutions that they had encountered. In the valley of the Senegal River in West Africa, in the region called Fuuta Tooro, a sector of the Islamic clerical elite led a movement that overturned the warrior aristocracy in the mid-1770s and forced into public debate the question of the legitimacy of selling fellow Muslims to Europeans as slaves. The Almamy (or imam) who ruled Fuuta Tooro after that revolution obliged the French to sign a treaty in which they agreed to refrain from transporting any of his subjects into the trade. Neighbors and rivals who refused the authority of the Almamy nonetheless continued to raid into his territory and seize captives to be sold for deportation to the Americas.[2]

The people of Fuuta Tooro, along with others who spoke the Pulaar language, were referred to by the French as the "Foules" or the "Poules," terms that in the Americas were often rendered as "Poulard." When a young woman being held as a slave in the French Caribbean colony of Saint-Domingue was referred to as "Rosalie, négresse de nation Poulard," it was thus an origin in Senegambia that was implied. The paper trail linking Édouard Tinchant to this woman called Rosalie involves two documents, each brought into being in a moment of struggle, and later deposited with local officials in an effort to secure a fragile status.

In order to prove that she could by rights adopt her father's surname, despite having been born out of wedlock, Édouard Tinchant's mother Élisabeth Dieudonné went to a public notary in New Orleans in 1835 with a copy of her baptismal record. According to this document, she had been born in 1799 in the colony of Saint-Domingue, in the midst of the Haitian Revolution. A free black woman named Marie Françoise, called Rosalie, was Élisabeth's mother. A Frenchman named Michel Vincent acknowledged in the baptismal act that he was Élisabeth's father. Having examined the document, the New Orleans notary authorized Élisabeth to take on the surname Vincent, and, as was standard practice, he saved a copy of the act in his bound volume of notarized records for the year.[3]

The names of Michel Vincent and Rosalie appear a second time in documents that they deposited in 1804 with French officials in Santiago, Cuba. They had fled to Cuba not as a result of the uprising of slaves in the northern plain of Saint-Domingue in 1791, but instead to escape the warfare that engulfed the countryside in 1802 when Napoléon Bonaparte sent a French expeditionary force to try to destroy the power of the black and brown generals who ruled the colony in the name of France, first among them Toussaint Louverture. Michel and Rosalie carried with them in their flight a set of freedom papers that identified her more fully as "Marie Françoise, dite Rosalie, négresse de nation Poulard"—Marie Françoise, called Rosalie, black woman of the Poulard nation. Together these documents confirm that Édouard Tinchant's grandmother Rosalie was a survivor of captivity, enslavement, and the Middle Passage from West Africa to the Caribbean.[4]

The words "of the Poulard nation" are suggestive, but they are not geographically or chronologically precise. As ship captains made their purchases on the coast of Senegambia, they rarely categorized individual captives with any precision. For the buyer and the seller in a West African port, the exchange of captives for goods was usually characterized by a generic phrase like "captifs jeunes pièces d'Inde sans aucun défaut" (young captives *pièces d'Inde* without any flaws). *Pièce d'Inde* was a unit based on the exchange value of a bolt of printed cloth from India, the cost of a healthy male captive between the ages of fourteen and thirty-five. Individual names and ethnic affiliations generally went unrecorded.[5]

It was instead on arrival in the Antilles that ship captains began to vaunt the "nationalities" of those whom they would sell. The ship *La Valeur,* for example, left the French port of Nantes on June 22, 1786, for Saint-Louis du Sénégal, where in February it loaded some seventy-four captives. Two months later, the *Affiches Américaines* described the cargo of *La Valeur* offered for sale in the port of Cap-Français, Saint-Domingue, as "a handsome load of blacks of the Yolof, Poulard, and Bambara nations."[6]

In some cases, such "national" markers were simply a rough-and-ready indicator of the African ports of call of a slaving vessel. The word "Sénégal," for example, was often used to refer generically to those purchased in the port of Saint-Louis du Sénégal, near the mouth of the Senegal River. But in many cases sellers used a label that attributed not simply a place of acquisition but a place of origin, designating a people by reference to a region, a language group, or a political entity. This system of designation rested on a flexible and to some extent imaginary European geography of Africa, one that assigned specific characteristics to particular groups, who were in turn associated with loosely defined places. Ship captains and traders often drew on these associations to describe Africans in terms that might evoke favorable images of skills, robustness, strength, beauty, or tractability. The colonist Moreau de Saint-Méry, for example, waxed enthusiastic about captives he referred to broadly as "Senegalese," evoking both the port of Saint-Louis du Sénégal and the valley of the Senegal River more broadly. They were "superior" slaves, he wrote, "intelligent, good, faithful, even in love, grateful, excellent domestic servants."[7]

Moreau de Saint-Méry identified a closely related set of captives with the term "Poulard," a word that he viewed as a popular deformation of the proper noun "Foule." The term "Foule," derived from the vernacular "Pullo" (plural: Fulbe), was used by French-speaking traders, administrators, and explorers to refer to a people, many of them cattle herders, often living in the middle valley of the Senegal River. Moreau distinguished the Foules, for example, from the Jolof (his term was "Yoloffes") who dominated the lower valley as well as much of the inland and coastal area farther to the south.[8]

Although in theory derived from places of origin, these designations also reflected conventional slaveholder wisdom about appearance: Moreau and others believed the Poulard to be characteristically tall, thin, and "copper-colored."[9] Ethnographers and historians have adopted a broader usage of the modern terms "Peul," "Fulani," or "Fulbe," distinguishing among many now far-dispersed populations who may speak variants of the language called Pulaar. Scholars generally eschew the attribution of timeless cultural attributes and specific physical features to the group, concentrating instead on the linguistic, cultural, and economic variability among those who migrated at different moments, and on the transformations that took place as they came into contact with other groups.[10]

For the eighteenth-century traders and planters who assigned "nations" to those in the human cargoes they sought to sell or buy, however, these subtleties were rarely to be seen. In Saint-Domingue the label "Poulard" seems simply to have carried a positive tone, signifying a group in which the men were expected to be good at handling animals, and the women characterized by domestic skills and beauty. For those thus labeled, of course, it might also correspond to some degree of shared history and language.[11]

Although a significant proportion of the captives during the very early years of the trade to Saint-Domingue had come from Senegambia, by the end of the eighteenth century most came from farther south in Africa. Even among the men and women who were from Senegambia, those denominated Poulard were outweighed by others designated Bambara, Sénégal, Soso, and Mandingo. The relative uncommonness of the designation "Poulard" makes it likely that when variants of the phrase "Rosalie de nation Poulard" were used in records from the district of Jérémie in Saint-Domingue to identify a relatively young woman, they do indeed refer to the same person.[12]

The designation "of the Poulard nation" may have been reinforced by Rosalie herself. To call oneself a member of the Poulard nation could, by the end of the eighteenth century, be a politically resonant act. The French who controlled the island of Saint-Louis du Sénégal were locked in conflict with a new régime in the middle valley whose policies posed obstacles to the deportation of Muslim captives for the Atlantic trade. Word had reached metropolitan France and England that there was a polity among the Poules now ruled by a man called the Almamy, who claimed the right to block the passage of slave traders through his territory. The English antislavery activist Thomas Clarkson, after interviewing a French botanist who had traveled in the region, wrote in praise of what he saw as the Almamy's forthright actions against the trade, contrasting them with the hesitations of European rulers.[13]

One French adventurer, M. Saugnier, who had abandoned the life of a grocer to try his luck as a trader in Africa, provided a meticulous account of his voyage along the Senegal River in 1785—almost an advertisement to those who might wish to follow in his footsteps. Describing the nation of the Poules as extending from below the town of Podor upriver to Matam, a fortified village occupied by both Poules and Saltinguets, Saugnier gave his readers a bitter description that reflected his own frustration as a slave trader with the uncooperativeness of their leaders, particularly the cleric named Abdulkaadir Kan: "Although the Poule nation lives in one of the most beautiful parts of Africa, it is however a very miserable one. . . . They are ruled by a chief of their religion—a miserable mixture of Mohammedism and Paganism—called the Almamy."[14]

Abdulkaadir Kan was a highly educated Muslim leader who had joined a movement denouncing religious laxity and the prevalence of slaving raids that took captive even the dependents of the most respected clerics. After victory in what would come to be known as the Revolution of the Toorobe, Abdulkaadir Kan took on the title of the Almamy and ruled over the area designated Fuuta Tooro, extending many hundreds of miles along the river and across the narrow band of rich lands on either side.[15] The subjects of the Almamy generally spoke or learned to speak the Pulaar language, and those who were not already Muslims converted to Islam. For the French traders and administrators on the island of Saint-Louis these people—on whom they depended both for food supplies and safe passage on the river—would be known as the "Nègres Poules du pays de Toro" (Poulard blacks of the land of Tooro), or simply as the Poules.[16]

Historically, the people of the middle valley had long participated in raids and battles in which they took captives, who in turn could either be ransomed by their communities of origin, or sold into the domestic, the trans-Saharan, or the Atlantic trade. The Almamy introduced a new policy, based on a more demanding reading of the Qur'an, and prohibited the selling of fellow Muslims into the Atlantic trade. Although domestic slavery continued to be practiced within his realm, by 1785 he was able to impose a treaty on the French that prohibited them from acquiring captives from his domain. The Almamy's control of a key segment of the river enabled him to inspect convoys, and he would not allow captives he judged to be his subjects to be sold to the traders on the island of Saint-Louis who supplied the European slavers. Given the difficulties of navigating the river, and the vulnerability of the convoy during the long voyage, traders had little choice but to observe the ban.[17]

After Abdulkaadir Kan's ascent to power it became less likely that the inhabitants of Fuuta Tooro would be transported to the Americas as slaves. There were, however, various paths to captivity, even during the time of the treaty between the Almamy and the French. Reversals in the Almamy's wars of expansion put captives in the hands of his neighbors; his rivals did not hesitate to attempt incursions into his territory; and he himself could use sale as a means of internal control. Armed groups of various kinds raided into Fuuta for captives, aiming to sell them to the Europeans at Saint-Louis, Gorée, or elsewhere. If not ransomed in time, Pulaar-speaking men and women among these captives would thus end up in the long-distance slave trade.[18]

The trader Saugnier provided his French readers with a picture of a sequence of events that could lead to such captivity. Describing the people he called the Saltinguets, the author wrote:

> They are commanded by a prince who by right of birth should have been the king of the Poules; but the priests who despoiled him chased him out of his land. This prince is courageous and makes frequent incursions into the lands of the Poules, and sells all of his captives to his neighbors the Moors, who take them to [Saint-Louis du] Sénégal.[19]

In effect, the Almamy's protection was effective only where and when he could impose his will, and there were plenty of competitors eager to circumvent his scruples on seeing his people sold into the Atlantic trade.

The designation of Rosalie, an enslaved African woman in Saint-Domingue, as "of the Poulard nation" almost certainly meant that she spoke—or had once spoken—the Pulaar language. In all likelihood, it also meant that she had been made captive somewhere in or near the valley of the Senegal River, including Fuuta Tooro, despite the formal protection offered by the Almamy Abdulkaadir Kan. It may also have signaled experience with written texts. Although the region was subject to disruption by war, supporters of the Almamy in Fuuta Tooro placed a high value on learning, on language, and on the placing of words on paper. Written verses prepared as amulets were widely believed to have protective power.[20]

The words "de nation Poulard," moreover, were inscribed on paper next to Rosalie's name as late as 1803 by Michel Vincent, the Frenchman with whom she had lived for several years and with whom she had borne children. The purpose of the document in question was not to increase her monetary value, but to identify her quite specifically in order to ratify her free status. It is possible that the term "Poulard" was a designation that her neighbors recognized and that she herself claimed with pride.

11

Some may have known that it linked her to a nation whose leader acted to keep his subjects from the Atlantic trade, and whose people ransomed captives when they could. On the other hand, *nation Poulard* was also a label imposed by slave traders, and it mirrored the language with which she would have been designated upon her first sale in the colony.[21]

Rosalie's age, as indicated in a subsequent act of sale, suggests an approximate birth date of 1767, so she would have been a young girl during the revolution in Fuuta Tooro. Her Atlantic crossing probably came during the 1780s or at the very beginning of the 1790s. The most likely port of her embarkation was Saint-Louis du Sénégal, where traders drew in captives from both the Senegal River and the overland trades and sent them forward to the French Caribbean colonies and elsewhere. Many captives were carried in French ships from West Africa to the Caribbean during the 1780s, but most slave traders no longer dared land in Saint-Domingue after the dramatic rebellion of slaves in the northern part of that colony in 1791.[22]

Saint-Louis du Sénégal was itself a thoroughly Atlantic spot, a narrow island along the coast of West Africa on which administrators, merchants, sailors, laborers, and captives coexisted under a fragile French colonial rule. The location was both perfect and precarious, for the island was situated in the Senegal River about eighteen miles upstream from the mouth, with the land of the Maures (Moors) to the north, that of Kajor and the Jolof to the south, Waalo to the east, and Fuuta Tooro and Galam reachable by boat up the river. The Portuguese had landed at the mouth of the Senegal River in the mid-1400s, and in 1659 an agent of the French Compagnie du Cap-Vert et du Sénégal had built a fort on the island.[23]

Saint-Louis' strategic location often tempted competing European powers to intrude. Eager for access to the river, the English captured and held the town for a few months in 1693, and then again for some years after 1758. Although actual control of the small island's heterogeneous population and varied trade did not necessarily track formal European declarations of sovereignty, the Treaty of Paris of 1763 conferred authority over the region on the English. During the period of English occupation of the island, local *habitants,* generally of mixed ancestry, exercised a substantial degree of practical autonomy. A subsequent treaty of 1783 reauthorized French dominion, but the *habitants* were eager to maintain the freedom of action they had acquired, including an important role in the river trade. Much of the middle valley of the Senegal River was by that point under the authority of the Almamy Abdulkaadir Kan, however, making access to trade very much a matter to be negotiated.[24]

In the years that followed, convoys of boats and barges, most belonging to the *habitants,* traveled upriver to a series of trading points *(escales)* along the banks, exchanging textiles, paper, alcohol, and other merchandise for ivory, gum Arabic, millet, and captives. At high water, between June and September, the river was navigable as far as the land of Galam, reaching into what are now Mali and Mauritania as well as Senegal, and merchants at the trading stations along the way sold captives drawn from even farther inland. Once finished trading, the convoy headed back down the river with goods and captives. Under the treaty signed by the French in 1785, however, representatives of the Almamy of Fuuta Tooro could inspect the passengers, freeing captives they deemed to have been illegally enslaved.[25]

The moment of arrival of the convoy back in Saint-Louis was a major occasion. Families were reunited, debts were repaid, deaths were reported, captives were sold. Throughout the year, residents of Saint-Louis had taken out loans, often promising to repay them in *pièces d'Inde* when the convoy returned. Now came the settling of accounts. For those who could not pay their debts, proceedings would be undertaken before the *greffe,* the office of the scribe *(greffier)* considered to be the "sole judicial officer" on the island. For the captives themselves, this was the moment of transfer, either into domestic slavery on the island, into the temporary depots where they awaited the Atlantic trading season, or directly onto ships standing offshore.[26]

Far more than a simple point of transshipment, Saint-Louis du Sénégal had long been a complex island society of its own—a classic West African trading post, but also a place of encounter and exchange. A small number of European men, generally living in customary unions with local women referred to as *signares,* had early on established webs of relationships in order to carry out trade in goods and people from the mainland. By the late eighteenth century much of the island's trade was in the hands of the *signares* and their descendants. The notarial records of Saint-Louis contain numerous contracts and transactions memorialized in French on behalf of women whose names reflect African and mixed ancestry. The total number of French men on the island was small, and most worked directly for the colonial government. Some commercial activities were nonetheless reserved to representatives of the officially recognized Compagnie du Sénégal.[27]

Many residents of Saint-Louis held slaves for their own use and generally kept them quite separate from the captives headed for the Atlantic trade. The labor of these enslaved men and women—estimated to number over 2,000—was used on the island in household production, transportation, or domestic duties, and men and women could also be rented out for immediate revenue. Skilled slaves, known as *laptots,* were essential to the annual convoys up the river, convoys that remained largely in the hands of the *habitants* based on the island, operating while en route under the protection of French forces. Wealth-in-persons was, in Saint-Louis as elsewhere on the West African coast, a fundamental element of status as well as a source of revenue and labor.[28]

The slaveholders of Saint-Louis could also bend French procedures to accommodate long-standing West African ideals of charity, protection, and patron-client relations. The formal legal *affranchissement* (manumission) of favored captives, as recorded by the official scribe, became a familiar act of highly visible charity, particularly common among women. At their request, the scribe would often include a requirement that the beneficiary of the freedom thus granted recognize the former mistress as his or her "benefactor." The *affranchissement* of a thirteen-year-old boy named Bouccari-Samba by a woman designated as the Signare Comba-Poule, for example, looks rather like the affair of an extended family, structured on paper to meet (more or less) the norms of French scribal practice.[29]

In addition to the complexities surrounding the Atlantic trade, transactions involving captives sold in the local marketplace could be politically fraught, since the leaders of the adjacent mainland African polities had both principles and interests at stake in what happened on the island. In one episode, a captive belonging to the the Damel of Kajor made his way to Saint-Louis, got drunk, and "sold himself" in the market, presumably pocketing the proceeds and occasioning a protest by the Damel. In an attempt to halt such sales of captives "by themselves," the French governor Blanchot ordered that sales could only be carried out under the supervision of the *maître de langue,* an authorized intermediary.[30]

The owners of slaves in Saint-Louis generally maintained a strict distinction between those who were their own *esclaves de case* or *esclaves de tapade* (house slaves) and would remain so, and those who were in transit and would go into the Atlantic trade. Captives held in the household were often recognized as having individual names and families. In the settlement of the inheritance of Marianne Fleury, for example, the captives whom she had owned were listed by the arbitrators as named individuals in groups designated as *familles*—such as Timac, sailor, age fifty-five, and his two boys ages fifteen and thirteen, one a carpenter and the other a

14

mason—and were kept together (at least on paper) in the course of the division of the estate. The threat of deportation into the Atlantic trade, however, shadowed even those who lived within households, and the records of the *greffe* confirm that individuals accused of crimes could be moved out of the protected status and sold to a trader headed for the Americas.[31]

For those destined for the Atlantic trade, unlike Timac and his sons, a stripping away of their names signaled a rupture with their past lives. There was not even the formality of a mass baptism and the conferring of a new name. By the time the woman later called Rosalie was in the hands of one of the traders of Saint-Louis, she had undoubtedly come to be recorded on paper not as an individual but as a commodity measured in *pièces d'Inde*.[32]

The records kept by the official scribes in late eighteenth- and early nineteenth-century Saint-Louis contain many traces of the French merchants and local *habitants* who gathered captives for sale to the Atlantic traders. One of the most conspicuous of them was an *habitant* named Paul Bénis, sometimes called Monsieur Paul, who bought and sold captives and gum Arabic for the Compagnie and for others. One can see his paper trail in the surviving contracts and sale documents, as he acquired land and buildings, made loans, and dealt with the Europeans who came and went from the island. He also outfitted ships for the trip upriver to Galam, and then housed the unnamed *captifs* in his buildings in Saint-Louis.[33]

When the season came for the Atlantic crossings, ships engaging in the risky pursuit of profit in the West Africa trade would arrive from Nantes, La Rochelle, Philadelphia, and other Atlantic ports. The vessels would initially stand offshore, beyond the intimidating line of surf along the coast, while the captains decided how best to approach their task. Sometimes they remained outside the sandbar that protected the island, and transferred persons and cargo to and from the ships into the long pirogues handled by African oarsmen. An alternative strategy was for the ship to attempt to follow the channel through the bar. This was a harrowing process, vividly conveyed in the subsequent formal depositions drawn up by surviving ship captains who had failed in the attempt.[34]

Even a skilled captain who took an experienced pilot on board ran a substantial risk in crossing the bar. If a ship laden with cargo drew, say, nine feet, and the water over the bar that day was just eight feet, then some of the cargo would first have to be offloaded onto a boat rented from the town—with the attendant risk of damage. Then came the moment to set the sails, pick up speed, and attempt to cross the bar itself. If the wind was too weak and the current too strong, it was simply impossible to make headway. If the calculation was wrong or the swell was too great, all would hear the terrible wrenching sound of the hull slamming the sand. Stuck on the bar in late July of 1804, the captain of the (appropriately named) Swedish schooner *Speculation* watched as the "natives of the mainland" gathered to gaze at his helpless craft. To the loss of the cargo to the waves was now added the risk of plunder.[35]

For captives like Rosalie, who were being taken on the outbound voyage, variations on the same drama were played in reverse. One particularly vivid description comes from a voyage made by the brig *Fly*, out of Philadelphia. The *Fly* had a difficult inbound crossing of the bar off Saint-Louis, but moored safely in front of the "town of the island of Senegal and tied up at the quay of Mr. Valentin" on April 3, 1805. Eight weeks later the *Fly* was ready to begin the journey back across the Atlantic. At 7:00 a.m. on June 4 they took a pilot on board, unmoored, "and made sail down the river; at 11[:00 a.m.] came t[o] along side of the guard ship about 6 miles below Senegal . . . the Supercargo came along-side with a boat load of slaves." They stayed five days at that place and took on "Guinea corn for the slaves." Then the *Fly* made sail down the river and anchored about two miles above the bar.[36]

The pilot and chief mate went out to sound the depth of the water over the bar and buoy the channel. But as the brig started across, the wind suddenly shifted, and "hauled in at N.W. took the sails all aback." This meant trouble. "Being then entered on the bar the vessel fell round off and struck among the breakers." They had no choice but to try to make their way into "smooth water, in towards the African shore," as "part of the crew and many of the slaves were employed staveing the water casks in the hold and heaving salt overboard to lighten the vessel, employed at the same time pumping."[37]

The captain now had to make a set of rapid calculations of profits, priorities, and lives. As the vessel hoisted a distress signal, the pilot boat took sixteen or twenty slaves to "the New York Brig that lay 2 mile above the bar." When the governor's barge came to the aid of the crew remaining on the ship, the captain began offloading slaves, the doctor, and passengers into the pilot boat and another small craft. But as the small boats began up the river they were attacked by "natives" from the mainland and "the boats were obliged to pull off towards the Brig, so as the Brig's guns should cover them so as not to be taken by the Africans but by coming too near the breakers both boats filled and capcised. . . . And a number of the Slaves at the same time drownded."

Then things got worse: "[We] found the vessel so far gone we were obliged to cut away the Foremast in order to keep her from going to pieces." The seas were breaking over the deck, fore and aft. They "got all the men Slaves upon deck and endeavored to knock them out of Iron's at intervails fiering off great Guns and small Arms during the night so as to keep the A[f]ricans from boarding us." The final calculation was stark: they cast off "and left the chief mate and 7 hands and 13 men slaves on board." Then, at noon, "the said Guard Ship's boat arrived on board the 2nd time and took out the Chief Mate and remainder of the crew with some luggage." That was the last offloading. The "13 men slaves," who may or may not still have been shackled, were apparently left on board as the ship broke up. In his deposition, the captain reported that of the seventy slaves originally taken on board the *Fly*, only twenty-four survived.[38]

Rosalie's own journey may have occurred on a French or a British vessel; we have no way of learning its name. But we do know that each ship's departure from Saint-Louis carried multiple challenges for captain and crew, and multiple terrors for the captives—of coercion, of abandonment and being abandoned, of the mountainous line of waves, and of the risk of drowning. Moreover, some of the circumstances of Rosalie's voyage can be inferred by looking at the records of other ships that set sail for the French sugar islands from the port at Saint-Louis during the 1780s.[39]

L'Amitié, for example, had left La Rochelle for Saint-Louis (referred to simply as Sénégal) at the end of 1786. Arriving in Saint-Louis in January 1787, the captain took three months to acquire 224 captives, many of them from the resident trader Monsieur Paul. The image of the loading is vivid: the captives were chained with "fers et menottes" (irons and shackles) and taken aboard one by one. Brought on deck for food that evening, they were subjected to a show of force: "at the same time we fired 12 shots of flintlock and three of blunderbuss" so that the captives would know that in case of revolt "we can defend ourselves." *L'Amitié* went south along the coast to Gorée to take on fifty-two more captives, and then set sail for Saint-Domingue on April 10, 1787.[40]

The show of force on deck at Saint-Louis, however, had not had the desired effect. On May 4, the crew discovered that a plot was being organized among the captives—or so the black quartermasters *(nègres quartiers-maîtres)* told the captain. The focus of the revolt was the misery of being physically shackled, and the captives were said to be planning to threaten the crew with death if their irons were not removed. Brought on deck one by one for punishment, the male captives eventually yielded up the name of a ringleader. He, after further whipping, provided a narrative of the alleged plot, in which both women and children were implicated:

> He confessed to us that all of the women were to have seized the moment of dinnertime when the officers were below and rebelled, that is that they would arrange among themselves to kill all the whites from the quarterdeck, while the men were to battle with the sailors in the bow. These women had consulted with the men through the children who worked in the kitchen, whom they exhorted to this task.

Having heard this account, the captain reported, "We acted against the women as against the men." Three weeks after this drama of plot and punishment, *L'Amitié* arrived in Port-au-Prince, and the 206 surviving captives were sold.[41]

Like the *Amitié*, the ship that carried Rosalie probably arrived first at Port-au-Prince, or at one of the other major ports in Saint-Domingue. The harbor at Jérémie, where Rosalie would eventually end up, was poorly protected from the sea and received only about a dozen ships a year directly from France. The continuing expansion of coffee production in the region virtually guaranteed a market for enslaved laborers, but the few transatlantic slavers that landed at Jérémie in these years generally brought cargoes of captives from Central Africa, particularly Angola. Most of the Senegambians who had reached this isolated district on the southern peninsula would thus have been carried there by smaller boats in the coastal trade.[42]

The reconstruction of Rosalie's likely Atlantic itinerary provides some clues about the knowledge that she brought with her into her period of captivity in the Caribbean. It is possible, though unlikely, that she had received the beginnings of training in literacy. If she was still unschooled, she would nonetheless have been familiar with the importance of writing. The same traders from Saint-Louis who sent ships upriver to find captives knew to load their boats with paper, a commodity much in demand because much in use in the communities along the way.[43]

Paper not only recorded crucial information for those engaged in commerce or formal study; it could in a quite different mode serve as the basis for a talisman or an amulet, something to provide protection in times of difficulty. Father David Boilat, writing of the Senegambian region some decades later, conveyed his own impression of the Pulaar-speaking peoples (including those called Toucouleur) and their customs. One of the watercolors that Boilat painted captured an image of a young widow seeking protection after the death of her husband. She is seated with a *marabout* (a holy man), who is putting ink on paper to create an amulet for her.[44]

Words could protect, and words could enslave. The young woman who was soon to be called Rosalie may or may not have seen the documents that were exchanged between the captain of the ship and the trader who had held her in captivity prior to her sale at the warehouse or on the wharf in Saint-Louis. The knowledge that writing confers power may nonetheless have accompanied her as she began her journey, leaving behind any claim to rights as a member of the Poulard nation, and heading toward a colonial society where she would be registered as property.

19

2

"Rosalie . . . My Slave"

When the woman who would soon be called Rosalie disembarked from a boat bringing her to the Caribbean colony of Saint-Domingue, those who had her in their control continued the process by which she was turned into a person held as property. Words were exchanged and papers were filled out, transferring to one or another resident of the colony the legal authority to exercise over her the powers attaching to the right of ownership. Categorized simply as some fraction of a *pièce d'Inde* when she was forced onto a ship in Senegambia, she was now designated a slave and given a name chosen by the purchaser. Perhaps young enough to be spared the pain of being branded with a hot iron, she was handed over to the person who would henceforth be designated her owner.[1]

Reconstructing the life story of a woman considered by law to be without rights requires turning to written records generated by those who laid claim to a property interest in her person. For Rosalie of the Poulard nation, five documents attest to her existence in Saint-Domingue. Three of these were drawn up in the southern port town of Jérémie, one in the nearby village of Les Abricots, and one in the parish church of Cap Dame-Marie, some leagues farther to the west. They record certain aspects of Rosalie's daily life, including her sale from one household to another and the potential change in her status initiated in several attempts at freedom through manumission. The one document reflecting her intimate life—the baptism of her daughter Élisabeth—exists only because by 1799 Rosalie had become a legally free woman, for whose child the sacrament would be recorded in detail by the officiating priest, unlike the baptisms of those born into slavery.[2]

The two men and one woman who held Rosalie as a slave left in the offices of the local notaries a paper trail of their own, providing a glimpse of the households in which she lived, and revealing the close connections to Africa of those who took ownership of her. They were all themselves the direct descendants of Africans; none had a French father; two were recently freed from slavery. For each owner, the purchase of Rosalie was part of a strategy of assembling "wealth in persons" within a household, a pattern familiar to those living in port cities in the slaveholding Caribbean and in many societies on the west coast of Africa. The passage from Saint-Louis in Sénégal to Jérémie in Saint-Domingue was long, but these structures of power and accumulation were well known to urban dwellers on both sides of the Atlantic.

Rosalie's years in Saint-Domingue encompassed the sequence of challenge, revolt, repression, and war that came to be known as the Haitian Revolution, finally triggering the French military expedition of 1802–1803 whose consequences would drive Rosalie from the island. From the vantage point of the households and the neighborhoods in which she lived, the dynamics of that revolution went far beyond the familiar struggle between "planters," "free people of color," and "slaves." The relationships of godparenthood, marriage, legal ownership, manumission, and inheritance cut across these categories and shaped the behavior of Rosalie and those around her. Although Rosalie first encountered the revolution as a slave, she would, across the decade from 1793 to 1803, become a freedwoman, a conjugal partner, a mother, and then a refugee.

The first document recording Rosalie's presence comes from Jérémie in the Grand'Anse, a district which took its name from the wide cove *(anse)* on the northwestern coast of the tongue of land that extends (along a massive fault line) to the south and west of Port-au-Prince. The hinterland of the Grand'Anse was intimidating, with rough and sometimes impassable trails leading to mountains and more mountains. The port of Jérémie looked primarily to the wider Caribbean, and the sailors entering and leaving it had long been as familiar with Kingston, Curaçao, and Santiago de Cuba as with the harbors of Léogâne and Port-au-Prince.[3]

Except for a few flat areas near the mouths of the rivers, the land of the Grand'Anse was not appropriate for growing sugar, and the early economy of the region was a modest one based on fishing, contraband trade, and small-scale farming. As a result both of its poverty and its geography, the Grand'Anse eluded much of the weight of direct control from French colonial officialdom. In the 1750s, however, the authorities had begun handing out formal "concessions" to lands in the southern peninsula. On the high ground there was plenty of rich soil in which to plant the tree crops of cacao and coffee. Claiming land either by settlement or by royal grant, newly arriving farmers aimed to gain an entrée into the Atlantic export economy. By the 1770s planters were shipping their produce out on the oceangoing vessels and coastal schooners whose skippers also facilitated a lively illegal trade with Jamaica.[4]

In maritime terms, however, Jérémie remained an unattractive harbor, with a shallow channel and an anchorage open to the northerlies. There was a tricky sandbar to cross, and no wharf other than the beach itself, so loading and off-loading had to be done by open boats known as *canots*. Economic inducements were nonetheless sufficient to attract some big ships, whether legal or contraband. Beginning in 1766, the English had authorized French and Spanish boats to call at ports in Jamaica, and merchants had hastened to Kingston to purchase cargoes of captives to be sold in Saint-Domingue. French planters worried that they might end up acquiring the "refuse" of their competitors, but they continued to buy.[5]

Most of the initial agricultural land grants had come without a labor force, and entrepreneurs scrambled to assemble *ateliers* (work gangs) of bound laborers to take on the tasks of planting, cultivating, and harvesting the crops. The traffic in African captives accelerated rapidly, though it relied heavily on foreign traders. In 1784 and again in 1786, the authorities offered French shippers a premium—first 100 and then 200 livres a head—for each *tête de nègres* introduced into the southern districts.[6]

French transatlantic ships that were engaged in the traffic in African captives responded to these incentives. The *Trois Frères,* for example, anchored in Jérémie in April of 1789 and disembarked 80 captives, most of them from Angola. *L'Émilie* arrived in September 1790 with 150. In September 1791 the *Nouvel Amour* delivered 339. Many captives also reached Jérémie in boats that brought people and goods from other ports in the colony, including Léogâne, Port-au-Prince, and Les Cayes, as well as some from Cap-Français.[7]

When the chronicler and jurist Louis Moreau de Saint-Méry visited in 1788 he found that just about everyone was obsessed with coffee. Speculators and ambitious farmers talked about the riches to be gained by planting in the interior highlands. In the *quartier* as a whole, Moreau counted 118 farms concentrating on coffee alongside cacao, 32 growing cotton, 10 producing indigo, and 7 growing sugarcane. There was also a lumber trade from the interior, particularly around the town of Plymouth.[8]

Economic activity brought administrative interest. Colonial authority in Jérémie was concentrated in the institutions known as the Sénéchaussée and the Admiralty, which held sessions on Fridays and Saturdays, assisted by five *procureurs* (state's attorneys), eight notaries, seven bailiffs, one *exempt* and one *brigadier* (both military officers), four policemen, one *étalloneur* (in charge of weights and measures), and one jailer. This was quite a bit of administration for a relatively modest town, but it reflected the size and increasing importance of Jérémie's hinterland and of the trade moving through the port. Moreau estimated that in 1788 the parish as a whole, which included rural districts, held approximately 2,000 whites and 1,000 people of color who were designated as free, alongside a population of 17,000 persons held as slaves.[9]

Some of Jérémie's 180 houses were quite pretty, in Moreau's opinion. The lower town, which stretched along the Rue de la Marine and the waterfront, was hot and crowded but convenient for business at the port. On the plateau a few meters higher, the upper town had a tree-lined main square and was expanding outward. The streets were alternately muddy and dusty, and Jérémie had many characteristics of a boom town. Some rents were said to have tripled in the previous ten years.[10]

The expanding economy of the region attracted not only agricultural colonists, but also those who saw potential in this urban economy. Around 1775 a freeborn black woman called Marthe Guillaume made her way westward from Port-au-Prince to Jérémie. Already the mother of four children (labeled *enfants naturels,* because they were born outside of marriage), the thirty-five-year-old Marthe Guillaume began in Jérémie with a small investment in a storefront shop, to be paid off over several years. From this base of operations she became a *marchande,* a female merchant, selling dry goods to city dwellers, including connoisseurs like the man who bought a length of fabric described as *queue de serein,* the canary yellow that was fashionable in Paris. She also acquired enslaved women, whom she sent out to sell goods in the street. These were her *pacotilleuses,* peddlers selling retail to small-scale buyers.[11]

In 1777 Marthe Guillaume placed her thirteen-year-old son Pierre Aliés as an apprentice for four years with a local mason, who in turn promised to behave toward the boy "like a good father of a family." Marthe Guillaume herself was considered to be a suitable godmother by her neighbors, including one Agnès, who gave the baby in question the name Marthe.[12] By 1784 Marthe Guillaume had expanded from petty commerce into buying and selling slaves, whom she marked with a metal brand that seared into their flesh the letters of her nickname, Marthone, with a "G" for Guillaume below. She purchased captives from "divers négriers" (various slave ships and their captains), then resold them at a profit. This woman born of an enslaved African father and a free black mother was soon well on her way to a position of financial power in town.[13] She developed links to the countryside as well, marrying her daughter Marie Anne Aliés into the Azor family, rural free property-owning people of color. Marthe gave five slaves as gifts to the newlyweds.[14]

Among the agricultural pioneers in the Grand'Anse were white Creoles from elsewhere in the colony, alongside some French colonists. The most prosperous among them brought capital, slaves, and pretensions to rural wealth and urban life. Some families—like the Galbaud du Fort or the Couët de Montarand—already owned large properties in the long-settled north, but invested in the newly opened lands in the south. Others, like a down-on-his-luck French immigrant named Michel Vincent, arrived more or less empty-handed, hoping to find success in the frontier region after failure elsewhere. Michel Vincent bought a small plot of land in Les Abricots, close to the large property of the Galbaud du Fort family, and set about planting coffee.[15]

Michel Vincent had emigrated from western France to Saint-Domingue decades earlier, settling near Les Cayes on the south coast. He had tried two of the classic strategies of a colonial adventurer: obtaining a royal privilege (in his case the *ferme de la boucherie,* collecting fees from local meat sellers) and marrying a rich Creole widow. He failed at both, losing the monopoly and being outmaneuvered by the widow, whose notary carefully secured her wealth to her children from a previous marriage. By moving to Les Abricots, acquiring a small property and building a house, he was presumably aiming to become a gentleman farmer. But his status had fallen since his days in Les Cayes, and he would continue to slip down the social ladder.[16]

No direct record of the first sale of Rosalie in Saint-Domingue seems to have survived, although there are some parallel sources concerning other young women from Senegambia who came to be held as slaves by free black residents of the town. In March 1787, for example, a woman named Élisabeth Zeila worked through Magloire Cabrocorso—himself designated as a *mulâtre* (mulatto)—to purchase a fourteen-year-old slave called Julie, labeled "of the Poulard nation." The seller was a white merchant, le Sieur Claude Collet; the eventual purchaser was a black woman of modest means. Rather than the classic picture of a prosperous planter who boards a slave ship to inspect the cargo, or who acquires captives as they are landed on the quay, this was a small-scale transaction, carried out through an intermediary who was a freedman.[17] Acquisition of a single captive by a person of African descent was a common pattern in Saint-Domingue, enabling a newly freed person to collect revenue from renting out the labor of that slave in an urban economy. The phenomena of accumulation and commodification were indeed at work in such circumstances, but on a scale that was small in terms of the overall colonial scheme—though potentially enormous for the person thus bound to labor.[18]

The initial household into which Rosalie was incorporated by sale was apparently that of an aged free man called Alexis Couba. In West Africa both Pulaar and Wolof speakers used "Cumba" as a female name, and it could then by extension be applied to the son of a woman carrying that name. The variant spelling "Couba," in Saint-Domingue, appears to be associated with Africans.[19] The cleric officiating at Alexis Couba's marriage, however, specified that he had been born in the parish of Jérémie, probably around 1712, and manumitted from slavery in 1778. At the manumission the notary had followed the law in force in ancien régime Saint-Domingue that prohibited freedpeople from taking the surname of a French family. He inscribed instead the name Couba, which may have reflected Senegambian origins on the part of Alexis's mother.[20]

Alexis Couba acquired a slave named Anne, and married her three years after his own manumission. Under the Code Noir regulating slavery in Saint-Domingue, such a marriage automatically rendered Anne free. Progressions of this kind were familiar in Jérémie, as men who had won their own freedom secured their rights of paternity and began to assemble households of free and enslaved dependents.[21]

Alexis Couba was building a family rather than a fortune. Four years after marrying Anne, he freed another slave, named Lisette, moving her from the status of property to that of free person. Judging by her age, it seems likely that Lisette was the mother of Anne, hence Alexis Couba's mother-in-law. What initially looks in a notarial record like accumulation begins to take on a somewhat different aspect. Alexis and Anne may have been partners for many years, but only when he acquired his freedom could he begin to move her and the other members of her family out of slavery as well.[22]

The household into which Rosalie was incorporated by sale, probably in the late 1780s, was thus one in which it was clear that slavery was not necessarily a permanent status. Seeing the examples of Anne and Lisette before her, Rosalie might logically anticipate that her own enslavement would be followed at some point by manumission, or at the very least that she would be treated in the ways expected by *esclaves de case* in West Africa, and perhaps insulated from further sale.

Alexis Couba had obtained for himself "wealth in persons" and access to Rosalie's labor or the revenue her labor could yield. But he may have overreached financially, and he soon relinquished the enslaved Rosalie to his more prosperous neighbor, the entrepreneurial *marchande* Marthe Guillaume. Perhaps he had to pay off a debt, or perhaps he needed ready cash. Either way, Rosalie now moved from a household headed by a recently freed black man to one headed by a prosperous freeborn black woman.[23]

With a house on the central Place d'Armes in Jérémie, several rental properties, and a daughter married into a well-known family of free people of color, Marthe Guillaume was by the early 1790s a woman of means. Nearly everyone in town owed her money, a sure sign of her standing in the network of reciprocities within the community. When she later had an agent draw up a list of all her debtors, it ran to some thirty pages.[24]

As a black person in Saint-Domingue, however, Marthe Guillaume had always to be prepared to prove her freedom. Each time she went to the notary—whether to sell captives or to harass a builder with whom she was unsatisfied—she proffered a document attesting to her free birth. Those who labored as domestics in her household presumably came to know the drill by which Marthe retrieved that piece of paper (perhaps kept in a trunk by the bed?) and took it carefully to the office of the notary. Rosalie, as a woman from Senegambia, already knew the power of talismans in her home country. She could now see in a new setting the efficacy of ink on paper.[25]

Marthe Guillaume's strategy for building a network of slaves, clients, and credit enabled her to prosper, despite the increasing hostility on the part of many whites to those they viewed as excessively ambitious persons of African descent. She had connections in Jérémie itself, in the countryside, and in the town of Les Cayes on the south coast. She could summon white artisans to answer to her dissatisfaction with their work, and collect rent from more distinguished white tenants. She was mother-in-law or godmother to children classed as free *mulâtres* in both the town and the countryside. Her wealth was enhanced by the labor of the enslaved women vendors described as *pacotilleuses*, as well as that of assorted additional slaves, of whom Rosalie was now one. The aftershocks of the French Revolution would nonetheless soon strain Marthe Guillaume's capacity to hold this network together.

Already in 1790 dramatic news was reaching Jérémie from Paris and from the town of Les Cayes. Julien Raimond and several other wealthy men of color from the colony had for years lobbied in France to try to enforce the guarantees of equal rights among the free that had been enunciated by the monarchy in the 1685 Code Noir. After 1789 they could extend this claim through a broad and inclusive reading of the Declaration of the Rights of Man. With the transformation of the French Estates General into a National Assembly came the call for local assemblies to send representatives to Port-au-Prince, where they would choose delegates to proceed to Paris.[26]

In March of 1790 the National Assembly issued a set of "Instructions" for constituting the local assemblies in Saint-Domingue. Worded ambiguously, the instructions seemed to offer the possibility of the franchise to some free men of color. The questions of status, standing, and ancestry—although not yet the question of slavery itself—were now on the table.[27]

Conservative white colonists, both absentees in Paris and those resident in Saint-Domingue, wanted at all costs to prevent the local assemblies from raising the public standing of free men of color, and from diminishing their own power. There was every reason to believe that they would try to hold the line when assemblies were convened, and the governor cued them to do just that. Not only free men of color, but *blancs mésalliés*—including white men who had married across the color line—generally ended up being excluded from participation.[28]

In the autumn of 1790 the wealthy Vincent Ogé, a man of color who had returned to the colony from Paris, mounted a risky movement calling for equal rights among the free, regardless of color. His followers initially succeeded in disarming the whites in the neighborhood of Grande Rivière, near Cap-Français, but were soon routed by troops led by the interim governor. Ogé fled across the border to Spanish Santo Domingo. Extradited back to the colony as a "chief of the brigands," he was broken on the wheel in the main square of Cap-Français. The brutality of the punishment meted out to Ogé and his colleagues undermined the possibility of a strategic alliance of property holders across the color line, in which white slaveholders would concede political rights to free persons of color in order to create a united front against the prospect of slave rebellion. Indeed, the colonists' killing of Ogé would be evoked in the coming struggles by both free men of color and the enslaved as an emblem of the fierce protection of a monopoly of power by the "aristo-cratic" white planter class.[29]

In November 1790 a group of men of color from the south also came together to demand the right to vote. Encamped at the *habitation* (estate) of one Prou, in the plain near Les Cayes, they were attacked by a large group of white men from the town, against whom they initially held on. Faced with reinforcements, however, the protesters backed down, receiving what at first seemed to be an amnesty from colonial officials. André Rigaud, a free man of color who would go on to become a major leader, later recalled the words uttered by the French official sent to repress them: "Men of color . . . You must *never* hope to cross the line of demarcation that sepa-rates you from the whites, your fathers and benefactors. Return to your duty. . . . I offer you peace with one hand, and war with the other."[30]

In these armed protests, free men who were often designated by their enemies as *mulâtres* or *affranchis* (freedpersons)—but who generally con-sidered themselves to be *personnes de couleur* (persons of color)—made demands for membership in the polity. They did not initially address the question of slavery. This position was consistent with the shared political grievances but quite varied class positions of those who constituted these early movements.

Some families of mixed ancestry owned coffee plantations and dozens of slaves. They were among the most vocal in decrying political distinc-tions on the basis of color, but as proprietors they also offered a potential bulwark against slave insurrection. Many freedpersons, however, like Alexis Couba and his wife Anne, simply worked in the countryside as farmers or in town as artisans and traders. They might own one or two slaves but they also had multiple social ties to those who were still held in slavery, who often included their own kin. Both wealthy and modestly situated free men and women of color could agree on the demand for equal public rights. Their responses might differ, however, in the face of an open call for an end to the holding of property in persons.[31]

Across these years, the terms used to designate individuals were com-plex, reflecting ongoing social processes, rather than fixed categories. The respect or disrespect implied could vary depending on the schema and the context. The triad *blanc/mulâtre/nègre* (white/mulatto/black), for example, generally stigmatized both of the latter categories, although the valence of a stigmatizing term could on occasion be challenged in moments of self-assertion. The terms "Européen," "Américain," "Créole," and "Africain" could be used in different ways for different purposes, and they overlapped rather than duplicating the various color terms. The legal distinction *né libre/affranchi/esclave* (freeborn/freedperson/slave) did not map smoothly onto the *mulâtre/nègre* dichotomy, since legal condition and designated color came from different category schemes. Finally, the term *affranchi,* although signaling free status, could be intentionally disrespectful, publicly recalling that an individual had once been enslaved. In certain moments of struggle the term *affranchi* was rejected by those thus labeled, in favor of the more encompassing *personne de couleur,* which affirmed personhood. It perhaps goes without saying that in seeking to understand the dynamics of the Haitian Revolution one cannot use any one set of these labels in isolation, as if they could by themselves denominate the relevant factions and groups of actors.[32]

While the struggle over the franchise brought division along lines of color among the propertied, news and rumors from Paris seemed to promise change for the enslaved. Although both the monarchy and the new National Assembly were very reluctant to touch the question of abolition, persistent reports circulated that "the king had given slaves three free days a week" and that whites were blocking this reform. Rumor began to assume its own power within slave communities across the French Caribbean. In Saint-Domingue, some versions of the rumor held that the free people of color in the colony had pledged to help the enslaved to achieve the promised rights, an inference that would later be reinforced by the actions of various leaders among the men of color, including André Rigaud.[33]

By early 1791 the conflict in the colony was taking a new shape. Around Port-Salut in the south, the scene of earlier protests by free persons of color, a man named Jean-Claude Lateste apparently spread the word to slaves of the imagined royal promise of three days a week to themselves. On January 24 these slaves were said to have gathered with others to plan an uprising in pursuit of this aim. The plot was uncovered before it could go very far, and left only a thin trace in the archives, but it prefigured events to come.[34]

On August 22, 1791, enslaved laborers on plantations of the northern plain around Cap-Français took up arms against their masters and torched the places of their enslavement. Although the slaves' initial demands may have been limited, the fact of a large-scale uprising terrified property holders. For conservatives, the catastrophe of burning plantations seemed to confirm long-standing predictions that any concession to the political rights of free men of color would bring social havoc. For convinced reformers, it made clear that the worst-case scenario was indeed possible, and thus strengthened their call for ameliorative changes in policy as a matter of prudence.[35]

In truth, it was difficult to be certain of the cause-and-effect relationship between the political movement of free persons of color and the acts of rebellion committed by the enslaved of the northern plain. Although conservatives characteristically hated them both, there was no automatic alliance between those who fought against the humiliations of what was called "caste" and those who fought against the circumstances of slavery. The capacity of the enslaved to wield weapons—either on their own behalf or in the struggles of others—was nonetheless clear. Indeed, property owners in the Grand'Anse had long used this capacity, arming their slaves against incursions by pirates or foreign invaders.[36]

The struggles that now ensued took on a particular bitterness in the Grand'Anse, where many free families of African descent were well established, and some white newcomers were particularly jealous of their own privileges. Across the south, property holders categorized as white, as well as those designated "of color," began to arm their slaves, in preparation for the coming contests. To conservative whites—who viewed their own arming of slaves as legitimate—it looked as though free people of color were inciting rebellion among the *ateliers* (enslaved workers) of the plantations. In December 1791 the town council of Jérémie described the opposition they faced from men they characterized as "brigands," and they attributed it precisely to the actions of free men of color.[37]

By late 1791, then, the position of Marthe Guillaume had become potentially delicate. Power in the town of Jérémie was held by a planter-controlled body sometimes referred to as the Coalition of the Grand'Anse, which was waging open warfare against men of color who had gathered their own forces in the highlands of the interior. Everyone presumably knew that Marthe Guillaume's daughter had married into the Azor family, and that it was Noël Azor and the web of interconnected neighboring families who were providing leadership to the free men of color in the hills. Some may also have known that Marthe's own son Pierre Aliés, now a young man of an age to bear arms, had close friends among the militiamen of color in town, men who were unlikely to bend to the efforts of white leaders in the municipality to bring them under control.[38]

During January and February of 1792 many men of color who had taken to the countryside in rebellion were captured by forces sent to repress them, and some were imprisoned on a ship anchored just offshore from Jérémie. A rumor spread through town that the victorious whites were intentionally inoculating the prisoners with smallpox. In these tense months, the record of Marthe Guillaume's economic activities in Jérémie, so dense for the earlier years, thins out a bit.[39]

News from metropolitan France added to the uncertainty. By the spring of 1792 revolutionaries in Paris had concluded that concessions to free people of color might provide a counterweight to the demands of the enslaved. In April 1792 the French Legislative Assembly decreed an end to formal legal distinctions of color among free people in the colony, conferring an equality of political rights on "les hommes de couleur et nègres libres" (men of color and free black men). News of what came to be known as the "decree of April 4" reached the colony in late May.[40]

Most whites in Jérémie, however, had no intention of relinquishing their capacity to impose social and political disabilities on the men whom they had so recently vanquished. They thus found themselves at odds with the colonial officials charged with enforcing the legislation arriving from Paris. To assert his authority, and that of Paris, against local opposition, the colonial governor, Vicomte de Blanchelande, turned to Les Cayes and the forces under André Rigaud, a free man of color. Through this alliance with armed men of color, the French authorities gained an appearance of submission from the whites in control of Jérémie, but only for a time. Fierce conflicts continued between white colonists and activist men of color, with each side deploying slave soldiers armed for their purposes. Tales of brutality circulated, including accusations against Noël Azor, the brother of Jean Baptiste Azor, husband of Marthe Guillaume's daughter.[41]

In early 1793, Marthe Guillaume—generally known to her neighbors as Marthone—began to take certain precautions. Declaring herself to be in ill health, she called a notary to her home to draw up a detailed last will and testament, carefully arranging for the disposition of her goods among her kin. Although many of those she held as slaves were simply to be allocated as property among her heirs, she made special provisions for a number of them. In particular, she declared that upon her death, her slave named Rosalie was to be freed.[42]

A week later Marthe Guillaume summoned the notary again and had him compose a second draft of the will. Rosalie's name did not appear in the new draft. Instead, a document of the same date formalized the sale of "une négresse Nommée Rozalie nation Poulard," about twenty-six years of age, to a neighbor named Jean Baptiste Mongol, a freedman categorized as *mulâtre* who worked as a butcher. We cannot know for certain whether this was a true sale, or a transaction designed to accomplish some goal

31

other than the one enunciated in the act. The stated price was high—2,400 livres. As was common in such cases, the money was said to have changed hands outside the view of the notary. It seems possible that someone who wished to move Rosalie out of the household of Marthe Guillaume may have provided the money to Jean Baptiste Mongol as an intermediary, but there is no way to be sure.[43]

The transfer of Rosalie to Jean Baptiste Mongol came at a moment of great tension in the town of Jérémie, where the municipal council was in more or less open revolt against the civil commissioners who had been sent to Saint-Domingue by the government in Paris. The commissioners were charged with exercising authority over those now seen as France's colonial "citizens." In principle, municipal councilors were required to observe the decree of April 4, 1792, mandating equal civil rights among the free, regardless of color. The municipal council in Jérémie nonetheless convened as an all-white body, though council members would later claim that two men of color had been elected but refused to serve.[44]

The council then announced that the local units of the Garde Nationale composed of and commanded by men of color should be dissolved and their members transferred to existing white units under white officers. Instead of extending rights, they thus appeared to undercut the respect that some men of color had gained as participants in the local defense force. As of early 1793, however, the council did not quite dare to order that the transfer actually be carried out.

One evening in the midst of this tense standoff, a white officer of the Garde Nationale tried to shut down a noisy celebration—a raucous *bal à bamboula,* a dance accompanied by drumming, according to the municipal authorities. The fête in question was apparently attended by both enslaved persons and free persons of color. Citizen Thomani, a celebrant who was himself a lieutenant in the Garde Nationale, exchanged sharp words with the officer who had come to shut down the party. The municipality summoned Thomani to answer for his actions, but decided for the moment to take no further steps.

The confrontation between the municipal authorities and men of color in the militia took place in the shadow of expanding conflict throughout the south, as the forces under the commissioners sought to contain insurrection by slaves, while at the same time facing insubordination from those hostile to the new French Republic, including the councilors in Jérémie. News had also recently reached Jérémie that the Republican army had attacked a stronghold of black insurgents in the Platons, between Jérémie and

Les Cayes. Additional "brigands" were said to be operating in the neighborhood of the community called Les Anglais. White authorities in Jérémie had imagined that they could still command the men of color among the Garde Nationale to join in securing the town against possible attack, but had been rebuffed. Now they would seek to reassert their control.[45]

Reporting on their confrontations with those they referred to as the men "formerly known as colored," the council members tried to argue that they were actually following the spirit of the declaration of civil equality by demobilizing units defined by color. To anyone observing the proceedings, however, it was clear that white officials were in fact trying to disarm men whom they deemed not entitled to constitute or command units of this kind. The result of forcing these men into militia units commanded by whites could be foreseen: officers of color would lose their commissions and would have to defer to commanders who might send them into battle against those they did not necessarily see as their enemies. A casual comment in one of the descriptions brings the story of unrest among the militiamen closer to home: present at the moment of the fracas with Thomani was not only Noël Azor, a resister of long standing, but also the young man designated as the "son of the Citizen Martone."[46]

Soon the municipal authorities accused Lieutenant Thomani of a physical attack upon another citizen, arrested him, and ordered that he be tried. This humiliation of a militia officer triggered further protests, and men of color from both the town and the countryside moved toward an encampment at La Voldrogue in the interior. Reports soon arrived in Jérémie that the men camped there were being joined by enslaved laborers from plantations that they had raided. They were also said to have opened up communications with Les Cayes, stronghold of André Rigaud, where the Republican civil commissioner Étienne Polverel was now in residence.[47]

The movement coming together in La Voldrogue had both a political and a military structure. Marthe Guillaume's son Pierre Aliés—whom some witnesses designated simply as "Pierre Martonne"—had taken charge of a "subscription" by which they would raise money for their efforts to demand the freedom of their colleague Thomani. A few days later Pierre was said by an informant to be in command, along with a colleague, of sixty-eight "seditious" men of color under arms who were going from plantation to plantation and exhorting (or intimidating) the enslaved to join them. When Marthe Guillaume's son signed a formal letter of protest to the municipality on February 23, he identified himself as "Pierre Aliesse, lieutenant," invoking the surname that the councilors had refused to accord him. He was now serving under a captain named Atlas, a man who would reappear as a leader in the years to come.[48]

The initial response of the municipal council was to convoke all the "peaceful" persons of color, those who resisted the appeal to "revolt," ordering them to appear at the town hall and inscribe their names on a list. The authorities then took some as prisoners—particularly women and children associated with free men of color. It is unclear whether Marthe Guillaume herself was imprisoned, perhaps as a means of putting pressure on her son. Probably not, given the number of people in town, many whites among them, who used her as their banker. But economic power was not likely to guarantee impunity indefinitely.[49]

As word of the renewed repression in Jérémie spread, the possibility of any cross-color alliance of the free against the enslaved looked more and more doubtful. From the enslaved men and women joining the *bal à bamboula* in Jérémie to those insurgent former slaves in the Platons who were willing to become soldiers in the newly formed Legions of Equality under André Rigaud, a fragile alternate alliance was taking shape, this one between the enslaved and those who were linked by color to a slave past. With the emissaries of the French Republic now turning to officers of color and troops drawn from the plantations, conservatives in Jérémie were soon placed on the defensive. The group of men of color that Marthe Guillaume's son had joined now swelled to some 300, including women, and was heading to Les Cayes to meet with Commissioner Polverel.[50]

As the drama of open rebellion moved forward, new possibilities emerged for some women in Rosalie's circumstances. Power in the countryside was shifting, and competing groups sought the loyalty of those held as slaves. The pattern nonetheless remains difficult to discern, in part because of an abrupt drop in the rate of survival of written records. For during the year of Rosalie's sale to Jean Baptiste Mongol, and of the uprising involving Marthe Guillaume's son, this northwestern corner of the southern peninsula of Saint-Domingue veered out of the orbit of French colonial authority, and into the sphere of inter-imperial rivalry.

To the most conservative planters and merchants of Jérémie, already thoroughly estranged from the authorities sent out from Paris, the only way to defend their interests seemed to be to negotiate their own antirepublican international alliance. Émigrés from Saint-Domingue who had made their way to London proposed a drastic step: inviting British troops to land at Jérémie to establish a foothold in the French colony in order to stop the radicalization of the revolution. These enterprising plotters had carried out a vigorous campaign of lobbying in London to prove their own credibility and achieve their ends. The British government was initially hesitant to commit itself to men who were obviously free agents, but the Grand'Anse region was still exporting temptingly large amounts of coffee, and the vast sugar plantations of Saint-Domingue made the colony the richest of potential prizes. Events in Europe, moreover, were pushing in the direction of renewed conflict between England and France. On February 1, 1793, England declared itself at war with France. A preliminary agreement with the Saint-Domingue émigrés was signed in London later that month. The dispatch of an expeditionary force from Jamaica was not out of the question.[51]

In the months that followed, disastrous conflict emerged within Saint-Domingue between the Republican civil commissioners and the newly arriving governor-general François Thomas Galbaud. The commissioners had been trying both to enforce the equal-rights decrees and to suppress rebellion in the colony. But Galbaud (brother of a landowner in Jérémie) had his own ideas about the best mode of pacification. On June 20, 1793, their struggle burst into open warfare, and the civil commissioners reached for an alliance with the slaves around the port of Le Cap to try to secure their authority. In a proclamation printed and distributed on June 21, the commissioners offered freedom to "black warriors who will fight for the Republic, under the civil commissioners' orders, both against the Spanish and against other enemies, whether interior or exterior."[52]

With Governor-General Galbaud in retreat and the city of Le Cap in flames, it became apparent that the abolition of slavery itself was now moving onto the agenda, grasped by the Republicans as the only way to keep the colony out of the hands of the nearby Spanish, the looming British, or colonists and Creoles whom they saw as counterrevolutionaries. In mid-August came an explosive set of announcements by Commissioners Sonthonax and Polverel: slavery would soon be ended throughout the colony—though many of those to be freed would be constrained to remain at their posts. The commissioners' decrees were scheduled to be extended to the south in October 1793. Officially, the law would soon recognize no claims to property in men or women in the town where Rosalie lived.[53]

Just as the news of the abolition declared by the Republican commissioners made its way to the south, however, the émigré planter Venault de Charmilly signed a formal agreement with General Adam Williamson, who commanded the British forces in Jamaica. On September 19, 1793, redcoats landed in Jérémie to welcoming cries of "Long Live the British!"

and "Long Live King George!" For two years planters in Jérémie had succeeded in maintaining their distance from Republican authorities, largely
governing the region on their own. Now, insulated militarily from the advance of the Legions of Equality under André Rigaud, they could constitute a Conseil Privé (a Privy Council) to advise the English, educating them
in the ways of the colony. In the treaty signed with the émigrés, Williamson
had agreed to roll back the Legislative Assembly's grant of civil and political equality to free men of color. The English more than made good on this
promise, allowing the execution of 160 free men of color held prisoner in
Jérémie. Conservatives could count on the new commanders to brook no
talk of abolition.[54]

The presence of an English occupation from September 1793 onward
shielded slaveholders in Jérémie from the direct legal effects of the abolition
of slavery decreed by the commissioners and later ratified on February 4,
1794, by the French National Convention. This was gratifying for planters
and merchants, but the town still held what one of their allies described as
"une masse de Canaille attachée à la République" (a crowd of scoundrels
still attached to the Republic)—that is, a population unwilling to shift its
loyalty to the British occupiers. The fracturing of the free population between those willing to welcome a foreign power and those still "attached to
the Republic" made enforcement of the rights of ownership over persons
quite delicate.[55]

The Legions of Equality under André Rigaud remained in control in
Les Cayes, and local men "formerly known as of color" had regrouped in
various encampments outside Jérémie. As the English tried to expand their
domain across the south and the west, they thus faced implacable opposition from those whom they characterized as "the Blacks," the "Banditti,"
or the "Commissioner[s'] Army."[56] Writing from Kingston, Jamaica, Henry
Shirley evoked the difficulty: "We have many Friends at aux Cayes, but
Rigaud a Mulatto who commands, not only keeps everything quiet there
but most likely will drive us from Jérémie."[57]

The British tried to keep enslaved laborers at work on the coffee plantations. The planter Venault de Charmilly bragged: "This Quarter having
never been in the power of the Banditti, nor of the Civil commissioners, it
has never been pillaged nor plundered; It is in a flourishing situation." He
predicted a harvest of fifteen to eighteen million pounds of coffee. But administering the areas under British control remained a huge headache, and
General Williamson would increasingly find himself obliged to offer freedom to some of those held as slaves in exchange for military service.[58]

The heterogeneous colonial society that the British found in place, moreover, did not make it easy to map the distinction between free and slave onto a dichotomy of white and black. As de Charmilly wrote, in a denunciation of what he saw as indulgence toward free people of color: "It is Difficult to Conceive of the number of free women of Color who now exist in St Domingue." Free women designated as *mulâtresses* or *négresses*—like the *marchande* Marthe Guillaume—seemed to de Charmilly to be an element of dissolution in the colony, and a disruption of the proper order of things. (Such denunciations, of course, did not prevent planters from taking women of color as "housekeepers" and bearing children with them.) A British officer nonetheless wrote quite bluntly to his superiors: "The Mulattos & all people of colour who are free, *must be made* equal with the whites, without this, the English cannot hold the colony." He thought it unlikely that "30,000 persons of this description will return to a state of degradation." The British imagined that they could extend to them only "the rights given to this class in the English colonies," but some officers on the ground could see that more was going to be required.[59]

During the first few months of the British occupation, Marthe Guillaume seems to have been able to keep her balance, although the participation of her son Pierre Aliés in the uprisings of men of color, as well as that of the family of her daughter's husband, the Azors, probably brought surveillance of her own activities. She had taken on responsibility for administering several farms, presumably those belonging to her kin, and the intense disruption of both the town and the countryside made it difficult for her to collect the debts owed her. By February 1794, Marthe Guillaume apparently decided that a strategic retreat was the better part of wisdom. She drew up a private power of attorney, conferring authority on a local judge to manage her affairs during her absence. She then disappeared from the town of Jérémie, perhaps to join her son or her daughter in some area of the countryside that was under the control of the Republican forces of André Rigaud.[60]

The military and political conflicts between the British and the Republican armies seem to have had consequences for Rosalie as well. Marthe Guillaume, who at some point reacquired ownership of Rosalie from the butcher Mongol, was now absent. Moreover, outside the areas of effective British occupation, slavery no longer existed in law, making the countryside south and west of Jérémie a zone of potential freedom. The circumstantial evidence suggests that around 1794 Rosalie herself left

Jérémie and moved in with the colonist Michel Vincent in the coastal village of Les Abricots.[61]

By October 1794 those the English called "the rebels from Les Cayes," the forces under André Rigaud, had made their way up to Cap Dame-Marie, where the parish church serving Les Abricots was located. With Rigaud as a potential enforcer of the decrees of abolition, it is an open question whether formal slavery itself could even be said to exist at this date on Michel Vincent's farm in Les Abricots.[62]

The relationship between Rosalie and Michel Vincent had little to do with the fantasy of romance between rich planter and light-skinned female slave that loomed large in the imagination of colonists like Moreau de Saint-Méry. Michel was neither young nor prosperous, and Rosalie was an African-born woman designated *négresse*, not *mulâtresse*. There is no evidence that she was ever legally held as Michel's slave. Somewhere along the line, the paths of the French colonist on his way down the social ladder and the African woman on her way up had crossed, and someone had arranged for her to work for him. Perhaps they had met in town while Rosalie was in Marthe Guillaume's household. (When Marthe Guillaume reappeared in Jérémie in August 1794 and summoned the holder of her power of attorney to draw up a full accounting of her financial position, the list included one debt owed to her by "Vincent.") Perhaps Michel, who had collected fees from butchers in earlier years, also knew Jean Baptiste Mongol, the local butcher to whom Marthe Guillaume had sold Rosalie in January 1793.[63]

Two documentary fragments from 1795 seem to sketch some of the lines of Rosalie's union with Michel. The first is a single sheet separated from the record book that it was meant to index. On it the curé of the parish church of Cap Dame-Marie, on whom those in Les Abricots depended for the sacraments, listed the baptisms he had recorded during the year. The names of two of those baptized jump off the page: Marie Louise and Jean Théodore. These are, with one small variation, the names of two of Rosalie's children, as they were listed in a later document: Marie Louise and Juste Théodore. It seems very likely that these are children—perhaps twins?—born to Rosalie and Michel, and baptized in the nearest parish church.[64]

The second document is a manumission paper for Rosalie drawn up in December 1795 at the request of Marthe Guillaume, who had at some point resumed formal ownership of Rosalie, at least on paper. Invoking the fidelity of "Rosalie négresse Poulard," the notarized text expressed Marthe

Guillaume's desire to grant full liberty to Rosalie, and enjoined her to follow all the laws governing freedpeople in the colony. Marthe Guillaume promised to obtain the official ratification of Rosalie's freedom from the British authorities, who were now in control of the region.[65]

With this notarized paper certifying her *affranchissement,* Rosalie inched quite close to a fully official freedom. But getting the required signature from the civil authorities put Marthe Guillaume into the position of a supplicant to the British general Williamson and his French advisers. The question of the status of people of African descent who sought formal recognition of their freedom remained in dispute. From his base of operations in Port-au-Prince, General Williamson was trying to suppress two groups of resisters, in part by persuading them to change sides: the Legions of Equality led by the Republican general André Rigaud, and those referred to as the "nègres révoltés" (the blacks in revolt) including a crew led by a man named Dieudonné, who was holding firm just outside Port-au-Prince. Williamson needed to continue conscripting colonial troops from the plantations, and when possible attract defectors from the ranks of the Legions of Equality. His advisers thought that in order to maintain this policy of attraction, freedom should only be granted to those who agreed to serve Britain under arms.[66]

Williamson's consultants on the Conseil Privé thus opposed approving any further manumissions "pendant la durée des troubles" (for the duration of the troubles), though they did not think it wise to inquire too strictly into the status of individuals who already exercised freedom. With André Rigaud issuing stirring calls to resistance from Les Cayes on the other side of the mountains, Williamson's planter allies advised caution, and acknowledged that some "abuses" would have to be tolerated from those who were claiming freedom, given the delicacy of the situation. Williamson was preoccupied with the risks posed by free people of color, and when the request from Marthe Guillaume crossed his desk, he refused to certify her acts of manumission, on the grounds that they were inopportune. Rosalie was out of luck.[67]

For the moment, Rosalie could still live as if free, given that Marthe Guillaume apparently proposed to make no further legal claim on her. But Rosalie had now become what we could today call a *sans-papiers,* a person with no papers to establish the legitimacy of her civil status. And when we look closely at her life and that of Michel Vincent, the lines separating the familiar categories of Saint-Domingue's population begin to blur. Rosalie was neither slave nor free. The widowed French colonist Michel Vincent was not really a "planter," though presumably no one referred to him as "rabble" either. Some might have called him a "petit blanc" (small white), but he was the thoroughly literate son of a notary, and he had a sheaf of documents attesting to his ownership of property and, once upon a time, slaves. Years earlier he had held a royal monopoly on the collection of fees for butchering in a district of Les Cayes, and had been married to a woman of wealth. That was all gone now, and Les Cayes was on the Republican side of the divide between the zone of British control and that of Rigaud's forces. The unofficially free Rosalie and the widowed Michel each found themselves in precarious circumstances, resource-poor inhabitants of an occupied territory within a colony in turmoil.

Over the course of 1797 and 1798, the British lost ground in the south to General Rigaud and were pressed from the north by General Toussaint Louverture, recognized by the French as the commander in chief of the colony. Equally important, the British were losing men to yellow fever, malaria, and typhus. By the end of 1798 Louverture had negotiated the departure of British troops from all of Saint-Domingue. With the British gone, the formal abolition of slavery by the French National Convention was now law throughout the colony. But occupation gave way to civil war, as Louverture and Rigaud vied for control of the southern peninsula.[68]

There may have been some refuge in the seaside town of Les Abricots, where by late 1798 Rosalie was pregnant again. On June 12, 1799, it was Michel Vincent who took the newborn to the parish church of Cap Dame-Marie to be baptized. He acknowledged his paternity and signed the baptismal register. The baby, named Élisabeth, was thus an *enfant naturel* (natural child) because her parents were unmarried, but she would not be listed as born of an "unknown father." Even without formal sanction, the union of Rosalie and Michel Vincent was beginning to look more like a family.[69]

The ceremony had both the form and the substance of a proper baptism. Rosalie herself was now identified with a baptismal name, Marie Françoise, presumably a reflection of a recent baptism of her own. The baby was called Élisabeth, but like many persons of African descent in Saint-Domingue she also had an informal nickname, in her case Dieudonné. There was a godfather—a man designated as Le Sieur Lavolaille, who worked as a ship's carpenter. The use of the courtesy title *sieur*—which was not extended to Michel Vincent—suggests that the curé considered the carpenter to be a man of some standing. There was a godmother, Marie Blanche, widow Aubert. She did not receive a courtesy title, but neither was she tagged with any color term—though in later years, and in another country, she would be described as a woman of color. Both godparents seem to have offered a degree of status or protection to the child—Lavolaille with his respectability, and the widow Aubert with her resources. The carpenter would soon disappear, perhaps back to France. But the widow would emerge several years later as the one to take custody of Élisabeth in another time of troubles.[70]

Once the 1799 civil war had been resolved by the victory of Toussaint Louverture, whose authority now encompassed the entire territory, life in the household of Michel and Rosalie seems to have settled into a modest routine. Michel held on to a house in the lower town in Jérémie, one estimated at an annual rental value of 300 livres. This put Michel far below his neighbor the *marchande* Marthe Guillaume, Rosalie's former owner, whose several rental properties in the upper town brought in thousands of livres each year. Indeed, Michel Vincent's property was estimated at the same value as that of Rosalie's still-earlier owner, the elderly Alexis Couba, and just one notch above that of the butcher Jean Baptiste Mongol. As of January 1802, when a census of the town was drawn up, the entire web of Rosalie's prior households was still in place in Jérémie, though it seems likely that she and Michel spent much of their time out on the little farm in Les Abricots.[71]

Michel occasionally went to a local notary to sell off another piece of his diminishing plot of land. In 1801 he sold land to purchasers listed as Tomtom and Olive, *cultivateurs* (agricultural laborers), almost certainly former slaves. Michel's household was apparently now composed of himself, Rosalie, their children, and perhaps an additional domestic servant, all living in close proximity to the newly freed *cultivateurs* of the adjoining Galbaud du Fort plantation. It would be anachronistic to say that Michel had in this way "crossed the color line," for during the conflict for military and political control of the south between generals Toussaint Louverture and André Rigaud neither party was seen as white, and whiteness itself was not, under the rule of Toussaint Louverture, a bastion of privilege. But Michel had certainly changed the structure of his alliances and his network of sociability from his days as the husband of a wealthy widow in Les Cayes.[72]

Rosalie's own role in the household is difficult to pin down. There had been no marriage, so she was not a lawful spouse. She seems to have received no pay, so she was not exactly an employee. But slavery was gone, so Michel had no legal authority to oblige her to remain with him.

The traditional term *ménagère* (housekeeper) may come close, with the twist that Rosalie perhaps helped Michel integrate himself into the changed social world of the south in revolution, rather than being simply his domestic servant and intimate partner.

In the town of Jérémie, Marthe Guillaume apparently continued to prosper. One of her houses on the Place d'Armes was occupied by Jean Baptiste Dommage, the Republican military commander of Jérémie who reported to Toussaint Louverture. Several of the notaries from before the revolution continued their work in town, though their records now carried the insignia "Liberté, Égalité, Fraternité," rather than the royalist formalities of the ancien régime or the British occupation. Buying, selling, and renting of property—but not of persons—continued apace.[73]

If Rosalie and Michel had achieved a certain stability after the birth of their children, things were thrown into turmoil once again by a test of wills between Toussaint Louverture and Napoléon Bonaparte. In July 1801 Louverture promulgated a constitution for the colony that reiterated the abolition of slavery and endorsed racial equality, while claiming more economic and political autonomy within the French empire than Bonaparte would tolerate. The first consul responded by sending out a military expedition aimed at humbling the black generals and imposing a régime friendlier to the interests of the wealthiest white colonists, many of whom were now in Paris and clamoring for restitution. Before Michel and Rosalie's daughter Élisabeth had reached the age of four, a French expeditionary force under General Charles Victoire Emmanuel Leclerc, Bonaparte's brother-in-law, arrived in Jérémie. The expeditionaries quickly defeated Toussaint Louverture's designated commander Jean Baptiste Dommage, Martha Guillaume's tenant.[74]

It was clear from Napoléon Bonaparte's behavior elsewhere that he intended to reestablish slavery in Saint-Domingue, though he did not acknowledge it. As a formal matter, the colony of Saint-Domingue was not mentioned in the 1802 French law that restored slavery in its pre-1789 form in the colonies returned to France by the Treaty of Amiens. To admit that reenslavement was a key goal of the expedition under General Leclerc would be to handicap the general in his relations with his own "colonial" troops, many of whom were men who had been freed by the earlier abolition. It would also have confirmed the worst inferences that could be made about French intentions, strengthening Louverture's appeal as he mobilized armed resistance.[75]

Leclerc's army succeeded in occupying the major port towns, and he was initially able to expand his control across large areas of the colony, while maneuvering to cajole, trap, or deport those who threatened his authority. Despite seizing and deporting Toussaint Louverture, however, Leclerc could not defeat local opposition to the assertion of metropolitan power. By early 1803 the expeditionary forces were faced with insurrection throughout the south, often led by officers who had served under André Rigaud. These resistance forces were able to rally veterans of various backgrounds, as well as thousands of *cultivateurs* intent on refusing reenslavement. On January 16 one group took the town of Tiburon, south of Les Abricots and Cap Dame-Marie, and was able to seize the ammunition stored there before being pushed back. By March various armed resistance groups were converging on Les Cayes, where they agreed to integrate their struggle into that of the Armée Indigène (the Native Army) under the authority of Jean-Jacques Dessalines.[76]

The conflagration in the south now drew the full attention of the French high command. General Leclerc himself had perished from yellow fever, and General Donatien Rochambeau took command of the French forces. He deployed 1,200 troops under General Sarrazin with orders to clear the overland route from Tiburon to Les Cayes, but Sarrazin's units were confronted by fierce resistance. French reinforcements arrived in Jérémie on April 10, but as these columns tried to advance from the town, they too were thwarted by resistance forces.[77]

As the fighting drew closer to the village of Les Abricots, Michel Vincent made plans to leave—alone—for France. His departure at this moment could have carried serious consequences for Rosalie. If the French expeditionary force were to triumph, slavery would in all likelihood be reimposed on those whom the revolution had freed. Indeed, General Rochambeau was already acting as though slavery was on its way back. But for Rosalie to flee to another colony in the Caribbean would be to run equally great risks. The decrees of the French Republican civil commissioners, the military achievements of Toussaint Louverture and André Rigaud, and the ratification of abolition by the French National Convention were all seen by other colonial powers as illegitimate acts of violence, not definitive transformations of law. It was not clear that any gain in status accomplished through the revolution would hold if one left the confines of the colony. But for a single mother of four children to remain stranded on what was rapidly becoming a battlefield was to risk death itself.[78]

With authority and sovereignty so thoroughly contested in Saint-Domingue, the very idea of status—slave or free—had broken loose from its usual moorings in law. But that did not mean that Michel and Rosalie ceased to attend to law. Perhaps to persuade Rosalie to remain with him until he departed, or perhaps out of a sense of obligation, Michel prepared a manumission paper that might serve her as proof of individual freedom once he left. Writing without the assistance of a notary, but drawing on the language that had been conventional in such documents prior to abolition, he declared that Marie Françoise, called Rosalie, "black woman of the Poulard nation," and her four children were his slaves, and that he hereby freed them all. He promised that if she chose to stay with him, he would henceforth pay her wages for her labor.[79]

The document, dated May 10, 1803, is in many ways a peculiar artifact. There is no evidence that Michel Vincent had ever "owned" Rosalie as a slave under French law, and he certainly did not own her in May of 1803, when everyone was still legally free under the acts of the French National Convention. But to confer freedom, he had first to claim ownership. He wrote that he wished that Rosalie and her four children might "enjoy the plenitude of liberty . . . like the other *affranchis* of this colony." The term *affranchi* (manumitted person) was in most respects archaic by 1803, having been widely replaced under the commissioners and under Louverture by the term *citoyen,* but it harked back to the language of the Code Noir, which had held that those who were *affranchis* by virtue of manumission should enjoy the same rights as those born free. The term had, moreover, been reintroduced when General Leclerc offered to declare *affranchis* those black men who joined his colonial troops. For Michel and Rosalie, the fictive ownership and the ancien régime formulas of this manumission paper were apparently intended to confer upon her and upon the children a freedom more durable, and more defensible, than the one declared by the French National Convention. A successor régime, or a neighboring polity, might be expected to defer to the written declaration of intent by a man describing himself as a slave owner, whatever the eventual policy on slavery itself.[80]

This improvised document also lacked the signature of a scribe—the official notaries had largely fled the neighborhood by May 1803, and some of them might have been reluctant to authenticate such a text in any event, since it offered official recognition to the legally extinct property right in a human being. To produce the text, Michel seems to have copied phrases from a standard notarized declaration of *affranchisse-*

ment, perhaps even the never-signed one that Rosalie had received from Marthe Guillaume in 1795, during the time of the British occupation. Without any official certification, this new declaration of freedom was effectively a text *sous seing privé,* that is, one drawn up by the parties but without authentication by a legal officer. It might only have full force if Michel Vincent were himself present to attest to its validity, or if it were subsequently registered in some way. But the circumstances were altogether desperate, and this was probably the best that they could do.[81]

The document also enumerated various elements of the freedom that Michel said he was granting to Rosalie—as if the simple fact of emancipation from slavery were not enough to assure that she could in fact come and go, attend to her own affairs, and receive wages if she continued to work for him. This explicitness reflected some of the reality of the situation. Already in 1793–1794 Civil Commissioners Sonthonax and Polverel had imposed various restrictions on movement that could oblige the newly freed to remain on plantations or to continue serving as domestics, and in 1800 Toussaint Louverture had developed his own rules constraining workers to labor. Then Leclerc had arrived, and the open secret of Napoléon Bonaparte's intentions began to spread. When Leclerc had promised freedom to those who enlisted to support him, it became perfectly clear that slavery was a renewed possibility for those who did not.

Rosalie and Michel were thus bringing this document into being in the shadow of contradictory laws and frightening wartime realities. To our own eyes, aware as we are of the eventual independence of Haiti and the long-term arc that would bend toward the destruction of slavery in the Americas, a "manumission" carried out a decade after the National Convention's declaration of abolition seems something of an absurdity, particularly since there was no evidence that Michel Vincent had ever "owned" Rosalie at all. But what the metropolitan government in France had authorized it could also invalidate, and those on the ground had no way of knowing how this fight would end. As the troops of the Armée Indigène acting in concert with Dessalines prepared the final assault against the French expeditionary forces in Jérémie in the spring of 1803, the fate of general abolition in Saint-Domingue was about to be decided. But to Michel and Rosalie, an individual manumission harking back to ancien régime practice could still seem more secure than the general emancipation declared by France under the National Convention, now undermined by Bonaparte's restoration of slavery elsewhere in the Antilles, combined with his reopening of the Atlantic slave trade. The days of the Republican civil commissioners and their decrees may have seemed a lifetime away. Moreover, if Rosalie found herself compelled to flee the island, a written declaration by a putative slave owner was likely to travel much better across jurisdictions than the decree of a contested revolutionary régime. In one of the last lines of the document, Michel declared optimistically that this private paper was to have the same force as if it had been drafted in front of a notary.[82]

Rosalie was not the only one to attempt to notarize her way to freedom in a moment of crisis. A few weeks later a carpenter, Charles Daromon, living in a parallel situation in the neighboring community of Grande Rivière, arranged for the crafting of a similar document. In this case a notary was available and provided him with language to formalize what he was seeking to accomplish, and what the woman who served him was hoping to secure. Charles Daromon, the notary wrote, had received from "the citizen Marie Jeanne, *négresse*" unspecified "important services in the time of the greatest alarms and terrors," and he wished to recompense her for her fidelity and good services by freeing her from any "commitment" *(engagement)* to him and to his heirs. The notary strained to avoid using the word "slavery," which was now a legal anachronism, but described Charles's actions using the terms *affranchir* and *manumission,* both of which were classic terms for grants of freedom from slavery. The text signaled an awareness of the shifting locus of authority, emphasizing that it would be up to Marie Jeanne herself to obtain any official certification of this notarized act. She was, moreover, to conform her own behavior to established laws and to "laws which may and will be established in the future for persons in the situation in which she finds herself and also for the reasons established above."[83]

When the notary from Grande Rivière entered the official copy of this text into his records, he did not title it an *affranchissement* or a manumission. He styled it simply a "Declaration establishing the civil status of Marie Jeanne." In effect, the question of civil status, *état civil,* had now become everybody's business. Going forward into an unknown zone of changing law—or perhaps interim lawlessness—relations that had contained a component of reciprocity, however asymmetrical, now needed to be formalized in a way that recognized this uncertainty. The carpenter might need to keep Marie Jeanne close to preserve his own health or life; Marie Jeanne might need to keep the carpenter at a legal distance to establish her own autonomy. Marie Jeanne, Rosalie, and many others negotiated in this moment of crisis with scribes, neighbors, and intimate partners, hoping to secure on paper something of what they had gained through revolution.[84]

Within a matter of weeks after Rosalie's own manumission document was signed, war reached the neighborhood of Les Abricots. A French prefect described the situation bluntly: "Le Nord est détruit; le Sud est en feu" (The North is destroyed; the South is on fire). Advances against the French by the forces of Dessalines were now compounded by a change in the larger geopolitics of empire. The Treaty of Amiens between the French and the British ruptured in mid-May, and hostilities resumed in Europe. The pattern of Atlantic shipping would be convulsed as war moved onto the seas. Michel had to abandon his plan of departing for France. Given British naval strength, moreover, it would now become nearly impossible for the French troops in Saint-Domingue to be resupplied from Europe.[85]

The combination of losses in the colony and the lack of supplies from France now left the expeditionary force on the defensive in the face of the troops advancing out of the stronghold of Les Cayes, moving north toward Jérémie. For many residents of communities in the war zone, sheer terror in the face of oncoming fire and fighting replaced any orderly process of choosing to stay or flee. Writing from later bitter exile in the United States, the merchant and planter Pierre Chazotte expressed fury at the French general Sarrazin for having failed to send troops to protect the population, and described himself as having supervised the evacuation in Les Abricots: "On my arrival . . . after a consultation with the inhabitants present, there being but two small vessels, it was agreed to embark first the white women and children, and then the colored ones." With no French reinforcements expected from Jérémie, he recalled, "we abandoned the small town of Abricots at the moment when a column of a thousand blacks rushed in it, with flaming torches in their hands. From the hills over it, on which stood the coffee estates of the heirs *Pauver,* we beheld the little town devoured by the fire, and all the valuables deposited in it by the neighboring planters reduced to ashes." British ships were prowling the Windward Passage, and refugees who had clambered aboard boats in Les Abricots could only hope that the captains would succeed in making a run for it to the nearest safe haven in Cuba. Those who could not find space on the boats trudged with their possessions along the dirt road toward Jérémie.[86]

From the point of view of General Dessalines and of subsequent Haitian historians, these battles in the south were part of an often pitiless war that arrayed their forces against those of a brutal colonial power. In early

July of 1803 the Armée Indigène marched in two columns toward the harbor of Jérémie, and the French troops, with a few unfortunate Polish allies, desperately stalled for time. Caught in the middle, many among the civilians who had taken refuge in Jérémie were already seeking to find passage on some kind of craft, hoping to reach either Santiago or Baracoa in Cuba. Soon the evacuation became general, with both troops and civilians scrambling to find a way out during a brief cease-fire. Formal capitulation by the French, making possible a relatively peaceful occupation of the city by the Armée Indigène, came in the first days of August.[87]

For the refugees who fled the colony during this spring and summer, the question of status and condition—and particularly whether a person once free could again be made a slave—would open wide as they made their way toward the Spanish colony of Cuba. Cuba had provided refuge in the past for exiles from the fighting in Saint-Domingue, but Spanish authorities there were now deeply suspicious of the revolutionary régimes of both France and its colony, and of the policies they had introduced.

Would the "natural liberty" regained by those who had been enslaved in the French colony survive a change of jurisdiction? If not, then for Marie Françoise, called Rosalie, freedom might soon be paper thin, secured only by the inked document penned by Michel Vincent.

3

Citizen Rosalie

The Spanish soldiers in the fort at the mouth of the bay of Santiago de Cuba were usually the first ones to sight the approaching sails. Napoléon Bonaparte's project to impose his will on the nearby colony of Saint-Domingue was collapsing, and many civilians left vulnerable as the final battles raged had boarded any available craft in the harbors to try to make their way to some safe haven. Cuba, a colony of Spain, seemed a potential place of refuge.[1]

For those on board, the crossing was a time of hunger, thirst, and fear. The fear that accompanied flight was magnified by the threat of capture by English ships in the Windward Passage. But in the midst of the tumult, those who fled also realized that they were leaving a jurisdiction that had abolished slavery, and approaching one that had not. As the Cuban shoreline loomed into view, so too did the possibility that a refugee might exercise—or be subjected to—the powers attaching to the ownership of one human being by another.

As of the moment of the departure of the boats from Jérémie and Les Abricots, no one could lawfully be held as a slave in Saint-Domingue, and those who had once been slaves had the right to be addressed as citizens. Workers in the countryside were designated *cultivateurs;* others were called *domestiques,* with all the ambiguity that term might carry. Former slave-holders, and some priests and notaries, might still apply the terms *nègres* and *négresses* to those in their employ. But no one was an *esclave.* General Leclerc had resumed the use of the term *affranchis*—freed persons—for men who would join his forces, which did imply a potential contrast with persons *not* freed. But Napoléon Bonaparte's scheme of reimposing slavery once his generals reconquered the colony was fast becoming moot, as the French expedition came to an ignominious end.[2]

Cuba was a stronghold of slavery, and its rulers had not the slightest desire to see a spirit of abolitionism land along with the refugees. This meant that for an arriving refugee of color to assert free status by virtue of the gains of Toussaint Louverture and the Haitian Revolution, or even the abolition decrees of the French National Convention, was to risk arrest, deportation, or sale into slavery. Into this space of enforced silence, those who had once been slaveholders could begin to slip a reassertion of property rights in men, women, and children they still viewed as rightfully their "slaves."

As the boats dropped anchor at the mouth of the harbor, the commandant at the fort sought guidance from Governor Sebastián Kindelán, in charge of the Santiago district. Kindelán initially made a blunt color distinction, refusing entry to the *negros* and *mulatos* whom he saw as posing an immediate potential danger to the colony. At the end of June 1803, he filed a report listing the boats that had arrived that month—from the French schooner the *Fidèle (Faithful)* to the more appropriately named *Último Recurso (Last Resort)*, both out of Jérémie. At the bottom of the page the scribe noted that of the passengers on these boats, the "persons of color, without distinction of sex or age," had been kept on board, while whites had disembarked.[3]

By July it was clear that Kindelán would have to cope with the arrival on his shores of hundreds—and soon thousands—of people. The captain of the schooner *La Nouvelle Société* (the *New Society*), Barthélémy Bouny, reported that the countryside around Jérémie was now in the hands of the "Negros rebeldes" (rebel Blacks) and that Jérémie itself was threatened with the same fate, causing families to flee and ask for hospitality from the residents of Santiago. One after another captain recounted the same story, with varying degrees of dramatic embellishment.[4]

The Spanish alliance with France, alongside the colonial government's interest in attracting "good white residents" to develop the island's agriculture, had quickly opened the door to refugees deemed white. The policy concerning refugees of color, however, emerged only over time, as the authorities tried to reconcile several competing considerations. In its eagerness to build up an enslaved labor force, the Spanish government had encouraged the trade in *bozales* (African-born captives) while prohibiting the landing of *ladino* slaves, those who had been for some time in one of the colonies, and who might transmit ideas of resistance from the French islands. The distinction between desirable "white residents" and presumably undesirable nonwhite ones, and the distinction between admissible captive *bozales* versus inadmissible *ladinos,* however, did not come close to fitting all those whose status had been reworked through more than a decade of revolution in Saint-Domingue. Authorities in Havana and Santiago would have to improvise a policy, and then inspectors would have to figure out how to apply it to the confusing array of people who were actually on those boats.[5]

The passenger lists of the boats represented a microcosm of the society from which the refugees had departed, and reflected the struggle to define the status of members of that society. On one schooner, for example, traveled a man named François Vallée, a master tailor from Les Abricots, accompanied by his wife, Marie Claire Cazenave, and their younger children.[6] Under French law, every passenger on this ship departing Saint-Domingue had been formally free for years, and no one could legally be bought, held, or sold as a slave in the Grand'Anse after the expulsion of the English in 1798. This did not stop François Vallée and his wife from declaring eight of the adults and children accompanying them to be their property. The passenger list prepared by the captain and delivered to the port authorities thus labeled these six women and their children *esclavos*—slaves. François claimed Josepha, *conga,* age fifty; Félicité, *conga,* age eighteen; Luisa, born in Jérémie, age twenty-two; and Ariete, also born in Jérémie. His wife Marie Claire claimed two black women and their children. By a sleight of hand, and with the cooperation of the captain and Spanish colonial officials, the couple had succeeded in reinstituting slavery en route. Their achievement would be repeated by hundreds of their fellow refugees.[7]

Although Kindelán's first impulse had been to refuse entry to refugees of color, the ship captains generally sought to disembark all those aboard, in order to return to Saint-Domingue and take on another boatload of passengers. One way or another, even the undesirables needed to be put on dry land. The governor soon came up with a temporary solution that would allow those designated as loyal domestics to come into town with their "owners," while those still seen as dangerous would be incarcerated offshore. In collaboration with a Catalan merchant (and slave trader) named Joseph Martí, the Spanish government placed a ship in the harbor, on which to imprison "all of the French Negroes, free as well as slave, over the age of 13." In the first instance these numbered 105, but more would continue to arrive. There was a vague plan to deport them all to Tierra Firme, the coast of Central and South America, though no one seemed to know quite how that would work.[8]

In the long run, Santiago de Cuba proved to be a receptive landing point for men and women who hoped to restore the social relations of slavery, and for their project of redefining others among the refugees as slaves. Authorized since 1789 as a port of arrival for the transatlantic trade in African captives, Santiago served an expanding hinterland of plantations producing sugar and coffee. Ships arrived regularly from the west coast of Africa, delivering bound laborers into the urban and rural economy. Men and women from Saint-Domingue who brought with them both financial resources and the habit of command could make a convincing case that they—and their "slaves"—offered something of value to a developing agricultural export sector. Those with more-modest resources, including men and women designated as *mulatos* or *mulatas libres,* could simply point out that they needed the labor of one or two slaves in order to avoid becoming a charge on the Cuban government.[9]

To avoid the seizure by the Cuban authorities of black men seen as potentially valuable "property," some captains tried landing groups of refugees on shore before reaching the fort at the mouth of the harbor. When caught, the captains would later claim that the problem had been lack of water and food, or that they had friends on shore at that point with whom they thought it wise to rendezvous. But it was hard not to be a bit suspicious when Captain François Berquier of the schooner *Almira,* arriving from Les Abricots with more than 100 people aboard, explained that he had almost run out of water two days before while near a port on the Cuban coast where he believed that there was water. He had therefore dropped off "el ciudadano Lepine" (citizen Lépine) and fifty-six male and female "slaves." He then proceeded to Santiago with the remaining passengers, who now more closely fit the criteria for entry into the city: white men, women, and children, some persons of color designated as free, and various servants.[10]

These crossings and landings became a sustained game of cat and mouse, played at sea but also played on paper, with the inscription of terms both ambiguous—*criados* (servants)—and blunt—*esclavos* (slaves). The approved procedure was for the ships to approach the fort at the entrance to the bay and wait outside the mouth of the harbor. After a first inspection, the captain would file a passenger list with the commandant at the fort, and then be rowed into the city to request permission to bring his boat into the harbor. A scribe was waiting to take the captain's deposition and to draw up the appropriately deferential petition to the governor. The captain communicated with the scribe, who in turn produced a formulaic request in Spanish, with added details depending on the circumstances. Captain Nicolas Dauvergne of the schooner *La Esperanza,* for example, claimed that he had been required by the lack of food and pursuit by an English frigate to land seven male *negros* and four female *negras* ten leagues away from the port of Santiago. He now asked that they all be returned to him. The men were to be put on a *pontón* (barge) in the harbor, the women to be turned over, accompanied by their children, to their "respective masters."[11]

When we see the word *esclavos* on passenger lists, then, we are often seeing a term produced in Spanish by a French captain to represent individuals not present—men, women, and children still back on the boat, and desperate to land, or on their way under guard from some remote beach. The word on paper does not tell us precisely how the tailor François Vallée had reconstituted his household as one with *esclavos,* nor does it tell us whether those thus labeled knew that in the eyes of Spanish administrators they had been transformed into slaves. Whatever exchange of labor for subsistence and protection Josepha and the others had envisioned when they left a war zone and boarded the boats with François Vallée and his wife, they now faced a permanent change in status. Their realization of the full consequences may have come if they suddenly found themselves offered for sale, or when they attempted to exercise one or another right denied to slaves—departure from the household, or autonomous employment on their own initiative.[12]

At the same time, Santiago de Cuba was a heterogeneous urban environment, one that could accord some chance of holding on to a freedom maintained or acquired in revolutionary Saint-Domingue. Numerous Cuban-born and African-born men and women in the city had over the years obtained their freedom, often by accumulating funds when their masters allowed them to hire out their own labor and keep a portion of the wages. There was also a long-standing militia composed of free men of color, which could provide a logical point of contact for their counterparts from Saint-Domingue. Marthe Guillaume's son, Pierre Aliés, implicated along with other militiamen in revolutionary action against the municipal administrators of Jérémie, had joined the refugees and now settled discreetly in Santiago as a free man of color, lodging with a Cuban militiaman. He may have been bereft of resources, but his freedom does not seem to have been challenged.[13]

If the household of François Vallée was swiftly reinscribed as being composed of masters and slaves, that of his neighbor and fellow colonist

Michel Vincent followed a different path. As of May 1803, Michel had intended to flee the Caribbean altogether, leaving behind his African-born companion Marie Françoise, called Rosalie, along with the children. But in the confusion attending the arrival in Les Abricots and Jérémie of the forces of the Armée Indigène under the orders of General Jean-Jacques Dessalines, Michel had never made it onto a boat for France. Instead, he tumbled into the chaotic evacuation to Cuba, and arrived safely in Santiago.

Michel and Rosalie's daughter Élisabeth Dieudonné was a four-year-old categorized as *mulâtresse*, hardly likely to appear dangerous to ship captains and port officials. She, along with her mother, also made it to Santiago, and they both avoided being characterized as slaves. The records concerning Rosalie's other children—sons Juste Théodore and Étienne Hilaire, and daughter Marie Louise *dite* Résinette—are, however, fragmentary and blurred. These three may have perished in the fighting or in the evacuation; they may have accompanied Rosalie to Cuba but left no archival trace; or they may have remained behind in Saint-Domingue on the eve of its transformation into the nation of Haiti.[14]

Each of the hundreds of refugee families arriving in Santiago faced the challenge of reconstituting a household and finding some means of support. Michel Vincent, who had once held a royal office back in Saint-Domingue, brought with him several bundles of papers documenting his prior ownership of land and slaves. But these provided little comfort and no revenue. In Santiago he was reduced to working as an artisan, a *mareschal* (farrier), attending to the health and hooves of horses. He and Rosalie found some kind of shelter in the crowded city, and a spot where they could raise pigs and chickens while he practiced his new trade.[15]

The fragile understandings by which Rosalie and her daughter Élisabeth could continue to be seen as free persons seemed to hold in Santiago. Rosalie still retained the manumission document that Michel had prepared for them before their departure from Les Abricots, the one that declared that he was her owner and that he freed her and her four children. This, however, was a private paper, without the signature of a notary. It was not clear how much force it would carry, beyond the continuing willingness of Michel to act in accordance with it. Both Michel and Rosalie thus had reason to try to certify the documents they were carrying: Michel to register formally his claims to ownership of property in Saint-Domingue and his testamentary intentions, for future reference; Rosalie to try to strengthen her claim to liberty.[16]

The French government was not permitted to have a consulate in Santiago, and Spanish authorities were adamant that no French emissary could exercise jurisdiction over the refugees. In keeping with reciprocal understandings concerning privateering, however, Captain General Ernouf of Guadeloupe had established in Santiago the "Agence des Prises de la Guadeloupe" in order to supervise the auctioning and taxing of the property of ships seized by French corsairs. These prize commissions had taken on increased importance with the resumption of war between England and France, as the flow of goods and money from Europe to the French islands was interrupted, and the proceeds from privateering became essential for colonial administrators. When refugees began to arrive in Santiago en masse, the officials of this agency improvised a temporary response to the problem of dealing with their affairs. The Agence did not legally have the authority to notarize documents or to undertake diplomatic tasks. But these bureaucrats were quite willing to copy or take deposit of relevant papers that the Saint-Domingue refugees might give them.[17]

On March 14, 1804, Michel submitted a last will and testament to the Agence in Santiago, where it was *homologué* (validated). Three days later Rosalie came to ask the same officials to register the freedom papers that had been drawn up in Les Abricots ten months earlier. With Michel apparently in ill health, Rosalie seems to have hoped that by causing this text to be written into a French register she could give it greater legal force, leveraging up the authoritativeness of her fragile proof of freedom. As Rosalie could see from events around her, other women arriving from Saint-Domingue, as free as she was under the decrees of the French Republic, were treated in Cuba as slaves and sold from one putative owner to another. Indeed, there was no guarantee that the revenue-hungry French officials would be immune from the same temptation. But she took the chance.[18]

The French scribe in Santiago began his task as if it were a slave owner who stood before him, and he wrote in the margin "Registration of freedom by." Then he stopped, inserted a period, and began again using a different preposition, clarifying that this text dealt with the registration of freedom *of* the woman named Marie Françoise, called Rosalie. At this crucial moment Rosalie was, in effect, authorized to attest to her own liberty. In a last gasp of revolutionary-era practice in France and Saint-Domingue, the official gave her the courtesy title *citoyenne* (citizen) as he transcribed her text into his records. He also provided her with a copy of the new document with his own signature added.[19]

In truth, however, these documents were still very fragile bulwarks against reenslavement. In the remaining French Caribbean colonies, slavery was back in place. There was little reason to think that Captain General Ernouf's men in Cuba would or could provide "citizen Rosalie" with any protection. The Agence des Prises was not a true consulate, and the courtesy title *citoyenne* carried very little content. If someone tried to take hold of Rosalie as a slave, she would have to hope that a Cuban court would accord her standing to appeal, and then treat as conclusive this unnotarized document, certified by a foreign bureaucrat who had no jurisdiction in Cuba.

For the moment, with the hybrid recopied text in hand, and the man who claimed to be her former master acknowledging her as free, Rosalie retained her liberty in Santiago. But within days, Michel Vincent was dead, and his designated executor was charged with carrying out the terms of the will. The executor was Michel Vincent's old friend the tailor François Vallée, the same man who had during the crossing from Saint-Domingue adroitly reimposed the constraints of slavery on those whom he claimed as his property.

Vallée's report as executor began by explaining what he had done with the movable goods belonging to the estate. He had sold "the little pigs" as well as the *serpes et haches* (billhooks and axes), yielding a modest seven and a half *gourdes,* equivalent to an equal number of Spanish piastres. He had given the red horse, along with the chickens and the *chaudières* (kettles), to citizen Rosalie, who was described as the *légataire particulière* (individual legatee) of Michel Vincent.[20]

Vallée then reported that he had been about to turn over to citizen Rosalie a *négresse* named "Marie Louise Désir," as called for in the will. This might possibly have referred to Rosalie's daughter Marie Louise *dite* Résinette. Such shifts in naming are common. But the daughter named Marie Louise was probably still quite young, and she had in the prior documents been designated as a *mulâtresse.* It seems more likely that the Marie Louise referred to by the executor was someone whom Michel had held as a domestic servant, and whom he treated as property subject to donation when he drew up his will. Because no copy of the will has survived, we cannot know whether Michel had in that text formally designated this Marie Louise as a slave. But he had apparently specified in his will that she should be transferred to the custody of Rosalie.[21]

Whatever Michel's intent, by the time of his death his estate was encumbered by debt. As executor, Vallée invoked these debts as the reason for his decision *not* to turn Marie Louise Désir over to Rosalie. The implication was that Marie Louise would instead either be held as a servant by the executor to cover his costs, or sold as a slave to pay off Michel Vincent's creditors.[22]

The summary disposal of Marie Louise reflects the pervasive general threat of enslavement and reenslavement that shadowed the community of refugees of color from Saint-Domingue. That process of enslavement, however, did not extend to everyone seen as being of African descent. A Spanish official, observing the situation, wrote a worried memorandum to the authorities in Spain, asking what to do with persons of color from French ports who looked to officials as though they ought to be slaves, but were behaving as if they were free. The refusal of these individuals to "recognize" slavery, he feared, created uncertainty about their "true" status and raised questions about their motives in coming to the slaveholding island of Cuba. At the end of July 1804, the Consejo Supremo de Indias in Spain finally addressed this concern about those they described as "individuals of color who, not recognizing slavery, arrive seeking asylum."[23]

The Consejo proposed that such persons be taken into custody and sent to the ports of Tierra Firme, on the Caribbean mainland of the Spanish Americas, to be supported there at the expense of the Royal Treasury until the king decided how best to deal with them. Officials in Spain instructed their counterparts in Cuba to figure out how large was the number of such persons, and what their intentions were. This then would make it possible to "rectify the judgment" on this matter of considerable "transcendence."[24]

Officials' preoccupation with people of color who refused to "recognize" slavery illustrated the continuing indeterminacy in status that was heightened by the changes in jurisdiction. Authorities in Cuba, like their counterparts in Jamaica and Louisiana, were very uneasy about the movement for general emancipation that had unfolded and triumphed in what was now independent Haiti, and they sought to exercise surveillance over the refugees from that conflict.[25] When significant numbers of men and women of color among the refugees asserted freedom, however, it was not easy for Cuban authorities to establish and enforce a contrary presumption. In some cases, a white colonist like Vallée might move quickly to assert ownership. But in others, there was no visible "master," no written title available to be produced by anyone, and a web of social solidarity behind the claim to free status.[26]

For colonial officials to assent to such assertions of freedom, however, was to create a risky precedent, for it implied that someone who might once have been a slave could declare himself or herself no longer bound by that institution. Deportation might diminish the risk, by removing such persons from contact with those of their neighbors who were again held as slaves, and with the African captives and their descendants who were being added to the workforce that sustained the rapidly expanding economy of Santiago. There is, however, very little evidence to suggest that the government actually carried out on a large scale the expensive solution of deportation to Tierra Firme.[27]

Some of the people of color whose deportation the Spanish authorities in Madrid had envisioned as imminent probably found their way into the city by coaxing or bribing officials into simply leaving them alone. Others who survived what must have been hellish conditions on the hulk anchored in the harbor may well have ended up being sold into slavery. The owner of that ship, Joseph Martí, was after all a slave trader, and he presumably knew how to slip men and women into the market for captives. A few may indeed have been deported, tossed into a world of itinerant witnesses and veterans of the Haitian Revolution whose presence the defenders of slavery throughout the region considered altogether unwelcome.[28]

Santiago de Cuba had long been a vortex of conflict as war in Europe was refracted into inter-imperial rivalry in the Caribbean. At the moment of the refugees' arrival, France and Spain had been allies. No alliance, however, was other than provisional, and in 1808 Napoléon Bonaparte's forces marched into Spain. Suddenly, the entire relationship between Spain and the French subjects residing in the Spanish colonies was cast into doubt. Across the Americas, as in the Iberian peninsula itself, Spanish officials had to decide whether to acquiesce to Napoléon's placing of his brother Joseph Bonaparte on the Spanish throne, or instead proclaim their loyalty to the deposed Ferdinand VII.

With the popular uprising in Madrid against the Napoleonic forces in May 1808, the geopolitical situation changed sharply, and Cuba found itself pulled into another set of great-power conflicts. As early as June 20, 1808, word of what was discreetly referred to as "modern news on certain occurrences in Spain" was filtering into the city of Santiago via newspapers from Jamaica. By the third day of August there was no doubt about it: Spain had declared war against the emperor of the French. England, from whom authorities in Cuba had long feared an invasion, was suddenly an ally.[29]

Local authorities had to turn on a dime. In a somewhat sheepish communication dated August 3, 1808, Governor Kindelán explained that shortly after the batteries of one town had fired on an English warship to protect a French privateer, authorities there had learned that Spain was now at peace with England. Reversing course, they seized the French privateer. Perhaps as a display of loyalty to the patriots in Spain, another such confiscated French ship would later be rebaptized with the name *Junta de Sevilla,* in honor of the recently convened assembly back in the Iberian peninsula.[30]

Once the news of war against France, and of Spain's alliance with England, had arrived in Santiago, the presence of more than 10,000 French nationals in the heart of Cuba's second city posed a challenge both to propriety and to security. In the face of relentless calls for expulsion led by the fiercely anti-French archbishop of Santiago, Governor Kindelán struggled to manage the crisis. The governor's life was not made easier by the stunts thought up by some of the residents, including one "ignorante Catalan" who had a portrait of Napoléon painted, hung it boldly over his posterior, and strolled slowly (and presumably provocatively) through the French neighborhood of Santiago. Governor Kindelán considered this an act of imprudence and subversion, but he decided to delete his description of it from the final draft of his report. Reflective of the popular spirit with which he had to cope, the story perhaps revealed a bit too much of the indiscipline that was surging in a city that was supposed to be under his control.[31]

The Spanish colonial government had initially offered the refugees in Cuba the possibility of swearing allegiance to the Spanish crown, and local authorities had been pleased with the rapid development of coffee plantations organized by émigré planters. In the months that followed the receipt of the news of war with France, however, the combination of patriotism and opportunism swelled demonstrations of anti-French sentiment. In April 1809, Spanish colonial authorities issued an order requiring the French to leave the island. The refugees needed rapidly to liquidate any landed property they had acquired and to find money for passage out of Cuba. Any claim of property in persons was now even more valuable, for such property could either be sold in a hurry, or taken on board ship and transported to some new land where the state would continue to recognize the rights of ownership in human beings.[32]

The most attractive destination was the nearby territory of Louisiana, with its substantial French-speaking population and expanding commitment to slavery. There was one catch, however. The United States Congress had declared the foreign slave trade to be illegal, and no captain could land enslaved persons in a U.S. port if they came from outside the United States, at risk of confiscation of his ship. Both the departing French, and the U.S. consul in Santiago, seem nonetheless to have expected that exceptions would be made.[33]

Once again, passenger lists were compiled with an eye to shaping future resolutions of ambiguities in status. The slippery term *criado,* like the French term *domestique,* could mean either servant or slave, and would serve to cover a multitude of relationships. The laconic list of ships departing from the port of Santiago in late spring of 1809 gives some sense of the process. The ships heading for New Orleans were the most conspicuous, and the scribe counted up their passengers. The schooner *Louisa,* Captain Daniel MacDonald, for example, headed for New Orleans carrying twenty-six men, twenty-eight women, six children, and seventy *criados.*[34]

When the *Louisa* reached Fort Plaquemine, at a bend in the Mississippi River en route from the Gulf to New Orleans, the territorial governor of Louisiana sent a message to the commanding officer of the fort. He instructed the commander to allow the ship to pass, but "to inform the Captain, that the Law does not permit the landing of the Negro's." Those among the refugees who wished to be admitted as slave owners, and who hoped that the *criados* accompanying them would be acknowledged as slaves, nonetheless anticipated—correctly—that there would be room for negotiation on this point.[35]

Rosalie herself did not board a ship destined for Louisiana. She was an African woman, and the risk of reenslavement in the slaveholding metropolis on the Mississippi would have been very great. Even if U.S. officials applied to the new wave of refugees the federal law that prohibited the importation into Louisiana of persons deemed to be slaves, that did not mean that such persons would be permitted to disembark as free. They might instead find themselves both rightless and stateless, ordered away from the shore on which they sought to land.

But what about Rosalie's daughter Élisabeth, now ten years old, freeborn and designated a *mulâtresse?* Élisabeth's godmother, the widow Aubert, had also emigrated from Les Abricots to Santiago de Cuba, along with a Belgian carpenter named Lambert Détry. Détry had bought some land in Santiago, and the widow had acquired a slave or two. The resulting household could presumably offer greater security than Rosalie's after the death of Michel. Placing the young Élisabeth with her godmother could carry grave risks, however. The lines between the roles of dependent, servant, and slave were blurred and malleable. Once incorporated into a household as a *criada,* a young woman could find herself being sold as an *esclava.* The widow Aubert, however, claimed to consider Élisabeth Dieudonné to be like a daughter to her. Before leaving for Louisiana, the widow took custody of Élisabeth, who then accompanied her in the crossing.[36]

For Rosalie herself, still under orders to leave Cuba, one possibility was to go to Haiti. In January of 1809 President Pétion, writing from Port-au-Prince, asked the governor of Santiago for permission to send a ship under a flag of peace (a *bâtiment parlementaire*) to Santiago to enable people of color to return from Cuba to Haiti. The Spanish colonial authorities, long fearful of the intentions of Haitian leaders, would not, however, allow the ship to enter the port. Governor Kindelán sent an exceptionally undiplomatic—that is to say, rude—message to President Pétion, informing him that he could not grant such a request. Kindelán prohibited anyone from the ship from setting foot on land.[37]

By May 1809, however, private initiative was achieving some of what diplomacy could not. Shortly after the departures of the larger ships for New Orleans, port officials in Santiago recorded some small boats headed for Haiti: the *güairo* called *Los Tres Hermanos,* for example, left on May 24 for Les Cayes. Its passenger list was distinctive: five men, eleven women, one child, but no *criados.* No one was foolish enough to try openly to transport someone else to Haiti as a slave, even under the euphemism of *criado.* Haiti was the destination of choice for a small subset of the refugees, those seeking to live as citizens in a nation without slavery. Eventually Rosalie would be among them.[38]

There are several paths by which Rosalie may have made her way there. On May 29, 1809, a small American schooner called the *Ana Bella,* under Captain D. Dixon, set sail from Santiago for Rosalie's former home district of Jérémie. Dixon took on just twenty-two passengers: three men, eleven women, eight children. No *criados.* A week later another American captain, in the schooner *Favorite,* made the same journey. And in July two English captains took additional small groups of passengers to Jérémie. These small boats departing for the Grand'Anse probably provided the best available option for Rosalie. If indeed any of her children had stayed behind in Haiti in 1803, she may have had some hope that she might see them again if she returned.[39]

This scenario, however, should be set against another possible one. The first documentary trace from which we can confirm Rosalie's presence in independent Haiti does not come until 1822. There were only a few spots on those boats leaving for Jérémie in 1809, and it may be that she did not in fact take one. Some refugees in her situation dodged the expulsion order and moved quietly out of sight into the poor neighborhoods of the city of Santiago, blending in with other African-born women, both slave and free. Rosalie presumably still had chickens, the kettles, and the red horse that she had inherited from Michel Vincent, and she could well have taken in laundry or worked as a food vendor or a domestic, living in a new web of friends and neighbors.

There was an ongoing community of African-descended women from Saint-Domingue who remained in Santiago. In 1817 the governor of the region sent an alarmed message to his superior in Havana, reporting on a new security risk that he had uncovered. A group of *negras esclavas francesas* (French enslaved black women) had formed a mutual-aid society, gathering "stipulated contributions" from each member in order to get together for dances, and to obtain the liberty of any of their number who was ill-treated by a master. The governor considered initiatives of this kind to be exceptionally dangerous. He rushed to investigate.[40]

Although there is something faintly risible about the governor's panic at the news of these dances, his alarm was in one sense justified. By agreeing to buy the freedom of any one of their number who was physically mistreated, the women in this mutual-aid association had redefined what it meant to be a slave. For them, the master's power over their labor might be acknowledged, but his power stopped at the boundaries of their bodies. These women took it upon themselves to define mistreatment, and let it be known that they would put together the funds to try to make sure that a master would lose all authority over any slave thus abused. Like the unnamed Saint-Domingue refugees whose status had puzzled authorities in 1804, these women did not "recognize slavery" in so far as it extended to the exercise of harsh physical force against them.

The society was apparently led by two women known to the members as *grandes madres* (great mothers) and by another known as *reina* (queen). These leaders distinguished themselves by wearing braided green bands; the members each wore an armband of the same color. The group had recently assembled for a meal together in the house of a white Frenchman who was the master of one of them. Present at that gathering were said to be ten free black men whom the governor described as their *concubinarios* (an awkward term implying long-term intimacy). The governor explained the presence of the men with a note that there had been at the time a ship from the Africa trade in the bay, with various sailors aboard. This seems to have been the schooner *Caridad,* whose captain was Juan Morales, and six of whose sailors were ordered to be arrested as soon as the ship returned to Santiago.[41]

The governor of Santiago thought it urgent to "frighten and repress these slave women" in order that their actions not inspire disturbance among the slaves in the city, whom he otherwise believed to be in a tranquil and subordinated condition. The governor of the island was even more emphatic, explaining in a letter to the Real Audiencia in Madrid the necessity of a punishment that would, without damaging the interests of the slaves' owners, be "humiliating" to the women. He aimed to persuade anyone who might be tempted that such associations were "detestable." While such gatherings might seem insignificant, he wrote, they in fact "always have the inclination or carry with them incendiary actions or effects."[42]

If Rosalie remained in Santiago for a few years, she may have known these women, who helped to enforce a self-declared rule that sought to limit the power of masters over those they claimed as slaves. The episode in any event uncovered a continuing presence of black women perceived as French, along with their French "owners," despite the expulsion order. Equally important, it linked some of the boldest of these women to free black sailors serving on ships making the journey to West Africa. A web of connections and communication across the Gulf to Louisiana, across the Windward Passage to Haiti, and even across the Atlantic to Africa remained in place, even if families themselves had been torn apart.[43]

The written traces left in Santiago by Rosalie confirm that she had learned the role of documents in a slaveholding society. She had seen that power and paper could turn a free woman into a "person with a price," as they had given sovereignty over her to a succession of owners in the town of Jérémie in Saint-Domingue. In Santiago she demonstrated that adroit maneuvering within that world of power and paper could occasionally turn such a "person with a price" back into a person of standing. By having a French official re-transcribe the private manumission paper signed by Michel Vincent, Rosalie transformed it into a semi-authoritative identity card, similar to the one that Marthe Guillaume had proffered to attest to her own freedom back in Jérémie. For a fleeting moment the recopied text verified her standing as "citizen Rosalie," confirming the recognition extended to former slaves by the French National Convention a decade earlier. And crucially, it created a deterrent against anyone who might try to reenslave her.

Rosalie had also seen the costs and potential benefit of shifting jurisdictions, and the strategic value and risks of cross-racial and cross-class alliances. By seeking out French authorities in Spanish Cuba, she had evaded the awkward questions that might be posed by a Spanish official, and held on as long as possible to the title *citoyenne*. But by 1809 to be French was to be a candidate for deportation from Cuba. If she boarded a ship in Santiago in 1809, heading for Jérémie, identification as a French refugee from Saint-Domingue would enable her to depart under a general passport given to captains to deport the "foreigners" whom the governor had ordered expelled. If instead she found some way to remain in Santiago, she may well have dropped the name Rosalie and begun to call herself Rosalia, moving into a community of other Africans who had survived both the Middle Passage and slavery to become part of the city's population of *libertos* and *libertas*.[44]

Rosalie's daughter Élisabeth was still too young to maneuver on her own in the world of paper. But in coming into the custody of her godmother and her godmother's partner she could see the indispensability of being integrated into a household, even as a dependent. The new crossing from Santiago to New Orleans, however, carried many of the same risks as the prior crossing from Saint-Domingue six years earlier. There was no guarantee of a safe landing, and for men, women, and children of African descent, there was again the prospect of being declared to be persons who could be held as property. This next shift of jurisdictions would reopen questions of status and standing, as it brought Élisabeth and her fellow passengers to the wharves of a slaveholding city, capital of the newly acquired Territory of Orleans, in the United States of America.

4

Crossing the Gulf

Once again, it was soldiers on guard at a coastal fort who first realized that an entire flotilla of ships filled with refugees was approaching. This time the fort was at La Balise near the mouth of the Mississippi River, and the ships had come from the ports of Santiago and Baracoa. By mid-May 1809, territorial governor William C. C. Claiborne in New Orleans acknowledged that he faced the arrival of hundreds and perhaps thousands of Saint-Domingue refugees, displaced from their original haven in Cuba. The prospect of accommodating these French migrants posed immediate legal, logistical, and political problems for the harried Claiborne. He initially tried to pass part of the responsibility on to the French consul in New Orleans, instructing him to contact the French ambassador in Washington, who would "doubtless furnish means" for the support of the refugees. This was, of course, an altogether overoptimistic assumption.[1]

It was clear that the French refugees included not only white colonists, but people designated black or of color, some acknowledged as free, but others claimed as slaves by individuals presenting themselves as their owners. Already in 1807 the first legislature of the Territory of Orleans, alarmed by the revolution that had taken place in Saint-Domingue, had envisioned that "serious inconveniences might arise, if measures were not taken to prevent the introduction of people of color from Hispaniola, and from the French American islands." The legislature had therefore banned the settlement in Louisiana of all such newly arriving men of color, requiring that they post bond and leave the territory. Free women of color and children were exempted, on the grounds that they "shall be supposed to have left the island above named, to fly from the horrors committed during its insurrection." In the next session, the legislature extended the ban to all arriving men of color of whatever origin, and provided explicitly for the enslavement of such individuals if they did not depart forthwith. The problem of perceived political risk from the free was soon compounded by the inadmissibility of the enslaved. As of January 1, 1808, federal law no longer permitted anyone to bring from outside the United States "any negro, mulatto, or person of colour, with intent to hold, sell, or dispose of such negro, mulatto, or person of colour, as a slave, or to be held to service or labour." The complex constitutional compromise on the international trade in captives had been superseded by a direct ban on the importation of bound laborers.[2]

Governor Claiborne's early orders to the naval authorities along the river suggest something of his anxiety in regard to this law. Informed that the schooner *Nuestra Señora del Carmen* had reached the fort at Plaquemine, he wrote to the commander:

> You will permit the Schooner ... with the negro's on board to pass the Fort; But you will inform the Captain that no slave must (until further orders) be landed on penalty of a forfeiture of the Vessel, and a heavy pecuniary fine.
>
> You will bring to at the Fort every Vessel with slaves on board coming from a foreign Port, and report the same to the Governor of the Territory; The propriety of permitting a Vessel with slaves to ascend, must depend upon the circumstances of each particular case.[3]

Governor Claiborne was trying to find some solution that would accommodate the recently enacted federal law as well as the long-standing preoccupation in Louisiana about "French Negroes" as dangerous carriers of revolutionary ideas. Although Claiborne did not conceptualize the problem as one of determining the status of individuals, such determinations were implicit in the way that he referred interchangeably to "negros" and to "slaves." Among the passengers on these ships were many black men and women who had been legally free at the moment that they left Saint-Domingue but then were claimed as slaves when they arrived in Cuba. Added to their number were African and Creole men, women, and children purchased from slave traders or Cuban owners in Santiago. Still others of the refugees had been free in Saint-Domingue and had maintained their freedom in Cuba but were now at risk of being categorized as slaves. The possibility of such enslavement made freedom itself quite fragile.

Because the refugees who claimed to be slave owners insisted that they depended on the labor of those they designated as slaves, Claiborne's preoccupation with providing a subsistence for the refugees he saw as free became entangled with the question of whether to admit others of the refugees as slaves. Upon reflection, Claiborne was evidently tempted to allow some among the migrants to make use of "the few faithful domesticks who had accompanied them in their misfortunes." For Louisiana's resident slaveholders, moreover, the emergency provided a nice rationale for trying to get around the recent ban on bringing new bound laborers into the country. On May 15, Governor Claiborne forwarded to the secretary of state a petition from "a number of a very respectable and humane citizens" concerning the ban on the landing of slaves. On May 20, he spoke directly with "white Passengers" from one of the ships from Santiago. On June 28, 1809, Congress authorized the president to suspend the penalties that would otherwise have been applied to captains who brought into the United States slaves accompanying free Saint-Domingue refugees.[4]

It was not yet clear whether the president would in fact decree such a suspension, but on July 8 Governor Claiborne sent the secretary of state a list of the boats that had thus far arrived in New Orleans from Cuba, with the implication that all their passengers had now disembarked. He reported that "the slaves have been all delivered to their Masters they giving bond with security to have them forthcoming when demanded." The ambiguous term *criado*, or servant, on the manifests of many of the outgoing ships (translated as *domestiques* in the French version) had now been rendered quite bluntly as "slave," thus imposing a presumption of slave status on thousands of refugees.[5]

The mayor of New Orleans reported, with an air of precision, that the arriving passengers included 2,731 whites, 3,102 free people of color, and 3,226 slaves. On the wharves of New Orleans, some process of attribution of status had taken place as the refugees disembarked. Words written on a ship's manifest, or tallies handed over by a captain, became numbers to convey to the governor. And once designated explicitly or implicitly as a slave, a person who had previously lived as free would require substantial resources and powerful allies in order to contest that label. However confusing the initial circumstances, if one refugee succeeded in exercising the powers attaching to the right of ownership over another, that action gave apparent solidity to the claim of ownership itself.[6]

How were the mayor and his scribes to know into which category of color and status an individual should be placed? Marie Blanche Peillon, widow Aubert, had carried no color label in the sacramental records of Cap Dame-Marie in Saint-Domingue in 1799, when she stood as godmother to Rosalie's daughter Élisabeth Dieudonné. During the Saint-Domingue revolution the labels *femme de couleur* and *homme de couleur* had been legally extinguished—though never fully abandoned in practice—as all free persons became citizens. Those labels now reemerged in the written record, once again made to seem natural and self-evident. In New Orleans, the widow Aubert was to be designated a free woman of color.[7]

Rosalie herself had avoided boarding one of the ships out of Santiago headed for Louisiana, but would instead return to Haiti. She thus did not confront the presumption of slave status that might well have attached to her, as an African-born woman, had she landed on the wharf in New Orleans. If she wished news of her daughter, however, she would henceforth need to count on the relay of information by sailors, travelers, and traders who carried goods between the various ports of the Caribbean and the Gulf of Mexico. Despite the refusal of the United States to recognize Haiti as an independent nation, boats from New Orleans did make the passage to what was often called "the Island of Santo Domingo." Voyages to Havana and Santiago de Cuba were even more frequent. Rosalie had relinquished custody of the ten-year-old Élisabeth, but she would not necessarily thereby lose contact.

Élisabeth's own status as free was the result of events in the 1790s in Saint-Domingue, specifically the emancipation of her mother Rosalie under the acts of the French National Convention and their enforcement by Toussaint Louverture and André Rigaud. At the time of Élisabeth's baptism, she was doubly freeborn, first because of her mother's inscription as a *négresse libre,* and second because of the abolition of slavery in Saint-Domingue. Could that status be reversed from free to slave in New Orleans? Would she need—and did she have—any proof of free birth that would hold up in a Louisiana court?

Both legally and socially, the question of color and status was a matter of rights, standing, and even survival. There were few clear rules, and ascriptions could be disputed and contested. We might therefore best hold the mayor's tally at arm's length, and describe the arriving immigrants instead as 2,731 people who in the context of New Orleans in 1809 could convincingly portray themselves as whites; 3,102 people who were deemed by observers to be "of color" but who managed to persuade those around them that they were free; and 3,226 individuals who were deemed by observers to be of African ancestry and in whom one or another arriving passenger—or someone else—could make a persuasive claim to a property interest, hence "slaves."

In effect, Governor Claiborne and the ship captains had turned crisis into opportunity, pulling off a legal sleight-of-hand and a large-scale circumvention of the congressional ban on the foreign slave trade. The population of the city had been nearly doubled by the settlement of the refugees. And more than 3,000 of the newly arrived men, women, and children, written back into slavery on the wharves of New Orleans, would henceforth perform unremunerated labor for various of the free residents of the territory and later state of Louisiana.

The footnote making the governor's improvisation permanent came in September, when President Madison's secretary of state Robert Smith instructed the district attorney Philip Grymes to drop all charges against the ship captains who had brought the French refugees from Cuba, since the president had decided that in all such cases "where vessels have been libelled for a violation of the Law prohibiting the Importation of slaves" the ships were to be released as soon as the captains paid the court costs. This was followed in March of 1810 by an act from Louisiana's Legislative Council lifting the bonds initially posted by those refugees who had entered the city claiming to hold others as slaves. These "owners" could now "possess, sell, and dispose of" those they had identified as slaves on arrival. Nothing in the federal law banning the importation of slaves actually conferred freedom on victims of those who had contravened it. Even less would it reverse the enslavement of passengers brought by the now-pardoned captains of the boats from Santiago.[8]

Not only had slave status been attributed to men, women, and children who had lived as free in Saint-Domingue, but even designation as free at the moment of disembarkation was insecure in an environment of large-scale reenslavement. The woman named Adélaïde Métayer, for example, arrived in New Orleans with her three children on one of the boats coming from the Cuban town of Baracoa. Free under French law after 1794, she had also paid money to her former master back in Cap-Français, Saint-Domingue, in 1801 in order to be released from any remaining labor obligations that she might owe him. She had obtained from him a signed receipt acknowledging her freedom. In Baracoa she had comported herself as a free woman and baptized both of her newborn daughters as free. Indeed, her neighbors agreed that she had been "at her ease" and enjoying her liberty at the time of her departure from Cuba. No one apparently disputed this freedom when she disembarked in New Orleans, and she was counted a "free woman of color."[9]

Once settled in the city, however, Adélaïde Métayer crossed paths with a tailor named Louis Noret, who had been the business partner of her former owner back in Saint-Domingue, Charles Métayer. Asserting that he was still owed a debt by the brother of Charles Métayer, Noret was able to persuade a court in New Orleans to authorize the sheriff to seize Adélaïde Métayer and her children and offer them for sale at auction, in order to pay the debt Noret claimed he was owed. Although Adélaïde was initially able to obtain a suspension of her own sale and that of her daughters, the court allowed the auction of her son to go forward, on the grounds that his name did not appear on the receipt signed by Charles Métayer back in Cap-Français nine years earlier. The proceeds of the sale of the boy turned out to be sufficient to cover the total debt claimed by Noret, and Adélaïde Métayer returned home, though without any definitive ruling on her status. A few years later the tailor Noret tried to repeat his success in extracting revenue by arranging to obtain a power of attorney from the son of Charles Métayer, and again claiming a property right in Adélaïde Métayer. It took seven legal proceedings before Adélaïde Métayer finally established her freedom to the satisfaction of the Louisiana courts.[10]

In territorial New Orleans and early statehood Louisiana, it seemed easy to assert ownership of another human being, and—if one were of African descent—difficult to prove ownership of oneself. The 1807 territorial statute on migrants from Hispaniola had provided a few hints as to how the distinction between slave and free might be made:

> Every man and woman of color from Hispaniola . . . pretending to be free, shall prove his or her said freedom, before the mayor of the city, or any justice of the peace, by credible testimonies, and shall take a certificate of such justification, attested by the said mayor or justice of the peace, and if such justification cannot be made, the said man or woman of color shall be considered as a fugitive slave, and employed at the public works, until they shall prove their freedom, or be claimed by their owner by virtue of good titles.[11]

The burden of proof fell on the individual claiming to be free; there was no presumption that abolition in Saint-Domingue in 1793–1794 had effected a general transformation in status. One could even be deemed a "fugitive slave" in the absence of any putative master. The mass disembarkations in 1809, moreover, left little time or space for formal inquiries, particularly if a given "slave" was promptly sold to a new owner.

The question of status became as much a matter of circumstance as of law. Most of the refugees had originally fled Saint-Domingue in groups and had been recorded by notaries and colonial officials in Cuba under myriad categories—slaves, servants *(criados),* blacks, whites, mulattos, etc. They had then set up households in Santiago, and it was with these kin and neighbors that they had re-embarked for Louisiana. Each person thus arrived in New Orleans enmeshed in relations of kinship and clientage—and in some cases alleged ownership—that would define that person's initial social world in Louisiana. As refugees settled in the city, they reworked those ties once again, in the shadow not only of their own hurried departures, but also of Louisiana's status as a territory of the United States.

For the young Élisabeth Dieudonné, daughter of Rosalie and Michel Vincent, security was for the moment guaranteed by the widow Aubert, who lived in a consensual union with the Belgian carpenter named Jean Lambert Détry. Once they arrived together in New Orleans, the stigma of the label "of color" was imposed on both Élisabeth and her godmother, but their freedom was apparently not challenged. Households composed of a white man, a woman of color, and a child were hardly unfamiliar in New Orleans and would now become even more numerous. Lambert Détry, moreover, seems to have been quite willing to serve as informal protector to his companion's godchild.

The widow and the carpenter had evidently brought with them from Cuba both ready money and persons they claimed as slaves, making it relatively easy to set themselves up in the city. The New Orleans bon vivant and entrepreneur Bernard Marigny was in the midst of subdividing his land to create the residential neighborhood called Faubourg Marigny and was eager to sell land on credit to the arriving immigrants. Détry bought two lots on the Rue Moreau (now Chartres)—no money down, fifteen years to pay. He then set up shop and acquired slave sawyers to assist him in his work. By the time of the 1810 census, Lambert Détry appeared as head of a household described as composed of one white man (Détry), three "other free people" (the widow, her goddaughter Élisabeth, and perhaps another child), and thirteen slaves. Between persons they succeeded in having classified as property at the time of their arrival, and those they acquired in the city, the pair had moved thoroughly into the ranks of slaveholders.[12]

The widow Aubert herself, now fifty years old, began to buy and sell land and slaves in her own name as well. She was not—and under Louisiana law she could not be—legally married to Détry, so she needed no approval from a husband to operate as a free agent. And operate she did. Over the next forty years she established herself as a cranky and formidable resident of Faubourg Marigny, making money, wrangling with her neighbors, and serving as surrogate mother to Élisabeth.[13]

The alliance between Lambert Détry and the widow Aubert was a cross-racial conjugal union, but it had nothing whatsoever to do with the (much mythologized) custom later referred to as *plaçage,* in which the mothers of young women of color are said to have "placed" their daughters with white men as a means of upward mobility or security. Détry and the widow Aubert were instead two aging survivors with substantial hardships behind them, and with an evident willingness to impose hardships on others, using the ownership of persons as a mode of upward mobility. Détry and the widow Aubert alike earned revenue through the unremunerated labor of the men and women they held as slaves. Their combined household also included young people of various statuses, including Élisabeth Dieudonné. There was soon at least one other young woman from Saint-Domingue, purchased by the widow as a slave in 1813 and called by the nickname Trois-Sous, or Threepenny.[14]

When Détry died in 1821, it was in a house that he owned and the widow Aubert occupied. In a "mystic testament"—that is, one placed under seal with a notary—he left the bulk of his property to two young women of color who were the daughters of his friend and executor François Xavier Freyd. He gave the widow Aubert the use and control of most of this property, however, for as long as she might live. He specified that two of his slaves were to be freed as soon as they attained "the age required by the law for manumission."[15]

Détry also designated a bequest of $500 to Élisabeth Dieudonné, who seems to have been known within the household by the name of Marie, the first name of both her mother (Marie Françoise, *dite* Rosalie) and her godmother (Marie Blanche Peillon, widow Aubert). Détry explained the bequest by referring to her as his own goddaughter, though this was not technically accurate. Perhaps long years of living with the widow Aubert had made him Élisabeth's godfather de facto.[16] Détry made no mention in his will of potential heirs-at-law who might be back in Belgium, but after his death a group of those kin hired a lawyer and tried to invalidate the will, invoking Détry's open "concubinage" with the widow Aubert. They quickly settled, taking a share of the proceeds.[17]

With the promise of the bequest from Détry in hand, Élisabeth (or "Marie") Dieudonné, now twenty-three years old, became engaged to marry a young man named Jacques Tinchant, the son of a Saint-Domingue émigrée woman of color. At the moment when the marriage contract was drawn up in 1822, it was the widow Aubert who appeared with them at the notary's office, claiming that she had been like a mother to the prospective bride since she was a child, and asserting that Élisabeth's actual mother was currently living not in New Orleans but in what the widow still referred to as "Saint-Domingue." The absent presence of the woman the widow called Rosalie Vincent was thus acknowledged, but subordinated to the wishes of the godmother whose familiarity with matters of property was reflected in the details of the contract.[18]

Élisabeth's partner in marriage was a young man whose birthplace was variously given as Baltimore, Maryland, or Halifax, Amérique Septentrionale (presumably Nova Scotia). Jacques Tinchant was designated a "natural child"—that is, born to parents who were not married—and was categorized as a free person of color. His father was apparently a French colonist from Saint-Domingue who had emigrated to Baltimore, taking with him at least one man whom he tried to claim as his slave. A rather plaintive advertisement in the Baltimore papers, signed by one Joseph Tinchant, appeals for the return of "my negro fellow" named Jack Zacharie, said to have spent "some time in Hispaniola, and who has for several years been employed as cook on board of vessels from this port." Joseph Tinchant warned ship captains not to hire the man. As Jack Zacharie's escape to sea suggests, New Orleans was not the only place where freedom once gained in Saint-Domingue could be reasserted. Joseph Tinchant himself left few traces in the records of Baltimore and seems to have played little or no role in his son's life in New Orleans, aside from the conferral of a surname.[19]

Jacques Tinchant's mother, by contrast, comes through the notarial records in New Orleans loud and clear. Her baptismal name was Marie Françoise, but she was often called Suzette. Her surname was any of a number of variants of Bayot, Bayole, Bailhot, or Bayotte.[20] A refugee from Saint-Domingue, she may have arrived in the United States (probably Baltimore) in the 1790s, accompanied by the senior Tinchant, and perhaps by a sister. At some point after giving birth to the child who would be called Jacques Tinchant, she made her way to New Orleans, where the notarial records designated her a free woman of color.[21]

Marie Françoise Bayot's itinerary illustrates the recurrent pattern by which refugees with modest resources established themselves by constituting new households. An unaccompanied woman with a baby to care for, Bayot joined forces in New Orleans with Louis Duhart, a Freemason from near Fort-Dauphin in Saint-Domingue who—like many other impecunious but educated white émigrés—was offering his services as a schoolteacher. Duhart's family on his father's side came from the southwest of France, in particular the region of the Béarn near the Pyrenees and the

Basque district of Saint-Jean-de-Luz. The Duhart ancestors included a long line of sailors and sea captains who shipped out of the port of Nantes.[22]

Louis Duhart and Marie Françoise Bayot thus formed a couple whose union, like that of Détry with the widow Aubert, could not be formalized in New Orleans as a marriage, given the prohibition in Louisiana law of the marriage of white persons with persons of color. They nonetheless baptized their first child together in the Cathedral of Saint Louis in June 1810, giving him the name Pierre Duhart. A second son was named Louis Alfred Duhart. Marie Françoise Bayot's son Jacques Tinchant thus acquired two younger half-brothers who would later serve as his business partners, and eventually as godparents to his children.[23]

The schoolteacher Louis Duhart had considerable standing among the Freemasons who had come from Saint-Domingue, but his financial situation was tenuous—New Orleans was full of refugees trying to survive by teaching French. In 1817–1818 Louis tried his hand at becoming a planter, buying cotton property in Plaquemines Parish in association with other investors (one of them a fellow member of his Masonic lodge). Apparently naïve in their business dealings, the partners found themselves cheated, undercapitalized, and generally beset with misfortune. They, in turn, visited misfortune on the urban slaves whom they consigned to plantation labor. The enterprise did not prosper, and the investors' group was dissolved amidst acrimony.[24]

When he returned to New Orleans after this debacle, Louis Duhart seemingly retreated from his identity as a single white businessman and openly set up a household with Marie Françoise Bayot. They continued to buy and sell slaves as their boys were growing up, and often engaged in complex notarized transactions that conformed to the legal restrictions on the goods that men could confer on women with whom they lived in what the law saw as "concubinage." Some of these purchases seem to have been shams, concealing arrangements designed to protect her future and the future of the children, or perhaps to keep property out of the hands of any potential creditors of Louis Duhart's.[25]

When Marie Françoise Bayot's son Jacques Tinchant married Rosalie Vincent's daughter Élisabeth Dieudonné in 1822, their union was thus emblematic of the creation of new "American" households by the second generation of the refugee population. Two resourceful women of color—Marie Françoise Bayot and the widow Aubert—had secured their young dependents' initial years in New Orleans despite the existence of hostile legislation, and had provided them with resources and connections. The next phase would require hard work on the part of the former dependents themselves, as well as the renegotiation of these family relationships.[26]

For the first year after the wedding, Jacques and Élisabeth lived with the widow Aubert and took meals at her house. The widow could be both a patron and a pill, exerting her control and taking her kin and neighbors to court in disputes over money. She was involved in at least four lawsuits between 1822 and 1840—including one triggered by her refusal to hand over the legacy of $500 from Détry to Élisabeth and Jacques. (She claimed to have spent it on their room and board.) Indeed, it seems that each wedding or funeral of someone close to her could become the occasion for a legal wrangle. Up to the time of her death decades later, the widow kept a sheaf of these legal records in an iron box in her armoire.[27]

On January 1, 1825, Élisabeth and Jacques, who had now moved out of the widow's household, took their first child to be baptized at the Cathedral of Saint Louis in the heart of the old city. Unlike his parents, the baby François Louis Tinchant, designated a *quarteron libre* (free quadroon), was a legitimate child, born of a legally recognized marriage. The family's network of support—and presumably the inspiration for the baby's name—was visible at the ceremony, with Jacques' mother Marie Françoise Bayot as godmother, and her partner Louis Duhart as godfather.[28]

For nearly all free people designated as "of color," however, the social room for maneuver in New Orleans had been narrowing. The 1825 Civil Code prohibited those who had lived in "open concubinage" from receiving substantial real property from their partners—a direct effort by the legislature to undercut long-standing unions between white men and women of color. This would not affect Jacques and Élisabeth directly, but it would affect Jacques' mother Marie Françoise Bayot, who was prevented by Louisiana law from marrying her white partner Louis Duhart. Soon, an additional statute declared that all free people of color who had entered the state since 1825 were obliged to leave. Again, Jacques and Élisabeth were not directly implicated, but the intensification of official hostility was unmistakable.[29]

Although Élisabeth and Jacques had themselves married within the category of "free persons of color," they each had been raised in a household that crossed what was now increasingly portrayed as a firm color line. The Louisiana legislature's assaults on cross-racial couples represented both a symbolic and a substantive attack on the milieu in which Jacques and Élisabeth lived, and would serve to restrict the choice of partners for their own children.

By March of 1830 the tone of the pronouncements issuing from the state legislature was fierce. Bundling together the potential threat of "discontent among the free coloured population" with the danger from "insubordination among the slaves," a new statute prescribed "imprisonment at hard labor for life" or the death penalty for those judged guilty of writing, printing, publishing, or distributing anything that might encourage such discontent. Indeed, anyone who made use of language "in any public discourse, from the bar, the bench, the stage, the pulpit or in any place whatsoever," including private conversation, that had a tendency to produce such discontent, or excite insubordination, was to be penalized with three to twenty years at hard labor, or death, "at the discretion of the court." Marie Françoise Bayot and Louis Duhart owned domestic slaves and were presumably unlikely to encourage insubordination among slaves more generally. But they were also a cross-racial couple with two sons who would have to face these menaces of stigma and suspicion. Around 1831–1832, Marie Françoise and Louis decided to abandon Louisiana and set sail for France. They were headed for the Béarn, in the foothills of the Pyrenees, near the area from which Louis Duhart's own parents had left for the colonies a generation earlier.[30]

Jacques and Élisabeth remained in New Orleans, where they prepared to thread their way through the maze of restrictive laws and try to take advantage of the buoyant urban economy. Their primary asset would be Jacques' own skill and labor, but they too would draw upon the system of slavery. It was common for free people of color in New Orleans to be entwined with slavery in several different ways—sometimes benefiting directly from ownership of domestic or other slaves, sometimes facilitating the freedom of slaves to whom they were bound through ties of kinship or shared experience. In the marriage contract of Jacques and Élisabeth, the widow Aubert had conferred on the new couple the ownership of an enslaved woman named Gertrude and Gertrude's twelve-year-old daughter. Gertrude's time continued to be hired out over the next years, bringing a steady income to the household. About a decade after their marriage, however, Jacques and Élisabeth took steps to manumit the slave Gertrude.[31]

Manumission of one slave could nonetheless be matched by the acquisition of others. In the mid-1830s the city of New Orleans was expanding rapidly, and Jacques Tinchant and his half brother Pierre Duhart formally agreed to combine their holdings and constitute themselves as a *société* to buy land and build houses. Piece by piece, they acquired properties in the city's suburbs of Faubourg Marigny, New Marigny, and Franklin. In 1836

Tinchant and Duhart spent $1,000 to purchase an enslaved black man named Giles, alias Clark, about twenty-one years of age. Thus, while Jacques Tinchant had in 1833 freed one of the two slaves of his wife's marriage portion, he now held a half interest in another person held as property.[32]

Over the next years Tinchant and Duhart sold deep, narrow lots to a variety of purchasers, many of them men and women of color. From one vantage point, Jacques Tinchant was a carpenter turned builder and developer, transforming white-owned rural land on the edge of the city into house lots and dwellings for a multiracial clientele. Blaise *dit* Blaise Léger, *nègre libre*, for example, paid Tinchant and Duhart $400 for a lot in Faubourg Franklin measuring 34 feet on Washington Street and 117 feet on Morales Street. The webs of kin and clientage in these communities were quite dense, however. Blaise Léger himself had recently been manumitted in accordance with the last will and testament of Jean Lambert Détry, the same Belgian carpenter who had provided for Jacques Tinchant's wife a decade earlier. Between Détry's death and the formal manumission, the young Blaise had lived in the house of the widow Aubert, including the year that Jacques and Élisabeth lodged there. The sale of a small house lot to Blaise Léger when he reached the age of twenty-three and acquired his freedom may well have involved the fulfillment of a family obligation as well as pure business logic.[33]

Jacques flourished as an artisan and businessman, and he and Élisabeth established a settled and stable family. With multiple ties to kin and allies who could provide resources and protection, and with a secure place in the building trades during a period of expansion, the couple had made steady progress toward modest prosperity. They had five surviving children between 1825 and 1836, beginning with Louis (François Louis), and then on through Joseph, Pierre, Jules, and Ernest.

As Jacques and Élisabeth progressed economically, they also sought to shake off some of the signals of individual stigma that added to their own social burdens. Jacques had from early on adopted the surname of his absent father, Tinchant, and no one seems to have queried that usage. Élisabeth, however, had arrived in New Orleans as the "natural child" of an African woman and a deceased Frenchman. In the marriage contract that her godmother supervised, she was thus given only the first name Marie and the nickname Dieudonné. Élisabeth would later say that the name Marie had been erroneously attributed to her, because it was the baptismal name of her absent mother. Whatever the Christian name she used, when Élisabeth signed without a surname, her lack of legitimate parentage—and, indeed, the possibility that she or her mother had been enslaved—became visible.[34]

Marriage to Jacques Tinchant did not erase the stigma. Standard practice in French-speaking civil law jurisdictions called for a married woman to be identified in legal documents with the name that appeared in her own birth record, generally her Christian name and her paternal (or "maiden") surname. Marriage did not change a woman's legal name; the use of the husband's surname was custom, not legal usage. Élisabeth's task, then, was to achieve the right to a respectable paternal surname in place of the nickname Dieudonné. When their first son Louis was baptized in 1825, she had taken a step in this direction, persuading the priest to inscribe her name with the words "Elisabette Vincent." Like her own mother, Élisabeth was now informally taking on the surname of Michel Vincent, who had died back in Cuba. Apparently nothing stopped her from doing so in front of Father Michaud at the cathedral.[35]

It would be a bit bolder to make this assertion in a document certified by a public notary, thus adding to its apparent legality. In 1834 Jacques Tinchant sold a piece of land, and the notary Octave de Armas formalized the sale, listing the buyer and the seller as *gens de couleur libres,* free persons of color. Under the terms of their marriage contract, Élisabeth held a general mortgage on all of Jacques' properties, and therefore her assent to the sale was needed. Presumably taking his cue concerning her legal name from that marriage contract, the notary first listed her as Marie Dieudonné. But he also acknowledged the way that she now styled herself, and expanded this to "Marie Dieudonné *dite* Élisabeth Vincent." It was common practice for a notary to convey some of the complexity of New Orleans naming through the use of the term *dite* (called)—with the *dite* signifying his own uncertainty as to the status of that second appellation. Élisabeth herself went right ahead and signed the document as "Elizabht Vincent." The spelling was shaky, but her implicit claim to trace her parentage to Michel Vincent was clear.[36]

The stigmatizing lack of a surname nonetheless remained visible on her marriage contract, a document that she had to proffer again and again when Jacques engaged in legal transactions. In November of 1835 Jacques and Élisabeth, however, found a way to notarize Élisabeth's way to respectability, turning the familiar proceedings to their own advantage. They went to the office of the notary Théodore Seghers to file a formal "rectification" of her name as it had appeared on their marriage

contract. The couple now presented a copy of Élisabeth's baptismal record, in which her father Michel Vincent had acknowledged his paternity. They asked that on the basis of this evidence her name be formally
"rectified" to Élisabeth Dieudonné Vincent.[37]

The sudden appearance of this piece of paper was certainly convenient. The document was apparently an official copy, dated 25 May 1823,
of the record of a baptism that had taken place decades earlier in the
French colony of Saint-Domingue. Someone had evidently arranged for a
Haitian civil officer to re-transcribe the 1799 sacramental record, which
had itself been drawn up in the midst of the Haitian Revolution. And now
someone had conveyed the new document to Élisabeth in Louisiana.[38]

A surviving ship's manifest suggests just who that person is likely to
have been. On April 20, 1835, a two-masted vessel, the brig *Ann,* landed in
New Orleans after a journey from Port-au-Prince, Haiti. On board was a
passenger whose name was listed as Rosalia Vincent. The Spanish form of
the name Rosalie may date back to the time in Cuba; the surname Vincent
came from her now-deceased partner the French colonist Michel Vincent.
It seems a good bet that Rosalie carried with her the carefully certified record attesting to the fact that Michel Vincent had brought their daughter
to the baptismal font in Cap Dame-Marie, Saint-Domingue, thirty-six years
earlier.[39]

These documents, however, were not necessarily enough to achieve
Élisabeth's goal. Under the 1825 Civil Code of Louisiana, free illegitimate
children of color were legally "allowed to prove their descent from a father
of color only." By 1835, however, Élisabeth's husband Jacques Tinchant was
a respected builder, known to the New Orleans notary Théodore Seghers as
a client who bought and sold land, and occasionally a slave. The notary was
now willing to overlook the slight irregularity in the proposed "rectification" of Élisabeth's name. Her father Michel Vincent, after all, was a long-
dead Frenchman, not a self-protective member of Louisiana's white elite.
He was not in any position to object to this assertion of paternity.[40]

Given the fine distinction made in the Louisiana Civil Code between
acknowledgment and legitimation, it is not entirely clear that establishing that Michel Vincent's name was on the baptismal record actually
conferred on his "natural daughter" the legal right to adopt his surname.
But once the "rectification" had been entered into the record, and cross-
referenced in the margin of the file copy of their original marriage contract, Élisabeth Dieudonné became for all practical purposes Élisabeth
Vincent. When her name appeared in legal documents, it now did not

resemble that of a child born out of wedlock to a former slave mother, but was instead indistinguishable from the names of those born to families who had always been free.[41]

The modification of Élisabeth's name was an important step toward formal respectability, but it could not mitigate the practical limitations imposed on people of color in New Orleans in the 1830s. Since their earliest childhood, Jacques and Élisabeth had lived in an artisan and professional milieu centered on Saint-Domingue refugees, many of whom showed a strong commitment to literacy and to education. Jacques's stepfather Louis Duhart was a teacher, and Jacques himself signed his contracts with a confident hand. Élisabeth's writing was more hesitant, but she had achieved at least a basic literacy. The prospects for their own sons, however, were clouded by the hostile scrutiny imposed on the few schools that did accept children of color, combined with the lack of accessible higher education for such children in New Orleans. Jacques and Élisabeth probably managed initially to adapt to the paucity of appropriate schools by arranging private instruction for their older boys Louis and Joseph, but there was a limit to this strategy.[42]

An additional discouragement may have been the prospect of more-rigorous enforcement of the law requiring all free persons of color in New Orleans, except those born in the state, to register each year at the mayor's office, providing evidence of their legal status as free and attestations of their reliability from some white person. Jacques and Élisabeth, like many other relatively prosperous members of the community, had apparently declined to comply with this rule in the first years. Jacques' name appears in the city directory and on tax lists, but does not figure on this humiliating registry. It was not clear, however, how long the privileges accorded to their modest wealth would hold. The Louisiana legislature was heading down the path toward the demarcation of a single and stigmatizing color line, and nativist meetings calling for restrictions on the employment of slaves and free persons of color suggested that further constraints were likely to be on the way.[43]

In the late 1830s, the couple began to consolidate their holdings and to prepare for another departure. Jacques' mother, Marie Françoise Bayot, had settled in France, and seems to have been in poor health. Élisabeth's mother, Rosalie Vincent, now in her late sixties or early seventies, had in all likelihood concluded her visit to the slaveholding metropolis of New Orleans and returned to Haiti, where she had rebuilt her life in the years since the expulsion from Cuba. Jacques now sold some of the couple's small urban lots in New Orleans, while retaining others for rental revenue. On May 12, 1840, he went for the last time to the family notary and filed a power of attorney for his half brother Louis Alfred Duhart to manage his affairs in his absence.[44]

There was an awkward transaction to complete first, however. Six years earlier the couple had manumitted the enslaved woman named Gertrude, who had served in the household of the widow Aubert when Élisabeth was growing up, and had been deeded over to Jacques and Élisabeth at the time of their marriage. But they still held as a slave Gertrude's daughter Marie Louise, who was now twenty-two years old. Louisiana's legislative restrictions on manumission made the freeing of a slave of this age cumbersome and difficult, and Jacques and Élisabeth seem never to have taken that initiative. Instead, just weeks before leaving New Orleans, they went to the family notary and officially sold Marie Louise to her own mother.[45]

Under the terms of the contract, Gertrude was to pay the couple 800 piastres (roughly equivalent to dollars) in several installments. Once the last payment was made, Marie Louise was to become free. Jacques and Élisabeth seem to have designed this procedure in order to circumvent the restrictions on manumission, while extracting an income in the process. The contract transformed Marie Louise into a particular kind of "person with a price," legally the slave of her own mother, who in turn had to pay a sum close to the market price for the young woman's freedom. Louisiana law would consider Marie Louise a *statu liber,* someone who held a recognized promise of future freedom. But a sequence of payments, and additional legal steps, remained before the promise would become real.[46]

Their financial and legal affairs in order, Jacques and Élisabeth were ready to leave. Their eldest son, Louis Tinchant, would remain behind, a link to the world of business in the growing city. Jacques may have faced a difficult moment when he sought a passport for himself and his dependents, for his nationality remained quite unclear. Probably born in Baltimore, this "natural son" of Saint-Domingue refugees would have had only a fragile claim to French nationality. His claim to U.S. citizenship was even more tenuous. Creole men of color like Jacques Tinchant were the builders of the city, but they could not count on rights or respect in return. The slaveholding states rarely accorded formal citizenship to persons designated as "mulattos" or "free men of color," though some of the practical attributes of citizenship could on occasion be exercised.[47]

In this period of loose categorizations of birthplace and residence, and of shifting definitions of nationality and citizenship, Jacques may in practice not have been required to produce much documentation in order to obtain a passport enabling them to board a ship for France. The Louisiana legislature had criminalized any encouragement of "discontent" among free persons of color. But, ironically, if the discontent was produced by the acts of the legislature itself, and caused a family of color to abandon the city, the authorities were unlikely to stand in their way.

5

The Land of the Rights of Man

Years later, Jacques and Élisabeth Tinchant's youngest son, Édouard, would denounce the injustices of the antebellum South and its "tyrannical aristocracy that forced our father to expatriate and which, ever since our earliest years, he has taught us to hate." In his letter to Máximo Gómez at the very end of the nineteenth century, Édouard averred that his father had left Louisiana for France "with the only object in view of raising his six sons in a country where no infamous laws or stupid prejudices could prevent them from becoming MEN." The implication was clear: as legal and social constraints closed in on Louisiana's "free people of color" in the 1830s, his parents had felt themselves driven out.[1]

By several measures New Orleans had nonetheless provided Jacques and Élisabeth with opportunities. Élisabeth had arrived in 1809 as a child refugee of war, separated from her African-born mother and her siblings and raised in the care of a demanding godmother. Jacques, a "natural child" born in Baltimore to the Saint-Domingue refugees Marie Françoise Bayot and Joseph Tinchant, had been raised and apparently tutored by his mother and her new partner, Louis Duhart. Literate, skilled, and well connected, Jacques was able, by the time he reached his twenties, to support a family in the expanding economy of New Orleans. His abilities as a carpenter and his sharp eye for real estate put him near the center of the wide network of free artisans of color who dominated the building trades.

What did France seem to promise, then, such that Jacques and Élisabeth would sell off most of their New Orleans properties, pack up the children, and set sail for Europe? Édouard's later reflections point directly to the question of rights, and indirectly to the availability of formal education. In a sharp contrast to Louisiana's multiple restrictions on persons of color, the French Civil Code of 1804 and its 1814 Constitutional Charter established the formal legal equality—within metropolitan France—of all citizens. The

Restoration régime of Charles X (1824–1830), despite its conservatism on other points, modified some of the harsh measures that Napoléon Bonaparte had put in place during his effort to suppress the Haitian Revolution, including the ban on the admission to France of "blacks, mulattos, and other people of color" without special authorization.[2]

After the adoption of a new constitution at the beginning of the July Monarchy in 1830, the French state also began to dismantle some of the distinctions that had been maintained in the colonies after their abolition in the metropolis. On April 24, 1833, the parliament voted a new statute governing the colonies of the Caribbean and the Indian Ocean, stipulating that every person "born free or who has legally acquired freedom" would enjoy both civil and political rights. The statute in its second and final article abrogated "all restrictions and exclusions that have been declared in reference to the exercise of civil and political rights on behalf of men of color and freedpersons." It did not go so far as to abolish slavery in those colonies—indeed, the statute was part of a package that increased the power of slaveholding colonists. For persons in Jacques and Élisabeth's situation, however, the liberal régime's policy signaled an explicit recognition that the constitutional provision that "Frenchmen are equal before the law, whatever may be their titles and rank" now encompassed those deemed to be "free persons of color."[3]

The news of the situation in France that reached Jacques and Élisabeth in New Orleans, moreover, came from a source they could trust. Jacques' mother Marie Françoise Bayot and her partner, the Freemason and schoolteacher Louis Duhart, had already chosen the option of emigration. Around 1830 Marie Françoise and Louis had left New Orleans for the region of France known as the Béarn, near the border with Spain, in the Basses-Pyrénées. Though born in Saint-Domingue, Louis Duhart traced his ancestry to the Basque country of France. His grandfather Martin Duhart had been a sea captain born in Saint-Jean-de-Luz on the Atlantic coast, later operating out of the port of Nantes. In the mid-eighteenth century Martin Duhart had built a link with Saint-Domingue through his slaving voyages, opening the way for the Duhart descendants to seek their fortune in the Caribbean.[4]

For Louis Duhart's generation of white refugees from Saint-Domingue, France remained a place of return when the appeal of the enterprises of the Caribbean and the Gulf of Mexico wore out. In effect, Louis and Marie Françoise, nicknamed Suzette, behaved like colonists who would eventually head back "home" to France, though it was a country that neither had ever seen. The surname Duhart was familiar in the Béarn, and the town of Pau and its environs offered them the possibility of landowning and social standing. As an aging couple whose union crossed what Louisiana's laws had portrayed as an unbridgeable color line, they stood to benefit from moving to a society where they could legitimate their children, one whose laws of inheritance would not place obstacles in their way.

Some people back in New Orleans had already perceived the two of them as a permanent couple, referring to her as Suzette Duhart, as though she were Louis' wife. But their union had no legal standing in Louisiana, for under the state's 1825 Civil Code, marriage between a white person and a person of color was null and void. In metropolitan France Napoléon Bonaparte had issued his own version of the ancien régime bans on the immigration of persons deemed black or mulatto, and he prohibited the marriage of a white person with a person judged to be black, often entangling those who were of mixed ancestry as well as those of direct African ancestry. At the time of Marie Françoise Bayot's flight from Saint-Domingue around 1793, and for years afterward, France would not necessarily have been a welcoming destination. In 1819, however, the marriage and immigration prohibitions were lifted. At least in law, by 1830 monarchical France offered a favorable contrast to republican Louisiana, helping to draw Louis and Marie Françoise across the Atlantic.[5]

Thus it was that on April 17, 1832, Jacques Tinchant's mother had finally become a respectably married woman, no longer vulnerable to the humiliation and deprivation of inheritance rights that had weighed on those construed under Louisiana law as "concubines." Having published the banns at the front door of the town hall during the two prior Sundays, as was proper, Monsieur Louis Nicolas François Duhart, *rentier,* and *demoiselle* Marie Françoise Bayot celebrated their marriage before the mayor of the town of Pau. Theirs was now a true, a public, and a legal claim to the married state. The marriage act simultaneously legitimated their sons Pierre and Louis Alfred Duhart, both born in New Orleans. These young men—the half brothers of Jacques Tinchant—could now leave behind the label of "natural child" that had appeared in their New Orleans baptismal records, along with the tag "of color." They would henceforth be designated *enfants légitimes,* legitimate children, able to marry without stigma and to inherit without obstacle.[6]

Louis Duhart and Marie Françoise Bayot could also report back to Jacques and Élisabeth on their considerable degree of economic success in rural France. Farmers in the Basses-Pyrénées had experienced subsistence crises in 1816–1817 and in 1827–1832, creating immense hardship for the poor but bringing opportunities for those who could afford to speculate on land. Because land prices fell during these periods of poor harvest, Louis and Marie Françoise found that a fully established farm was within their reach. In 1833 they had purchased the agricultural establishment called La Hourcade in the small community of Gan, near Pau.[7]

Production at La Hourcade was organized along the familiar lines of *métayage*, with landless *métayers* (sharecroppers) who worked the fields, and *domestiques*, *servantes*, and a governess who worked in the house. Rapid wealth of the kind that Louis Duhart had once sought in his brief and unsuccessful plantation experiment back in the Mississippi Delta was not likely; that was a colonial-style dream that he had now abandoned. But he could supervise the work of tenants and laborers, rather than having to round up clients for his tutoring business as he had in New Orleans. Harvests in the Basses-Pyrénées were abundant in 1833. For Louis and Marie Françoise the gamble of moving to France was paying off.[8]

In both substance and in social identity, moreover, Louis Duhart had finally become a *propriétaire*, a landowner, rather than a schoolteacher. As his *métayers* worked the land and the farm's revenues increased, Louis solidified his claim to the status of *rentier*, one who lived off the labor of others and income from property. The final social triumph may have come when their son Pierre Duhart, now freed from the stigma of illegitimate birth, wooed and won a young woman from Pau. His bride, Zoé Bonnafon, came from a prosperous family with its own colonial ties. Her father, a merchant and proprietor, was in Guadeloupe at the time of the wedding. Her mother, like many wives of men who had gone to the colonies, was listed as a *propriétaire* and *rentière* in her own right. When this alliance was formalized in January 1840, all three members of the Duhart/Bayot family present at the ceremony—Louis, Marie Françoise, and Pierre himself—were designated in the record as *rentiers*. No color terms signaled mixed ancestry for Marie Françoise and Pierre, as they had in Louisiana, and the witnesses who signed the register were two local notables: a captain from the *gendarmerie* of the town of Tarbes who held the rank of chevalier de la Légion d'Honneur, and Joseph Raymond Nogué, mayor of Pau. News of the fine marriage that Jacques Tinchant's half brother had managed may have been among the communications that reached Jacques and Élisabeth in New Orleans as they prepared their own departure.[9]

On balance, then, the family news reaching New Orleans from Pau in the 1830s had probably been quite upbeat, and doubtless included the specific intelligence that in the Béarn there were local schools open to all, and land for sale in the foothills and valleys. Minister of Education François Guizot had in 1833 ordered the formation of a boys' primary school in each *commune* in France, so basic schooling was now widely available at modest cost. The town of Pau also held a *collège royal,* offering a classical education. France's constitutional monarchy conferred formal civil equality on most adult males. The prospects, in short, seemed to be good.[10]

Jacques and Élisabeth had no way of anticipating that the moment of the older couple's arrival in the Basses-Pyrénées had been an unusually propitious one, or that the good news from the parents' household papered over certain likely limitations for the next generation. Louis Duhart was a white man from Saint-Domingue whose family ties to the region presumably made it easy to resume French nationality based on birth in the colonies. Jacques Tinchant, by contrast, was an American-born man of color. France, moreover, remained emphatically a slave-holding empire, although slavery was concentrated in the colonies. Racial prejudice was persistent, reflected in the episodic bans on the immigration to the metropolis of persons designated black and mulatto, including the brief renewal in 1817–1818 of the old restrictions. Formal changes in the rules did not necessarily mean the end of the spirit that had led to the restrictions.[11]

Following the revolution of 1830, the French state had established broad civil equality, and Louis-Philippe of the House of Orléans ruled as "king of the French," bound by a revised version of the earlier Constitutional Charter of 1814. The régime nonetheless continued to impose sharp limitations on suffrage. Without wealth, one had no claim to a formal political voice. Only a few dozen men out of the several hundred households in the town of Gan reached the property threshold to be eligible to vote. Louis Duhart had indeed accumulated—perhaps just barely—the property required for suffrage, and his name was inscribed as an *électeur censitaire* on the list of qualified voters. Jacques Tinchant would never make it onto that list.[12]

No one could know, moreover, that by the late 1830s the region of the Basses-Pyrénées was on the verge of another series of bad harvests. A new migrant purchasing a farm in 1840 would face an entirely different economic situation from the one that had enabled Louis and Marie

Françoise to shift successfully from American urban activities to French rural ones.[13]

However imperfect their understanding of the challenges that lay ahead, Jacques Tinchant and Élisabeth Vincent had nonetheless been persuaded by the prospect of education and respect for the boys, and rights for themselves, as well as the possibility of landed proprietorship. Within a few months of their Atlantic crossing and subsequent arrival in the Basses-Pyrénées in 1840, they bought a farm called Pédemarie, located on the other side of the hills from the Duhart establishment at La Hourcade. Once again, harvest failures had lowered land prices, and wages had fallen, making it easy for a newcomer with ready money to buy in and hire laborers. Jacques and Élisabeth paid 27,000 francs for the land, the house, the barns, the animals, and some furniture and kitchen equipment.[14]

The city of Pau offered the hoped-for prospect of education at all levels, far different from the personal tutoring that would likely have been their only option for advanced studies in New Orleans. Once Jacques and Élisabeth settled in, their sons Joseph (age twelve) and Pierre (age seven) could begin their formal schooling with the October *rentrée,* the start of the new academic year. There was a local *école communale* in the village of Gan itself for the children of rural laborers, but the Tinchant sons attended the more exclusive *collège royal* in Pau, where they embarked on studies in Latin along with the children of local notables. Brothers Jules (age four) and Ernest (eighteen months) would in a few years be able to do the same.[15]

The anticipated family reunion, however, was soon struck by mourning. Jacques' mother Marie Françoise Bayot died in November of 1840, just a few weeks after the beginning of the school year. Louis Duhart was now a widower, and he would soon turn the administration of La Hourcade over to his son Pierre, who was settled permanently in France. Relations between the two half brothers—the well-established Pierre Duhart and the recently arrived Jacques Tinchant—seem to have remained steady. But one of the anchor lines attaching Jacques to the land in the Basses-Pyrénées, the presence of his mother, had been broken almost at the moment that the family's rural adventure began.[16]

With an eldest child back in New Orleans, but the four younger ones with them in France, Jacques and Élisabeth presumably had their hands full. Then, in December 1841, Élisabeth gave birth to Édouard, the sixth and last of the Tinchant sons. If questions of citizenship were to arise later—and they did—Édouard would be the only son who could assert birth on French soil. The attribution of a formal *qualité de français* (French nationality), however, depended crucially on parentage as well as birthplace. It is unclear whether Jacques Tinchant, who was almost certainly born in the United States, ever attempted to assert French nationality through his own father, the elusive Joseph Tinchant, senior. Throughout the pre-1848 period, naturalization was both expensive and difficult to obtain, and it seems that Jacques did not try for it. In the eyes of the law, therefore, Édouard was a child born in France of a presumptively foreign father. Under the rules in force in the early 1840s, this would give him insufficient grounds on which to claim French nationality.[17]

Édouard's mother Élisabeth, born in colonial Saint-Domingue, might have had a stronger claim to French nationality on her own. Her status as a child born out of wedlock made any tracing of nationality through her French father Michel Vincent tenuous, but since Saint-Domingue itself had been French at the time of her birth, proof of birth there might by itself be sufficient. Refugees born in Saint-Domingue had in the past successfully appealed for "reintegration" in their *qualité de français*. As a married woman, however, Élisabeth was instead very likely seen as having taken on the (quite unclear) nationality of her husband Jacques.[18]

For the moment these questions of nationality and citizenship did not pose an obstacle to the achievement of the family's immediate goals. The boys could go to school. The parents suffered no sharp civil disabilities. And when Jacques and Élisabeth recorded their land purchase, no stigmatizing label designated them as *gens de couleur libres*. The French notary did, however, take the trouble to transcribe the complicated path by which Élisabeth, designated as an *enfant naturel* with only a Christian name and nickname at the time of her marriage contract, had later produced a baptismal record before a New Orleans notary to establish her paternity and adopt the surname of her father, Michel Vincent. The "rectification" of her name on that original marriage contract had been efficacious, but it did leave a trail.[19]

The farm called Pédemarie was a large and handsome establishment of twenty-one hectares situated on the flank of a hill, with one boundary touching the route to the town of Eaux-Bonnes, on the royal road to Spain. A stone house and two adjacent barns defined a rectangular courtyard, and the lands around the house included pasture, fields for planting, chestnut forests, vineyards, woodlots, and groves of ferns, used as fodder. Jacques and Élisabeth had acquired the six cows in the stable, the large supply of grain and hay already in the barns, and a quarry yielding stone that was in demand for road repair. In Gan and its vicinity, the grape harvest of 1840 was of particularly high quality, so the enterprise presumably got off to a good start.[20]

Pédemarie was not a simple family farm. Though much of its acreage was in woods rather than fields or vineyards, its size put it into the top third of rural properties in France. Without prior experience of farm management themselves, Jacques and Élisabeth conformed quickly to the local norm of employing sharecroppers. Like Louis and Marie Françoise a decade earlier, the couple began by operating their farm on the system of *métayage*, contracting out the agricultural tasks to local cultivators who worked the land with their own tools, and sometimes animals, and who received a fraction of the harvest as payment. Directly under the authority of the landowner, the *métayers* of the Basses-Pyrenées had neither the autonomy nor the security of independent farmers or rent-paying tenants on long-term contracts. The initial *métayer* at Pédemarie was an older single man named Péguille, soon referred to in the census with the possessive designation *Péguille à Tinchant*, Tinchant's Péguille. Péguille was assisted by two *domestiques*, Jean-Pierre Adam and Jean Paya, also designated as *à Tinchant*, both presumably farm laborers. Although employing a *métayer* could give the proprietor the status of a notable, by the 1840s the system was coming to be perceived by many observers as archaic, discouraging of investment, and likely to yield meager benefits to both parties at the end of the year.[21]

Three female servants worked for the family, bringing the household to thirteen people. Asserting authority over dependents was not an unfamiliar role for Jacques and Élisabeth, fresh from the slaveholding society of New Orleans, where they had controlled the enslaved woman Gertrude and her daughter, as well as the enslaved carpenter who had worked with Jacques. Their shift from urban to rural activity, however, was not an easy one. Supervising the profitable running of a vineyard, a dairy, and the production of grain was a specialized responsibility for which they had little preparation. Things soon began to falter.

In each successive census—1841, 1846, and 1851—the identities of the *domestiques* working on the farm and of the *servantes* (female servants) working in the house were different from those of the census before. The *métayer* named Péguille soon disappeared from the list of residents on the property, which suggests that the Tinchants were now trying to have the land cultivated directly, perhaps using day laborers who did not appear in the census. By 1846, the household was down to one *servante*. The experiment in agricultural enterprise seems not to have been yielding the expected financial benefits.[22]

Jacques did not reach the rank of a substantial taxpayer, eligible for suffrage, that his stepfather had quickly achieved, a position for which Jacques' lack of documented French nationality would have posed an additional obstacle. It is also possible that Jacques and Élisabeth were seen by their neighbors as persons of color from elsewhere, and in some sense outsiders. In later years his postal address included the phrase "Jacques Tinchant, Américain," distinguishing him from the locals. But American connections were common in this region of frequent out-migration to South America and the Caribbean, and were unlikely to carry any uniform stigma. Moreover, although their social standing may have been fragile, the pattern of education Jacques and Élisabeth sought for their sons suggests both the breadth of the parents' aspirations and the milieu into which they succeeded in placing their children, despite the financial difficulties the family encountered in the transition to rural life.[23]

The Vincent/Tinchant household had arrived in France as the country's educational system was being transformed into one that widened access while reinforcing social distinctions. Minister of Education Guizot had indeed ordered that a school for boys be established in each commune, and those who enrolled in these simple establishments learned to read, write, and count at a modest cost, with the poor exempted from payment altogether. But to go to the *école communale* was a mark of low status. In the towns, more-prosperous families had the option of enrolling their children in a *pension,* a private school that offered a curriculum centered on modern languages, history, and geography. The very best students from the *pensions* might go on to higher education, including the *grandes écoles* that were designed to train engineers, miners, and other professionals in the sciences. French immigrants to the Caribbean had sometimes sent their children back to France to attend boarding schools like these, where they were educated alongside the children of merchants and of wealthier artisans. At the top of the hierarchy sat the public but expensive *collèges* and *lycées* that offered a classical education to the sons of those who were referred to as *rentiers,* families living off of rents and revenues rather than their own labor. With the French Revolution, access to classical education had come to encompass more than just the sons of aristocrats, but enrollment in these schools remained both a symbol of status and a costly investment for parents. In the 1840s, only about 5 percent of children attending school were enrolled in *collèges*.[24]

The *collège royal* in Pau (called a *lycée* after 1848) was regarded as a school of high quality, and it is to that elite institution that Jacques and Élisabeth sent their sons. Following in the tradition of the ancien régime establishments run by the religious orders, these postrevolutionary schools began with boys of age seven or eight and embarked them on a long education devoted to classical languages, humanities, and Christian culture. Students were introduced to the secrets of rhetoric and formal writing that had long been seen as the foundational studies for men who would enter public life. By the mid-nineteenth century some sons of merchants and artisans were making their way into these institutions, where they often suffered the mockery of their classmates from *rentier* families. Indeed, the fiction of the period—including most vividly Flaubert's *Madame Bovary*—is filled with portraits of these strivers, risking humiliation in pursuit of advancement through education.[25]

By 1845 government educational inspectors judged the *collège* in Pau to be one of the best in the region. Joseph Tinchant had been a student there at least since 1843, and traces of the other Tinchant boys' enrollment appear in the local newspapers. Young Édouard in particular would in later years appear frequently as a winner of prizes for his academic achievements.[26]

Elementary studies in these schools had long been centered on French and Latin grammar taught through "passages extracted from the classical authors." In 1839, a formal list of French and Latin authors appropriate for instruction was issued, and it remained in force with a few variations until 1851. Students in the very early elementary years (*huitième* and *septième*) were to study, in addition to their grammar books, the *Fables* of La Fontaine and Fenelon. For their Latin they would embark on *De Viris illustribus urbis Romae,* the lives of illustrious men of the city of Rome, a famous pastiche of easy passages borrowed from Plutarch. When the most successful and ambitious students moved on into *sixième* and *cinquième,* they would continue with Fénelon and La Fontaine, and add a sacred work by the Abbé Fleury, as well as new Latin texts. Things got very serious by *quatrième,* with Virgil, Cicero, and Plutarch himself, as well as some Voltaire (the historical rather than the philosophical works), and the best-selling *Télémaque* of Fénelon.[27]

It was a curriculum that could encourage a visionary young man to see himself as following in the footsteps of the greats, and could provide the rhetorical skills to try to make that vision real. For a young provincial, moreover, it encouraged aspiring toward Paris, the place where culture itself seemed to be located. By his own account, Joseph Tinchant—the eldest of the Tinchant sons to have come to France—finished his studies at the *collège royal* in Pau at the age of eighteen, thus in 1846. The official history of the school confirms that despite his late start within the French educational system, he had won a prize for his performance in *quatrième*. With his formal training in Latin, in rhetoric, and in history, he was ready to leave the foothills of the Pyrenees and strike out on his own for the capital.[28]

Young Joseph Tinchant had become accustomed to the full enjoyment of civic equality in France, in marked contrast to the deference that was required of free men of color back in New Orleans. The abolition of the formal legal privileges associated with aristocracy and what was referred to as "caste," one of the accomplishments of the French Republic, was still respected under the constitutional monarchy. Class differentiations remained sharp and visible, but were now often determined by fortune rather than by birth. In theory, social difference also resulted from differences in talent, though critics were skeptical on that point. What allocation of substantive rights would accompany formal civic equality, moreover, remained a question very much up for debate.[29]

If upon arrival in Paris Joseph gravitated toward the milieu of educated and ambitious young men who occasionally attended classes in law or philosophy, he likely heard various opinions on this issue. The jurist who held a chair of political economy at the Collège de France, the Italian liberal Pellegrino Rossi, offered a course in constitutional law that explicated the boundaries of rights and liberties under the monarchy by proposing a tripartite division of civil, political, and public rights. Civil rights—including the ownership of property—should be available to all. In Rossi's typology, "public rights"—including rights to self-expression and assembly—should also be open to all members of society. Political rights, however, could be constrained on the basis of variation in presumed capacities (hence, for example, denied to women or limited by a property requirement).[30]

The learned Pellegrino Rossi had been obliged to handle questions of color somewhat gingerly as long as slavery still existed in France's colonies.

Reflecting the tense relationship between liberal theory and the interests generated by colonization, Rossi spoke disapprovingly of slavery, but apparently did not openly use his position to call for abolition. He adopted the era's conventional stereotypes concerning "races" (referring, for example, to the "handsome proportions" of Caucasians), though he remarked on the ascent of men of color in the Antilles to positions of public authority, and expressed hope that the "quarrel of the white race and the black race" would soon end.[31]

Direct criticisms of slavery and of racial prejudice were nonetheless becoming increasingly audible in Paris in the 1840s. The activist Victor Schoelcher, the Romantic poet Alphonse de Lamartine, and others, building on the earlier campaign against the slave trade, now turned their attention to the abolition of slavery itself. Cyrille Bissette, a man of color banished from the French colony of Martinique, had begun in 1834 to publish an antislavery journal, *La Revue des Colonies*. These activists fused romanticism with reformism, pushing at the limits of permissible political criticism under the monarchy. Joseph Tinchant may well have crossed paths with their followers, even if he was primarily concerned with finding opportunities to develop his career, rather than taking a public stance on the issues of the day.[32]

Paris in 1846–1848 was politically exciting, but it was not easy. Like Gustave Flaubert's fictional Frédéric Moreau in the novel *L'Éducation sentimentale*, Joseph Tinchant had good schooling behind him, but no specific professional studies, no particular occupation, and no certainty of an inheritance ahead. He nonetheless lived through an intense education in republicanism and repression in the city, one that shaped his political persona in the years that followed. A key element of that education was the acquisition of a language (and a practice) of rights and of civic equality.[33]

These ideas were, both in theory and in practice, soon being pushed beyond earlier boundaries. In his lectures at the Law Faculty in Paris, Pellegrino Rossi had noted with pleasure that his typology of civil, public, and political rights was "beginning to be generally adopted." Rossi viewed public rights as rooted in human nature, but capable of emerging and expanding as societies became more developed—hence his interchangeable use of the terms "public rights" and "social rights." Rossi's concepts of rights were both sturdy and flexible, potentially encompassing more and more spheres of public life.[34]

The public rights of assembly and expression were increasingly being turned aggressively to the cause of reform, as writers and orators decried the privileges and corruption associated with the monarchy, and a few uttered the seditious call for a return to republicanism. Property limitations on the suffrage were challenged, slavery itself was being questioned, and activists suggested that the legitimacy of the régime had been exhausted. The abolitionist organizer Cyrille Bissette moved from journalism to direct action, and carried petitions against slavery door to door in 1847 to obtain signatures from Parisian workers.[35]

Faced with the evidence of misery in the cities and the countryside, activists began to speak not only of social rights but also of social equality, as they tried to envision a world in which such misery would be banished. Moving beyond Rossi's liberal framework, they envisioned a "social republic," one that would guarantee work and wages for all. The most Romantic of the political activists sought to confer broad new rights and power on the *peuple*, envisioning France's "people" as the only source of true authority.[36]

Beginning in early February 1848, events accelerated rapidly. Vast public banquets were convened in the name of reform, and then thwarted by the prohibitions imposed by a fearful monarchy. Crowds took shape in the street and were joined by students marching in line, singing a full-throated "Marseillaise" to reawaken memories of the great Revolution of 1789. Sent to repress the increasingly assertive *peuple*, some National Guardsmen were ready to fraternize rather than fire. Barricades went up across the city; crowds pressed against the palace; the king abdicated. An attempt to establish a regency failed, and within a matter of days a coalition provisional government had been formed. France was once again a Republic.[37]

There ensued a complex struggle over the question of whether this new government would indeed become a "social republic," or whether the overturning of the monarchy and the reestablishment of republican government would be sufficient to define its core principles. Radicals clamored for a red flag rather than the tricolor, and wore red sashes around their waists as they joined the crowds in the street. Immersed in this milieu, Joseph apparently came to identify with the principles of public rights and social equality, combined with an intense hostility to what were often called "caste" distinctions.[38]

The ferment of 1848 extended far beyond Paris, finding echoes in rural areas that had suffered harvest failures and low wages. The 1840s were difficult for farmers, with only occasional good years for those who produced grains and potatoes, the fundamental foodstuffs of rural France. At Pédemarie in the Béarn, Jacques and Élisabeth Tinchant had by 1846 already reduced the paid personnel on their farm, despite being unable to count on family labor, since Joseph had been in school and the other boys were too young to be of substantial help. Then, in 1848, a cycle of agricultural depression set in that would last through 1852.[39]

These years define the era of "the Republic in the village," when debate about republican ideas blossomed—and was repressed—in towns and hamlets across the country. Schoolteachers in particular were conspicuous among the supporters of the ideals of the Republic, though the instructors at the *lycée* in Pau attended by the Tinchant brothers may have been a bit more reticent than those of the village *école communale*, which served the laboring classes. When Édouard Tinchant recalled, somewhat romantically, that his father had always taught him to detest "aristocratic tyranny," the phrase echoes the terms of denunciation in 1789 more than that of 1848. Édouard, however, would update it to draw a parallel between slaveholding and aristocracy.[40]

In the town of Pau itself enthusiasm for the broad suffrage instituted for the elections of 1848 was accompanied by exuberant civic celebrations, including processions, meetings, and the planting of a tree of liberty. Gone was the property requirement that had narrowed the franchise so sharply. An announcement posted in public spaces explained that every adult Frenchman was now a "political citizen": "Every citizen is an elector. Every elector is sovereign. Law is equal and absolute for all." The elections were announced in Pau with an early-morning drumroll, the sound of trumpets, and the arrival of infantry and cavalry of the National Guard to protect the polling places. There was drama here to fill the republican imagination of young observers like Édouard Tinchant, as well as adult voters.[41]

The results of those elections, however, were a setback for the most radical proponents of a "social republic." Many in the rural population resented the taxes they had to pay to support the National Workshops that were used by the radicals to expand employment in the city; others were unconvinced by the individual socialist leaders. Although some rural departments continued to support the "social republic," when the tally from the late April elections for the Constituent Assembly was complete, it was clear that the majority in the countryside had opted for a liberal republic, and not for socialism.[42]

Before that Constituent Assembly could be seated, however, a crucial step was taken. Echoing the radicalism of the revolutionary generation that had voted the first decree of abolition in 1794, the French state again aligned itself with abolitionism and the campaign for equality. Pushed forward by popular ferment in the metropolis and slave initiatives in the colonies, the new Republic decreed the formal abolition of slavery on April 27, 1848, to be enacted across the entirety of France's empire two months later. Indeed, under the new laws, no French citizen could own slaves, even outside of France's jurisdiction—a step that eventually caught the attention of observers in New Orleans.

A striking declaration in the texts accompanying the metropolitan decrees held that no laws should be established that created obstacles to "social equality." Again, these steps resonated across the Atlantic. The Haitian minister resident in France saluted the advent of the Republic with "enthusiasm" as an event representing immense progress for humanity, and welcomed the decrees that would bring emancipation to "our unhappy brothers," in reference to those still held as property in the French Antilles.[43]

The events of early 1848 in Paris were exhilarating, and the moment of abolition was a high point. But the months that followed were marked by division and frustration. Then came the terrible June Days of insurrection in the capital, in which workers thrown out of work by the closing of the National Workshops massed in the streets. They were met by repression and massacre at the hands of an army of peasant conscripts under a general who had learned the intricacies of urban warfare in colonial Algeria. No sooner had the Republic been consecrated than the implications of its core principles were bitterly disputed, both in the capital and in the countryside. In Pau, radical schoolteachers were soon brought under the direct orders of the local prefect, and in February 1849 the head of a local *école communale* was fired. In 1850 the national government cut suffrage back sharply, and in 1851 Louis-Napoléon Bonaparte carried out his coup d'état, beginning the transformation of the republic into an authoritarian regime marked by episodic plebiscites. Republican activists were "proscribed" and sometimes exiled.[44]

If events in the city were frightening, times in the countryside were very hard. No amount of debate about the "social republic" could alter the fact of bad harvests. Joseph could see that there was no future in following in his parents' footsteps in the Béarn. Their agricultural enterprise was shrinking rather than expanding, with the possibility of worse yet to come. After a wave of fierce state repression swept Paris in the last months of 1848, Joseph Tinchant apparently concluded that he had seen enough.

True to the Vincent-Tinchant Atlantic tradition, he pulled up stakes rather than putting down roots, and looked across the sea for a path away from danger and toward greater opportunity. He had accomplished one of his parents' primary goals for the family's move to France, achieving an unusually high level of formal schooling. But however much he appreciated educational opportunity and civil equality in France, and whatever his sentiments about the advent of the Second Republic in 1848, he had begun to look back to Louisiana as a more promising field of economic opportunity. It had been nearly half a century since Louisiana was actually a colony of France, but for enterprising young metropolitans it still held out the classic colonial dream of wealth to be made easily. In his own family, rental income from New Orleans had continued to flow to Jacques Tinchant in Pau, even when profits from the family's new agricultural enterprise in France were faltering.[45]

His parents and his uncle Pierre Duhart may have told Joseph something about the difficulties of life in the Americas when one was labeled an *homme de couleur,* but perhaps they were discreet when speaking around the children and refrained from narrating the humiliating experiences to which one could be subjected under Louisiana's "infamous laws and stupid prejudices." Joseph was still quite young, and under no obligation to figure out in advance just how the equal-rights principles of a *quarante-huitard*, an eighteen-forty-eighter, could be sustained in a slaveholding city in the heart of the Mississippi Valley. He would face that problem when he had to. For now, the most important thing was to move on.[46]

There was, moreover, a clear route back to the Americas. Joseph's older brother Louis had stayed in New Orleans and helped to maintain the family's link to that world of commerce, serving as their father's agent in renting or selling off their remaining urban properties while setting up a small business of his own. The census enumerator in New Orleans held Louis Tinchant to be a "grocer," suggesting that he probably ran a corner store at which clients could find drink and sociability as well as foodstuffs. Perhaps Louis's shop could use a younger assistant?[47]

In late 1848 Joseph booked passage out of Bordeaux on the *Mount Washington,* sailing for New Orleans. He was twenty-one years old, he carried one trunk, and he traveled in steerage. No color term accompanied his name on the passenger list filled out by the captain at their port of departure in France. A year or so after the ship landed, however, the census-taker in New Orleans would inscribe Joseph Tinchant in his brother's household in the fourth ward of the third municipality of New Orleans, and place next to the name the letter *M* for mulatto.[48]

6

Joseph and His Brothers

It was something of a gamble in 1849 for a young man of color to seek resources and respect by moving to Louisiana. Picking up the remaining threads of the family's earlier life in New Orleans, Joseph Tinchant initially found employment as a clerk, perhaps working for his brother Louis, who had recently married a young Louisiana-born woman named Octavie Rieffel.[1] Their father's half brother Louis Alfred Duhart was still in town, and their mother's godmother the widow Aubert had just passed away. In an early letter home, Joseph wrote to his mother about the complexities of settling the estate of the widow, the astute but entangling businesswoman in whose household Élisabeth had been raised.[2]

A long-lived survivor of the refugee generations of Joseph's parents and grandparents, the widow had stayed on for many years in the dwelling left for her use by her former partner, Jean Lambert Détry. She finally relinquished her legal claim to the use of the house in January 1848, enabling the executors to begin the process of passing it on to Détry's heirs. A few months later she died, having reached the age of ninety. When the appraisers arrived at the house, they were welcomed by the widow's former slave Marie-Antoinette Lambert, who escorted them through the rooms as they proceeded to compile a notarized inventory of the widow's belongings.[3]

When writing to his mother about the settlement of the estate, Joseph Tinchant did not refer to the widow by any of the names that appear in the official record of the proceedings. Instead, to him she was "Madame Lambert." Élisabeth Vincent's children had apparently been taught to address their mother's godmother as a proper married woman, attributing to her one of the surnames of her companion Jean Lambert Détry.[4] Like the relationship of Suzette Bayot and Louis Duhart, or even that of Rosalie and Michel Vincent, the union of the widow from Saint-Domingue and the carpenter from Belgium was retrospectively transformed into a marriage by some of those around them. The surname Lambert was then extended as well to the freedwoman Marie-Antoinette with her manumission.[5]

Those who, like the widow Aubert, were characterized as *gens de couleur libres* are often imagined to have remained aloof from those who were enslaved. The reciprocities developed over a long life, however, could on occasion create complex relations of dependence. In her last will and testament, the widow left many of her possessions to Marie-Antoinette Lambert, whom she herself had held as a slave. Indeed, most of the furniture in the house in which the widow died belonged to the young woman, now married to a local brick mason. On the inventory of goods compiled by the executor, Marie-Antoinette signed in a firm hand, as she had on her own manumission document sixteen years earlier.[6]

At the time of the widow's death, the primary assets inventoried in the estate consisted of persons held as property: Louis, also known as Jean-Godo, twenty-three years old; two young women, each designated "négresse Créole"; and the older woman nicknamed Trois-Sous (Threepenny), "créole de Saint-Domingue." Several of the slaves were listed as "statu-libre," meaning that they held a promise of freedom, reflecting manumissions called for in the widow's will.[7]

On the second day of the inventory of the succession, the executor (a white attorney) and the heir turned to the widow's papers. Here, carefully saved, was a trail of petitions and lawsuits, as well as many purchases of slaves, beginning with Trois-Sous in 1813, and continuing through to the slave named Amanda in 1831. The widow's will left another slave, Marie Jeanne, to a niece who she thought might be living in Tampico, Mexico, and two slaves to her executor, on condition that he free them. And finally, the will declared, "Je donne la liberté à ma négresse esclave Trois-sous, agée d'environ Cinquante-cinq ans"—I give freedom to my black woman slave Trois-Sous, about fifty-five years old. This woman from Saint-Domingue, held as a slave by the widow for thirty-five years, with a written promise of freedom deposited with a notary, was finally to be freed.[8]

Or so it seemed. Official documents concerning last wishes are rich sources of information, but they do not necessarily determine the events they seek to control. The text of the widow's will—which had been witnessed by Joseph's older brother Louis—held that Trois-Sous was to be freed. But in the event, when the estate was actually settled, Joseph Tinchant reported to his mother, "we bought her." The most generous interpretation of the purchase—for which they paid just thirty-seven dollars—would be that the former slave was in need of care or a place to live.

Joseph referred to her as still "quite alert" *(bien alerte)*, suggesting that she was aging but still active.[9]

As the fate of Trois-Sous suggests, the line between slavery and freedom, like that between concubinage and marriage, was not necessarily a clear one in the New Orleans of the mid-nineteenth century. The form of a sale could conceal a de facto manumission; or an apparently legally mandated manumission could be averted by a sale. For a proper manumission to be finalized, the owner or agent had to complete a complex set of requirements, including the posting of notices, obtaining of clearances, and appearance before a judge. For Trois-Sous, this seems to have been a task that no one would take on. Once the executor Edgar Montégut authorized a purchase by the Tinchants, Trois-Sous had no mechanism for enforcing the manumission on her own. By paying thirty-seven dollars for the property right over her, Louis Tinchant moved her from one household to another, exercising whatever degree of concern he thought appropriate for a woman who had very likely helped to raise his mother. But Trois-Sous remained legally a slave.

By reporting on their acquisition of Trois-Sous, Joseph signaled his ability to help follow up on his parents' connections and responsibilities in New Orleans. But by itself this was not a very productive avenue of economic activity. Their father already had an agent who collected rents on the family's remaining properties in the city, and sent the money directly to France. Nor would serving as a clerk yield much status or benefit. Something more promising had to be found. Louis and Joseph were not carpenters like their father, able to add value to small plots of land in an expanding city. They did not have the capital to deal in real estate on a substantial scale. They needed a business open to those of modest means, but with the prospect of profit. While sugar and cotton were bringing vast wealth to the city's planters and merchants, these were not sectors in which small operators were likely to flourish.

By the early 1850s, the city directory signaled their choice: Louis and Joseph Tinchant began to be listed as "segar makers." Much of the tobacco exported from the United States passed through the port of New Orleans, and cigar-making skills were common among the free and enslaved populations of color in the city. A resourceful entrepreneur could roll cigars on his own to get started, or buy cigars from others who rolled them, and later purchase leaf tobacco in bulk and hire workers to do the rolling. The increasing constraints imposed by Louisiana's laws on free people of color were both galling and humiliating, but they did not prevent the Tinchants from engaging in commercial activities. The city's notaries happily officiated (for a fee) at sales, contracts, loans, and mortgages—though they generally recorded the brothers' designation as *hommes de couleur libres* alongside the details of each transaction.[10]

As their ambitions grew, Louis and Joseph sought to persuade their parents to advance them some capital to help expand their project. Five years after his journey from Bordeaux to New Orleans, Joseph Tinchant made a trip back across the Atlantic to appeal to Jacques and Élisabeth for support for the new enterprise. Rental revenues from the Tinchants' New Orleans properties had been subsidizing the family's life in France, but now the sons hoped to sell those holdings. In January 1853, Élisabeth Tinchant issued a power of attorney before a notary in Gan to her son Joseph, who signed the document in an elegant copperplate hand. Given the terms of Élisabeth's marriage contract with Jacques, her permission was needed each time a property was sold. Her power of attorney was thus essential to carry out transactions concerning the remaining properties in New Orleans, in order to apply the proceeds to the new enterprise. In the spring of 1853, three of these holdings were indeed liquidated, as Jacques sold out to his former partner (and half brother) Pierre Duhart for the substantial sum of $3,250.[11]

Louis and Joseph were now able to expand their operation to a warehouse at 15 New Levee Street in New Orleans and to purchase (at cut-rate and with no guarantees) a single forty-five-year-old enslaved cigar maker named Martin Mitchel. Because Martin Mitchel survived his years as a slave, we catch a more detailed glimpse of him in later records. He was a black man, born in North Carolina. After the Civil War, he lived as part of an extended household that included another cigar maker, as well as a woman named Nancy Mitchel (perhaps a sister?), also from North Carolina, who by 1870 was listed as "blind." Both had almost certainly been victims of the massive domestic slave trade that had moved men, women, and children out of the upper South and into the expanding economy of the Southwest.[12]

The Tinchant brothers presumably supplemented the labor of the enslaved Martin Mitchel with their own and that of free men working either as employees or as independent contractors. In several neighborhoods in the city, small-scale artisans acquired boxes of leaf tobacco by purchase or on consignment, and then rolled the cigars at home. Indeed, cigar making could be the occupation of last resort for men in the city who were down on their luck. In 1854 Benito Juárez, the lawyer and former governor of the Mexican state of Oaxaca, spent a year in exile in New Orleans, lodging in a boardinghouse and supporting himself by rolling cigars. André Cailloux, a Louisiana-born black man who would later achieve distinction in the Union army, was another cigar maker.[13]

By the time the 1854–1855 New Orleans city directory was published, Louis and Joseph Tinchant had been upgraded from "segar makers" to "segar manufacturers," with a wholesale and retail business in the warehouse district. The brothers were now beginning to put into place an even more ambitious plan—one whose very possibility built on the web of connections woven during the household's Atlantic travels. Their parents' farm at Pédemarie in Gan had tied up most of the family's capital. If Pédemarie were liquidated, it would liberate funds that Louis and Joseph could then use to expand the tobacco business internationally. Along with their younger brothers, they could seek to occupy different points in what economic historians refer to as the "commodity chain," dealing successively in leaf tobacco, imported cigars, cigar rolling, and the boxing and merchandising of the finished product.[14]

The regions where cigars had traditionally been produced, including Cuba, were in the mid-1850s beginning to lose some of their dominance in the market, as the export of leaf tobacco enabled manufacturers elsewhere to produce the cigars themselves. In 1855–1856, the Liberal government in Mexico—in which the former cigar maker Benito Juárez served as minister of justice—opened the field for expanded production and for export, culminating in the dissolution of the state monopoly on tobacco. The way was clear for entrepreneurs to move into a now more-diversified market.[15]

A family with an anchor at each end of the process—the Gulf and the Caribbean for the tobacco, Europe for the consumers and perhaps later the manufactory—might be able to benefit as this shift accelerated. The port of New Orleans, which looked in both directions, was an excellent vantage point from which to see the possibility of this strategy. And a family accustomed to moving from place to place, multiplying connections rather than abandoning them, could give it a try.

Events in rural France were pushing Jacques and Élisabeth to divest themselves of the farm in the Basses-Pyrénées, just as their elder sons were trying to persuade them to underwrite the tobacco proposal with a long-term loan. In 1852 the oidium fungus attacked vineyards throughout France, destroying one vineyard after another. For Jacques and Élisabeth, whose property included large areas of vineyards, this was a serious blow. They began to take steps to withdraw from farming altogether.[16]

In February 1854 they found a buyer who would purchase Pédemarie for 26,000 francs (somewhat less than they had paid for it), but only in installments over several years. They retained their furniture, the firewood already cut, some chickens, and a horse, and moved to a small house in the nearby town of Jurançon to wait for the final payments on their property. They were both now in their mid-fifties, and apparently ready to pass the torch of entrepreneurship to the next generation.[17]

It cannot have been easy to step down from being *propriétaires* of Pédemarie to spending the winter in lodgings down by the bridge over the (often-flooded) river in Jurançon. In 1856, Jacques, known in town as "Jacques Tinchant, Américain," signed a power of attorney allowing his sons to sell or mortgage his remaining properties in New Orleans. The shift from landed property into commerce was both a financial gamble and a generational transition, but in the depressed French agricultural economy of the mid-1850s it may have seemed unavoidable.[18]

Louis and Joseph could now lay the groundwork for an Atlantic version of their enterprise, one that would tap into the expanding European market for cigars. But where to establish their Continental base? France and most other European nations had strict and long-standing national monopolies on tobacco, making them inhospitable to a beginner. The kingdom of Belgium, however, taxed tobacco products rather than monopolizing their sale. Its port of Antwerp had direct links with a variety of destinations on the Gulf of Mexico, and a modest tobacco-processing industry. Ships from Antwerp often landed in New Orleans, bringing German immigrants and Northern European manufactures. Perhaps one or another Belgian ship captain or merchant had told the Tinchant brothers about the growing market and cheap labor available in Antwerp.[19]

The Kingdom of Belgium was in other ways a potentially accommodating environment for a family like the Tinchants. In the community of merchants and in official business, French remained the dominant language. Though socially conservative, and riven with class tensions, Belgium was a stable, highly urbanized democratic nation with a relatively free press. Among the exiles who had found refuge there (in addition to Karl Marx) were a variety of activists who had been involved in the 1848 revolution in France and suffered during its repression, including many of the so-called *proscrits du Deux-Décembre*, those banned by Napoléon III because of their opposition to his 1851 coup d'état. Belgium, moreover, was a young state (independent only since 1830) and not yet a colonial power, one with a substantial immigrant population and no history of formalized color discrimination. For Joseph, the boldest of the sons, it seemed worth a try.[20]

In June 1856, Joseph Tinchant took out a passport in New Orleans and prepared to sail back across the Atlantic. His initial destination may well have been the port of Bordeaux, allowing him to visit the family in Pau and consult with his parents and siblings about the next move. The project depended on the willingness of Jacques and Élisabeth to continue to underwrite the substantial loan to their older sons, and on Joseph's finding some way for the whole family to regroup in a new city.[21]

By autumn of the same year Joseph Tinchant was in Paris, where he met up with a musician and cigar maker friend from New Orleans named Edmond Dédé, who had traveled to France from Veracruz in Mexico. Edmond Dédé was probably aiming to make enough money to enroll in the Paris Conservatory, and he joined Joseph as they proceeded on to the great Belgian trading city of Antwerp. Registering with the Belgian police upon arrival, Joseph declared himself optimistically to be a "fabricant de cigares" (cigar maker) who lived by his own *commerce*. Edmond described himself as Joseph's "bookkeeper."[22]

At the same moment, back in Louisiana, Louis Tinchant divested the enterprise of the enslaved cigar maker, Martin Mitchel, whom they had acquired two years earlier. The price was twice what they had paid—$250 as opposed to $125—but still quite low. From this point forward, the family apparently no longer held anyone as a slave, unless perhaps Trois-Sous was still alive and living with Louis and Octavie. It seems likely that the manufacturing activities of "L & J Tinchant" in New Orleans were now carried out by free artisans.[23]

For the crew in Antwerp, the first winter months must have been miserable. Joseph and his friend Edmond moved into rented rooms at 188 Book Alley (Ruelle du Livre/Boeksteeg), in a poor neighborhood near the port.[24] They faced the double difficulty of finding workers to assist them in cigar making, and of developing a market for the finished product. Antwerp in the mid-1850s was a magnet for impoverished workers from the countryside. The collapse of the putting-out system in textiles had flung men, women, and children out of rural production and into the city, desperate for work. The two newcomers shared crowded living conditions with these poorer migrants, though if they could manage to get far enough ahead to hire workers to assist in the production of cigars, they could do so at low wages. Early in 1857 they incorporated into their household a teenage cigar maker named Salomon Benni, from Holland.[25]

With the beachhead in Boeksteeg established, the contingent from France began to arrive in Antwerp—first brother Ernest in March 1857, then brother Jules in May, then Jacques, Élisabeth, and Édouard in August. (Édouard was not yet sixteen years old, and the parents may have stayed in Jurançon through the spring so that he could finish the school year.) There was by now push as well as pull to this migration—the family no longer owned a house in France, and they had shifted the bulk of their capital to their sons.[26]

As the whole crew crowded into the rented rooms, Edmond Dédé took his leave, returning to France and what would eventually become a distinguished career as a composer and conductor. The Antwerp household, which now consisted of at least six Tinchants and the young Salomon Benni, struggled to get a foothold in the economic life of the city. Joseph in Belgium and Louis in Louisiana would have to move decisively to put their transatlantic projects into effect.[27]

First, they re-assorted the brothers in order to take advantage of the skills of Louis, who had the longest history in commerce, both as a grocer and as a tobacco manufacturer. In March 1857, acting on behalf of his father, Louis sold off yet another of Jacques' tracts of land in New Orleans—this one on Barracks Street, between Bourbon and Royal—for $2,000. Then, in the spring of 1858, accompanied by his wife Octavie Rieffel, their three children, and a servant, Louis boarded the steamship *Philadelphia* for New York. From there the family proceeded on to Antwerp, where Louis began to direct a small-scale export-import business under the name Maison Américaine.[28]

The arrival of Louis in Antwerp freed Joseph to go back to Louisiana to develop the tobacco component of the brothers' overlapping plans, building on the enterprise they had established in New Orleans as L & J Tinchant. Brothers Pierre and Jules joined forces with Joseph in New Orleans, where they lodged with a carpenter named Félix Azéma. Like their father before them, the brothers built their ties with artisans in the city's free population of color, as well as with clients from the white population. The census taker counted Azéma as a mulatto and registered Pierre and Jules as working in a "cigar store and factory."[29]

On June 20, 1859, Joseph Tinchant carried this alliance a step further, marrying Stéphanie Gonzales, daughter of a carpenter named Vincent

Gonzales, and sister to a half-dozen artisan brothers. Both Joseph and Stéphanie were designated as free colored persons on their marriage record. The young couple moved in with her parents, and their first child was born in April 1860.[30]

Free persons of color in New Orleans were now facing renewed legal assaults on their autonomy. They nonetheless maintained a very substantial network of institutions, including the Société Catholique pour l'Instruction des Orphelins dans l'Indigence, which administered a school for free children of color. The board of this society was an important point of associational activity, and Joseph Tinchant joined it, making himself useful through his ties to Belgian purveyors of French-language school supplies. He was soon named treasurer.[31]

By 1860 it might well have been possible to declare the family's tobacco venture a modest success. The R. G. Dun credit ratings agency noted that L & J Tinchant, cigar manufacturers, located at 9 New Levee, New Orleans, "met their engagements promptly" and were good for loans of a modest amount. The raters judged the firm, soon styled Tinchant Brothers, to be a "small but safe business." The Tinchants primarily sold wholesale to the trade, advertising rather suggestively to "grocers, bar keepers, and all dealers in Cigars" that their "imitations of the most reputed brands" were so perfect that "it is impossible for the best connoisseurs to perceive any difference, except for the prices, which are extremely moderate."[32]

Back in Antwerp, the elder Tinchants and the younger brothers were able to move out of Boeksteeg and to the more respectable address of Schuttershof 59/3. Jacques and Élisabeth, now in their sixties, could properly call themselves *rentiers,* and hope to live off the proceeds of the loan repayments and rental income from their modest remaining properties in New Orleans. On the recommendation of Joseph Tinchant, brother Louis was able to arrange schooling in Ghent for the son of family friends from Alabama. The young Augustus Clément Joseph of Mobile thus followed, as had the younger Tinchants, an established European pathway to overcome the limitations on educational opportunities for people of color in the southern states. Overall, the Tinchant family strategy of building networks across the Atlantic was working, though it did not yet yield any very great profits.[33]

As the year 1860 came to a close, however, it became apparent that all of this might come crashing down as a result of the rapidly accelerating sectional crisis in the United States. The most aggressive of the slaveholding states began to secede following the November election of Abraham

Lincoln, and as the momentum of disunion grew, Louisiana's voters (all of them by definition white) elected a secession convention. The state left the Union on January 26, 1861.[34]

Like other relatively prosperous men of color in New Orleans, Joseph Tinchant was now in a very delicate position. His colleague Armand Lanusse of the Société Catholique chose the path of ostentatious loyalty to the Confederacy, welcoming the formation of a Confederate militia of men of color, which then paraded in front of the school that Lanusse directed. Although Joseph himself had for a time held a part-interest in an enslaved cigar maker, his political sympathies lay with the Union, and he seems to have been willing to bide his time. The younger Tinchant brothers, Jules and Pierre, by contrast, did not wait to see what war might bring, and left to try their luck across the Gulf of Mexico in Veracruz.[35]

Joseph Tinchant's brothers-in-law Armand, Gustave, and Paul Gonzales, whatever their private convictions about the war, followed the lead of many of the most prominent free men of color in New Orleans and offered their services to the Confederate units organizing to defend the city. Scholars have struggled to interpret this initiative, evoking motives ranging from elitist self-interest on the part of a relatively "privileged" property-owning and artisan group, to sheer fear in the face of a proven pattern of bitter hostility to free people of color by the pro-slavery secessionists who were in power in the state. It is reasonable to suppose that individual decisions to enlist arose from many different motivations. Moreover, as one historian has recently pointed out, at a time of crisis refusal might have looked like cowardice, "and the fear of appearing less than fully a man was a worldview that seems not to have been tempered by the color of one's skin."[36]

Joseph Tinchant faced the challenge of maintaining good relations with the white clientele of his retail store on St. Charles Avenue, all the while concealing his hostility to the Confederate régime and managing a delicate set of relationships within the population of color. By early January 1862, he had discreetly withdrawn from his position as treasurer in the Société Catholique in which Armand Lanusse played a conspicuously pro-Confederate role. He kept his head down as the war news conveyed the very great uncertainty of the outcome of the conflict between the Union and the Confederacy.[37]

The Union blockade limited trade through the Confederate port of New Orleans, and business became increasingly difficult. Across the Atlantic in Antwerp, the press followed the unfolding of the Civil War in the United States with interest, watching the debate over slavery and trying to anticipate the consequences for their own port as well. Louis Tinchant continued to direct the Maison Américaine, which depended on such trade, but his financial situation deteriorated. The war made it more difficult to receive funds from the United States, and soon the principal of the school where they had placed the son of their friends from Alabama began to demand payment from the Tinchants, who had been the intermediaries. It was all very embarrassing.[38]

There was more serious embarrassment yet to come. The youngest Tinchant—Édouard—was the last one left at home with his parents at Schuttershof 59/3. Although he had been a star student in the *lycée* in Pau, he seems to have been at loose ends in Antwerp, rapidly becoming a troublesome romantic. Between April and September of 1861 he frequented bars down at the port, fell in love, and generally put his family's reputation at risk. After six months of this unmanageable behavior, something dreadful happened—or at least something that his father Jacques deemed to be dreadful. It is at this remove impossible to determine what the transgression was, although it seems to have been obliquely related to a young woman. Perhaps drinking and gambling entered into it as well; the tone of Édouard's subsequent apologies suggests that he may have incurred debts that his father had to cover.[39]

The stiff-backed Jacques Tinchant apparently had no intention of waiting to see what other harm to his reputation Édouard might come up with. He arranged for the young man to be spirited out of Belgium to Holland and to be put on a sailing ship headed for the Americas, where it was hoped that he might make himself useful to his brothers. No record of Édouard's departure from Antwerp seems to have been filed with the Belgian authorities, but on September 29, 1861, he set sail from the Dutch port of Vlissingen. From the first port of call, Dover, he sent a repentant letter to his mother, in which he reported that he was doing fine on board, reading a chapter of *The Imitation of Christ* every Sunday, and practicing Spanish two hours a day. He pronounced himself eager to reach his brother Jules, now located in Veracruz, and to begin to make up for the terrible things he had done.[40]

For years to come, Édouard would beg his father's pardon for his "follies." But once at sea in the fall of 1861, repentant though he might be, he seems to have been thrilled by the journey. The crossing took seventy-three days and brought the ship within view of Madeira and the Canary Islands, then across to Guadeloupe, Puerto Rico, and Cuba. A storm delayed their arrival in Veracruz, but they were able to land on December 15.[41]

There, however, Édouard stumbled into the rapidly escalating consequences of an international economic and diplomatic wrangle. When Benito Juárez emerged victorious in the three-year War of the Reform and assumed the presidency of Mexico in 1861, he faced a crushing international debt contracted by his predecessors—including the conservatives who had taken out loans in Europe in order to wage war against him. On July 17, 1861, the Mexican Congress suspended payment of interest on the national debt. A joint British, French, and Spanish military expedition to Mexico was mounted, ostensibly to persuade the Mexican government to change its mind.

The ambitions of Napoléon III, emperor of the French, however, would prove to be considerably more far-reaching. Intervention in Mexico offered the possibility of challenging the regional power of the United States—a prospect made more feasible by the possibility that the Confederacy might succeed in fracturing the nation altogether. At the very least, the Civil War would tie down the U.S. military and leave considerable room for action by European powers in Mexico.[42]

The troops of the Three Powers were meant to arrive simultaneously in Mexico, but in practice the Spanish navy stole a march on Spain's allies and sailed directly from Cuba to Veracruz. There the Spanish, French, and British intended to seize the customs house and begin collecting the revenue they believed that their nationals were owed. On the day that Édouard Tinchant landed at the port, the city of Veracruz had just been taken by the Spanish navy, and the French and British joined them shortly thereafter. The Mexican army held the territory a few leagues from the city, cutting off trade and communication with the interior. It was all very exciting to narrate in a letter home, but not very promising for a French-born young man hoping to make his fortune in trade.[43]

Édouard's older brother Jules, moreover, had received a bitter letter from their father giving his side of the story of Édouard's follies, which were said to include frequenting the port in Antwerp with "ce qu'il y a de plus crapuleux" (the lowest of lowlifes). Jules showed no interest in taking on the irresponsible Édouard, whose "character" he found distasteful. On the grounds that business was bad and that Édouard spoke no Spanish, Jules packed him off to the United States, hoping that brother Joseph would be able to deal with him. The Confederate city of New Orleans was under a Union naval blockade, but no matter: Édouard could take a boat to Texas and make his way to Louisiana overland. This did not promise to be an easy journey, but Édouard had been mortified to learn of his father's letter telling Jules and his colleagues about the episode in Antwerp, and he was apparently eager to leave.[44]

Thus it was that Édouard Tinchant, age twenty, arrived in the Confederate metropolis of trade and slavery in the spring of 1862 and walked into the midst of the Civil War. Édouard moved in with his brother Joseph's in-laws, the Gonzaleses, at 256 Prieur. He reported that they were gracious and generous with him, and he seems to have been excited by the whole enterprise.[45]

In later letters home, Édouard portrayed this as a moment of great political tension in Louisiana, in which he was obliged to conceal his own abolitionism from Confederate sympathizers who frequented Joseph's cigar store. In April 1862 the Confederate city fell to the Union forces of Flag Officer David G. Farragut, giving control of the outlet of the Mississippi to the Union. Activist men and women of color could now step onto the public stage, though they would quickly be challenged there by conservative Unionists, and reviled by pro-Confederates. The questions of race, respect, and standing that had troubled the generation of Édouard and Joseph's parents came again to the fore—but now with the prospect that Union occupation might help to change the ground rules.[46]

A foreigner in an occupied city in a country at war, Édouard hastened to register at the French consulate in September 1862. The consul was willing to accept his declaration of birth in Gan, Basses-Pyrénées, as sufficient evidence that he was indeed French. Édouard, who was about to reach the age of twenty-one, was probably aware that any future claim he might make to French citizenship could depend on his having taken this formal affirmative step.[47]

Under the French Civil Code, a son born in France of foreign parents was required by law to make a declaration of loyalty to France in the year following his achievement of majority if he wished to secure citizenship. A law of 1851—aimed at increasing the ranks of the military—had expanded this access by declaring that the son born in France of a foreign father automatically became a French citizen—*if* the father was himself born in France. But Édouard's parents, each the "natural child" of a French colonist settled in Saint-Domingue who later left the colony, seem to have had no clear nationality. Édouard's father Jacques had apparently been born in Baltimore. Édouard's primary claim to "French birth" on the part of a parent would thus have been his mother's baptism in Saint-

Domingue, something for which she did have documentary evidence, but which she may never have formally reconfirmed once in France. In any event, inscribing his name on a consular register was a wise move for Édouard, in case questions of citizenship were to arise later. The alternative could well have been the vulnerability of statelessness.[48]

This was an era in which citizenship for young men was rarely separable from the question of compulsory military service—and indeed some expatriates explicitly renounced their French nationality in order to avoid conscription in the French army. Édouard may have believed that by registering as a Frenchman in the United States he could instead exempt himself from compulsory military service in the occupying Union army. Certainly other residents of Louisiana with a claim to French nationality had earlier sought to avoid Confederate service through this mechanism. (In the end these men had been conscripted anyway, with only the promise that their service would be confined to the limits of the city.) Édouard later vigorously denied that avoidance of Union service had been his motive, and over the long run his behavior suggests that he saw French citizenship as having a value in itself.[49]

Sheltering under French nationality, however, was an uncertain strategy for a young man from a family identified in town as *de couleur*. It would earn no goodwill from the occupiers: Union officials in New Orleans suspected the French population and the French government of sympathies with the slaveholding regime. Aligning himself with the French consulate, moreover, would make for an uncomfortable political allegiance for Édouard. As the political debate heated up, the French consul expressed increasing suspicion of the population of color and hostility to the abolitionist currents that were, in his view, gaining strength.[50]

Across 1862 and 1863, moreover, a clash of imperial goals added to the tension. The Spanish-English-French coalition in pursuit of debt repayment in Mexico had broken down, and the original incursion in Veracruz was now replaced with a full-scale expedition under the orders of France's Napoléon III, aimed at a durable implantation of French power on the North American mainland. For Édouard, who despised Napoléon III as a tyrant, this aggression of an empire against a republic was repellent, opening up a further gulf between his views and those represented by the French consul. Within New Orleans, young men hostile to the French invasion had joined together as a group, calling themselves the "Defenders of the Monroe Doctrine." There was thus now a second major issue, in addition to slavery, on which Édouard Tinchant's avowed principles distanced him from France, and brought him closer to the views of radicals in the city.[51]

Édouard's older brother Joseph Tinchant was becoming highly visible as a spokesman for radical Creole men of color of the city. Jean-Charles Houzeau, a Belgian émigré who worked as a journalist in New Orleans, described such political commitments as the logical result of the experience of Joseph Tinchant and others with civil equality in Europe. The contrast between equality in France and inequality in Louisiana, Houzeau argued, made such men impatient with the burdens of Louisiana's racial discrimination. Invoking a favorite metaphor of the radicals, one that likened their spokesmen to the eloquent popular representatives of the Roman Republic, Houzeau wrote that Joseph Tinchant "had the fire of a tribune."[52]

In the spring and early summer of 1863, Union forces, including a unit of men of color from New Orleans, were besieging the Confederate fort at Port Hudson, while a major Union offensive was under way against Vicksburg. No one knew whether the Union would succeed, and the French consul reported that it was nearly impossible to get reliable military news. Union general Nathaniel Banks, fearing a possible Confederate attack on New Orleans, called for loyal men in the city to come forward as "sixty-day volunteers" to stand guard against such an assault. Édouard Tinchant, who portrayed himself in letters home as an ardent abolitionist *(le plus enragé des abolitionnistes),* now prepared to shift his self-identification from expatriate Frenchman to radical American.[53]

Joseph Tinchant—born in the city and well known to his neighbors—quickly took on an important role in mobilizing military support for the Union, closing down his cigar store to devote himself to the task of recruitment. The eloquence of which Houzeau later spoke was visible in a meeting held at Economy Hall in late June 1863. Nelson Fouché, who a few years earlier had organized the emigration of free men of color from New Orleans to Mexico, had convened a mass meeting drawing together a large roster of activists including Paul Trévigne, of the "African Unit" of the Loyal National League, and Joseph Tinchant, along with honored veterans of the companies of men of color who had fought under Andrew Jackson in 1815. The key agenda item was a declaration of desire of men of color to serve under arms to defend the Union and the city. To give voice to the bitterness of long-standing political exclusion, Joseph Tinchant reached for a classic family analogy. Until now, he told the crowd, persecution had suffocated their love of *patrie* (homeland). That homeland had been like a stepmother, pushing them away from the breast.[54]

To rouse his listeners to action, he shifted the metaphor to one of renewal and flourishing, and then back again to family: Patriotism wilted by slavery could revive in the sunlight of liberty; the stepmother had repented of the wrongs she had committed. The Code Noir, the lash, the stocks would never return. Would men of color now leave themselves open to the charge of cowardice? Would they have the world believe that their race was destined to be servile? ("No! No!" from the crowd.) If it were true that honor was a man's greatest good, they could now leave to their children the knowledge that their fathers, though they might perish, had chosen death rather than infamy and dishonor. ("Prolonged applause.")[55]

On July 4, 1863, Governor Shepley commissioned Joseph Tinchant as second lieutenant in the Union army's Sixth Louisiana Volunteers (Colored).[56] Among those who enlisted in the same regiment were Armand, Valcour, and Paul Gonzales, all brothers of Joseph's wife Stéphanie, and fellow residents of the Sixth Ward of New Orleans. Armand, who became a sergeant, was a mason, Valcour a shoemaker, and Paul an apprentice. Armand and Paul were veterans of the earlier Confederate Native Guard, but like many members of those units, they seem to have made a smooth transition to service for the Union.[57] Édouard Tinchant, who had lived with the Gonzales family when he arrived in the city, apparently joined up as well.[58]

The Sixth Louisiana soon stood guard on the ramparts of the city, in preparation for a possible Confederate attack. Although the unit did not participate in great battles, the fact of widespread recruitment among men of color altered the balance of forces within the city. Jean-Charles Houzeau, who had participated back in Europe in the 1848-era Republican "banquets," saw the dynamic as one in which a new political reality imposed itself on pro-slavery residents of New Orleans, obliging them to renounce "counter-revolution." He was a bit overoptimistic on this score, but his colleagues shared his sense that things were changing, and the publishers expanded the size of the radical newspaper *L'Union*.[59]

Soon the news arrived of Union victories at Vicksburg and Port Hudson. A Union unit of Creole men of color had participated in the siege at Port Hudson, and the courage of Captain André Cailloux, a black Union officer and New Orleans cigar maker who had fallen early in that campaign, became emblematic of the contribution of men of color to the Union cause. Édouard identified these men who fell at Port Hudson as "nos créoles" (our Creoles), a term that was often used within the French-descended population of color. Cailloux's sacrifice was embraced by

English-speaking black men and women as well. On July 29, 1863, Édouard and Joseph Tinchant's unit, the Sixth Louisiana, embodied martial
dignity as two companies of its men accompanied Cailloux's coffin
through the streets of the city in the immense public funeral procession.
Thousands of people of color, both free and enslaved, lined the way, vis-
ibly taking their part in the public sphere of the city of New Orleans.[60]

This may have been the peak of the public career of the Sixth Louisiana. The victories at Vicksburg and Port Hudson gave Union forces control of the Mississippi River, and the risk of a Confederate attack on New
Orleans diminished sharply. The regiment was therefore demobilized in
August without having seen combat. Édouard spoke vaguely in a letter to
his parents of having been invited by his colonel to take the rank of captain and help raise a Union regiment for an expedition to Texas, but there
seems to be no further trace of a second enlistment. Édouard told his parents that he had resigned after a month, having seen the way the Union
command was treating soldiers of color. His brother Joseph, as a lieutenant, was indeed directly affected by the hostility to officers of color on the
part of General Banks.[61]

What Édouard did not tell his parents was that while armed and in
uniform, he had suffered a humiliating incident. He was riding the streetcar toward Carrollton when a Union sergeant—apparently believing that
a "colored" soldier did not belong in the same car as his white fellow
soldiers—shoved him off. A Union lieutenant then put Édouard under
arrest. The streetcars were a focal point both for racists and for equal-
rights activists, and the right to ride them on equal terms raised questions
not only of color and respect, but of the policies of the Union army. Édouard protested to his superior officer and was apparently vindicated by
the colonel commanding the unit.[62]

The problem, however, was not confined to individual sergeants with
racist impulses. President Lincoln and the Union high command had still
not settled on a policy concerning slavery in the occupied states, or the
military service of men of color. General Banks himself, though he needed
the manpower offered by the men of color of Louisiana, refused their
claims to respect and recognition as leaders and citizens. The question of
eligibility for commissions was a flash point, and Banks had forced the
resignations of men who had been commissioned as officers in the Union
army in the first phase of recruitment. Although their loyalty to the
Union was unquestioned, some of the men associated with the "colored"

regiments—including Joseph Tinchant—began to take their distance from the Union high command and its complicity with the prejudices associated with a slaveholding society.[63]

The tobacco business optimistically named Tinchant Brothers, moreover, was faltering under the pressure of war and occupation. Joseph's original partners—Pierre and Jules—had now both left Louisiana. Édouard, recently arrived, had little to offer by way of experience and nothing by way of resources. Joseph apparently helped Édouard get started in a very small-scale business buying and selling firewood, but did not invite him into the partnership.[64]

Édouard tried to put a good face on the situation, explaining to his mother that he was a bit of a rolling stone, working on his own but not accumulating very much (he spoke of earning six dollars a week). At some point in 1864 Édouard moved in with the family headed by François Xavier, a shoemaker in Faubourg Tremé. Linked to Édouard's mother Élisabeth by ties of actual or fictive kinship, the family was struggling in wartime New Orleans, and Édouard reported that he was doing his best to help these Xavier "cousins." Like his brothers, Édouard was drawn to the cigar trade, but in his case the enterprise was limited to buying a batch of cigars at wholesale in New Orleans, traveling upriver to Memphis to sell them, and then coming back again to New Orleans.[65]

Although his commercial career was hardly brilliant, Édouard Tinchant was making his first moves toward a place in the public political life of New Orleans. The newspaper *L'Union*, established and funded by the Creole doctor Louis Charles Roudanez, and edited by Paul Trévigne, offered a tempting platform. The paper published literary and political essays in addition to news, and managed to number among its contributors both strong Unionists and former Confederates, including Armand Lanusse, who was a poet as well as a school principal.[66]

The essay that would provoke Édouard Tinchant's entry into the world of political polemics was one in which Armand Lanusse championed the cause of Emperor Maximilian, who had arrived in Mexico in June 1864, to be declared head of state of Mexico under French auspices. Lanusse wrote to praise the French intervention and urge his fellow francophone men of color to migrate to Mexico. In doing so, Lanusse was endorsing an option that had long been apparent to free people of color in New Orleans. Already in 1857 a group of free persons of color from Louisiana had proposed to establish a colony they called Eureka, on the

Gulf Coast of Mexico near Tampico. Drawn by the pro-immigration policies of the Liberal regime, and led by Joseph Tinchant's subsequent ally Nelson Fouché, the settlers had been scheduled to acquire land and Mexican citizenship. The enterprise was ultimately unsuccessful, but Mexico's antislavery reputation and open land continued to be a draw.[67]

In the summer of 1864, however, the question of moving to Mexico was taking on a quite different valence. Some Confederates advocated endorsing the claim of Maximilian to be the legitimate head of state, in exchange for his recognition of the Confederate States of America. Many northern Republicans, by contrast, supported the recently deposed Liberal Benito Juárez.[68]

Maximilian and his conservative allies now made a bid to attract white migrants from the Confederacy as settlers. French-speaking families were thought to be particularly appropriate for the imperial project of "regenerating" Mexico through immigration. In early August 1864 a French-language newspaper in Mexico City appealed for supporters of the Confederacy to come to Mexico, and adduced evidence from a "Louisianian" who had already established himself there.[69]

Armand Lanusse's timing thus precisely matched that of Maximilian's publicists in Mexico, but given his audience, he adopted a different set of arguments. Addressing the readers of *L'Union*, a newspaper known to be a strong supporter of equal rights, Lanusse charged that the federal authorities in New Orleans were failing to serve the interests of men of color. French-occupied Mexico, he argued, was a more appropriate home for Louisiana Creoles of color. Mexico had long been known to be a nation in which, its supporters argued, "whatever the color of their skin, all men are equal before the law."[70]

Criticism of Union policy from this direction rankled Édouard Tinchant, who counted himself a fierce abolitionist, a proponent of equal rights—and an absolute enemy of Napoléon III. Tinchant's argumentative position was handicapped, however, by the fact that the federal government of the United States indeed provided no effective guarantee of equal citizenship to men of color. As of the summer of 1864, despite the practical collapse of slavery in Louisiana, the larger question of the legal fate of slavery was still in debate.[71]

For President Abraham Lincoln, Union-occupied Louisiana provided a prospective example of reconstruction of a former Confederate state to be carried out in a spirit of amnesty and cooperation. White Unionists would be allowed to take the lead, and the question of equal suffrage would be deferred. In April 1864 an all-white constitutional convention assembled, charged with framing a constitution with which the state could reenter the Union. Although it was understood that the new constitution would need to recognize the abolition of slavery, a Louisiana judge had recently issued a ruling that implied that as a matter of law slavery still existed in the state. Delegates to the convention continued to wrangle over the question of monetary compensation to former slaveholders deemed loyal to the Union, and many denounced the very idea of black political participation. On the floor of that convention one delegate proposed to adopt as part of the new fundamental law of the state the proposition that "No negro shall be permitted to vote." He was ruled out of order on the grounds that "under the report adopted, only free white male citizens can be voters, and that is strong enough." Governor Michael Hahn eventually ordered that the judge who had declared slavery to be still in force be removed from office, and the final text of the proposed constitution confirmed the abolition of slavery. But it was certainly possible to make the case that the Federal occupiers and their white Unionist allies had temporized on the question of slavery and were far from granting the full enjoyment of civic equality to men and women of African descent.[72]

At the federal level, the Senate had passed the proposed Thirteenth Amendment abolishing slavery, but the House of Representatives had rejected it, so it was not yet available for possible ratification. The high command of the Union army in Louisiana, moreover, often behaved disrespectfully toward the Unionist men of color in the city. There was plenty for Armand Lanusse to point to when he argued that northerners would not respect the rights of men of color in the South.[73]

For Édouard Tinchant, however, the political call to emigrate to Mexico ran precisely contrary to what it had meant for him to choose citizenship in the United States—the burst of enthusiasm in 1863 that had caused him to relinquish his claim to French nationality by joining the Union army. The United States was not in any literal sense Édouard's *patrie;* he had been born and lived for twenty of his twenty-three years in France. But he was now convinced that in order to end slavery once and for all, men of color had to remain in Louisiana to stand and fight for the Union. And so in July of 1864 he took up his pen to denounce the idea of expatriating to Mexico, and to challenge the eloquent and accomplished Armand Lanusse. He would do so in the pages of *L'Union* and its successor, the bilingual *Tribune,* sophisticated radical newspapers read as far away as Washington, D.C. He would need to deploy all the rhetorical training that he had acquired at the *lycée* in Pau, while re-situating himself firmly as an American patriot. And he would have to do all of this in the knowledge that his own older brother Joseph, a widely respected former lieutenant in the Union army, was just about ready to give up on the cause and depart for Mexico himself.[74]

In the Senegal River Valley in West Africa a *marabout* (cleric and teacher) is preparing a protective talisman containing Qur'anic verses for a young Pulaar-speaking woman. Rosalie "of the Poulard [Pulaar] nation" was the designation given to Édouard Tinchant's grandmother as she was sold into slavery around 1785–1790. (Lithograph from Abbé David Boilat, *Esquisses sénégalaises* [Paris, 1853], Musée du Quai Branly, Paris.)

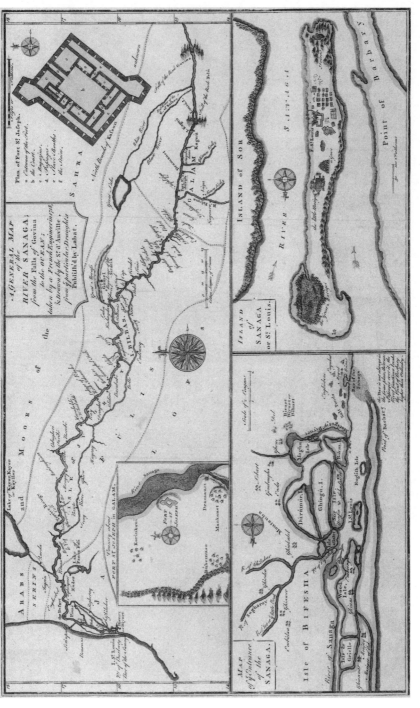

The island of Saint-Louis, occupied by the French, served as a point of departure for the annual convoy that went up the Senegal River to exchange textiles, metal goods, and paper for millet, gum Arabic, and captives. A treacherous sandbar stood between the island and the Atlantic, however, adding the risk of shipwreck to the many hazards that faced men and women deported from Saint-Louis into the Atlantic slave trade. (*Map of ye entrance of the Sanaga [Senegal]*, ca. 1718, private collection.)

Pictured at anchor in the harbor at Le Cap, Saint-Domingue, the *Marie Séraphique* receives visitors wishing to inspect the captives offered for sale as slaves in the French Caribbean colony. The wooden structure located amidships served as a barricade behind which the crew members could defend themselves against the captives in the event of insurrection during the crossing. (Watercolor, Musée des ducs de Bretagne, Nantes.)

After arrival in the Caribbean, Rosalie "of the Poulard nation" was sold to Alexis Couba, an elderly freedman, and then resold to a black woman named Marthe Guillaume, a prosperous trader in Jérémie, Saint-Domingue. In this engraving the lower town of Jérémie is visible along the beachfront, its upper town above and its battery to the right. (Nicolas Ponce, *Vue de la ville de Jérémie*, in M. Moreau de Saint-Méry, M. Ponce, and M. Phelipeau, *Recueil de vues des lieux principaux de la colonie française de Saint-Domingue* [Paris, 1791]. Clements Library, University of Michigan.)

In the midst of the Haitian Revolution the trader Marthe Guillaume sold Rosalie, now about twenty-six years old, to her neighbor Jean Baptiste Mongol, a free man of color. Two years later, during the British occupation of the town, Marthe Guillaume reacquired Rosalie and filed a manumission letter granting her freedom. The British authorities, however, refused to ratify the act of manumission, leaving Rosalie's status uncertain. ("Vente par Marthe Guillaume a Mongol de la Négresse Rozalie," File 6C-119, Jérémie Papers, Department of Special and Area Studies Collections, George A. Smathers Libraries, University of Florida, Gainesville.)

With the expulsion in 1798 of the British from Saint-Domingue by Republican forces under Toussaint Louverture and André Rigaud, and the extension of abolition to the entire French colony, Rosalie became a legally free woman. The following year she gave birth to a child baptized with the name Élisabeth and the nickname Dieudonné, and recognized by the impoverished French colonist Michel Vincent as his daughter. The portrait is of Élisabeth Dieudonné [Vincent] many years later. (Photo courtesy of Marie-Louise Van Velsen.)

In 1801 Napoléon Bonaparte ordered an expeditionary force to the colony of Saint-Domingue, aiming to wrest power from the black generals who had consolidated their authority in the course of the Haitian Revolution. The ensuing war created thousands of refugees, including Rosalie, Michel, and their four-year-old daughter Élisabeth, who fled across the Windward Passage to Cuba. When these refugees were expelled from Cuba in 1809, Élisabeth's godmother took Élisabeth under her protection to New Orleans, where they settled in Faubourg Marigny. (*Plan of the City and Suburbs of New Orleans from an actual survey made by J. Tanesse in 1815.* Engraving, April 29, 1817. The Historic New Orleans Collection. Detail. Accession no. 1971.4.)

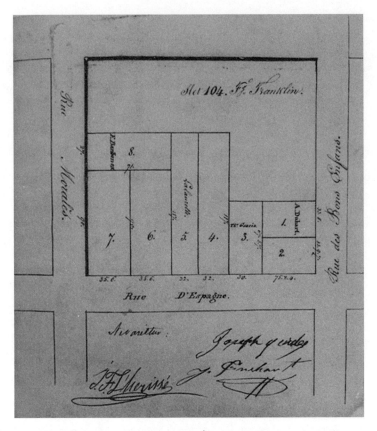

When she reached the age of twenty-three, Élisabeth Dieudonné married a carpenter named Jacques Tinchant, himself the son of Saint-Domingue refugees. Jacques became a successful builder, buying house lots in the expanding city of New Orleans and constructing wood-frame dwellings for sale in an active market. This document shows his signature. ("Vente de terre par Jacques Tinchant," January 18, 1842, Notary Cuvillier. New Orleans Notarial Archives Research Center.)

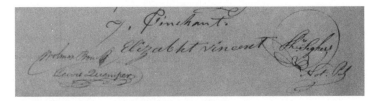

Civil law practice required that a married woman sign with her maiden name, and Élisabeth Dieudonné, born out of wedlock, thus carried a visible stigma as a result of her lack of a paternal surname. In 1835, however, she produced a copy of her baptismal record and persuaded a New Orleans notary to "rectify" her name so that she could adopt the surname of her father, Michel Vincent. Her spelling remained hesitant, but she could now legally sign her name as Élisabeth Vincent. ("Vente de terrain par Tinchant à Macias," 20 October 1838, Notary Théodore Seghers, New Orleans Notarial Archives Research Center.)

Increasingly pressed by the restrictions imposed on free persons of color, in 1840 Jacques Tinchant and Élisabeth Vincent left New Orleans for France with four of their children to settle near Pau, in the Basses-Pyrénées. The family migrated again in 1857, this time to Belgium, where their elder sons established a small trading business in Antwerp, and began to manufacture cigars. In 1861, at the age of 21, their youngest son, Édouard Tinchant, headed to the Americas and sent this portrait home to his parents from Memphis, Tennessee. (Photo of the young Édouard Tinchant courtesy of Marie-Louise Van Velsen.)

By 1862 Édouard Tinchant counted himself an ardent abolitionist, and in 1863 he volunteered for service in the Union army. After the Civil War he directed a school for freed children in New Orleans and was elected to the Louisiana Constitutional Convention of 1867–1868. A strong proponent of a state constitutional guarantee of equal "public rights" for all citizens, Édouard also advocated the recognition of the civil rights of all women, independent of color. Following the collapse of Reconstruction he left the U.S. South and rejoined his brothers in Belgium. (Photo of the older Édouard Tinchant courtesy of Marie-Louise Van Velsen.)

Maison Américaine
Louis Tinchant.
Fondée en 1857.

Édouard Tinchant,

Anvers.

Adresse Télégraphique et Postale
Édouard Tinchant Anvers.

Thursday September 21st 99

General Maximo Gomez

H A V A N A

General,

In early and ardent sympathy with the Cuban
cause,I have been always and pride myself in being still one of
your most sincere admirers.

I would be highly honored,should you have the kindness to
authorize me to use your illustrious name for a brand of my best
articles,your portrait adorning the labels whereof a proof is
enclosed.

Allow me to add as an excuse for the freedom of my request,
that I may not be altogether unknown to some of the survivors of
the last struggle.They may still remember me as a member of Compa-
-ny C 6th Louisiana Volunteers,Banks Division in 1863;as representa-
-tive of the 6th Ward of the city of New Orleans,at the Constitu-
-tional Convention of the State of Louisiana in 1867-68 and as a
cigar manufacturer in Mobile Alabama from 1869 till 1877.

In 1899 Édouard Tinchant, now established as a cigar manufacturer in Antwerp, wrote to
General Máximo Gómez in Havana, asking permission to use the general's name and
portrait on "a brand of my best articles." Addressing himself to the surviving hero of Cuba's
war for independence, Édouard supported his request for this favor by evoking his own
solidarity with the Cuban struggle and his family's opposition to the "infamous laws
and stupid prejudices" of the slaveholding societies of the Americas. (Fondo Máximo Gómez,
Archivo Nacional de Cuba, Havana.)

During all these years, I have been an humble but a steady
contributor to the Cuban fund and many are your countrymen, the
Cubans and your followers to whom I have lent a helping hand.

Born in France in 1861 I am of Haïtian descent as both my fa-
-ther and mother were born at Gonaïves in the beginning of this
century. Settled in New Orleans after the Revolution, my father,
although in modest circumstances left Louisiana for France with the
only object in view of raising his six sons in a country where no
infamous laws or stupid prejudices could prevent them from becoming
M E N .

More than many well rounded sentences these simple facts of
our family history will give a fair insight into my true sentiments,
and show you how deep may be my sympathy for your cause, not yet
won unfortunately, but for the success of which I devoutly pray,
wishing with all my heart to live to see its ultimate and lasting
triumph fitly crowning your noble existence.

Should you for some unforessen reason, choose not to grant the
great favor sollicited at your hands, kindly oblige me by acknowled-
-ging never heless receipt of this and, happen what may, believe me,
General wi h sincere thanks,

Very devotedly Yours

E. A. Tinchant

Édouard Tinchant's older brother
Joseph had lived in Paris during the
Revolution of 1848 and then crossed
the Atlantic to try his hand at trade in
Louisiana. There he married Stéphanie
Gonzales, from an extended family of
New Orleans artisans, and became
part of a community of aspiring free
persons of color. Commissioned a
lieutenant in the Union army in 1863,
Joseph was distressed by the treatment
of officers of color by the Union high
command and left New Orleans for
Mexico after his term of military
service was over. (Photographs
courtesy of Françoise Cousin.)

Converging back in Antwerp after their time in the Americas, four of the Tinchant brothers (Louis, Joseph, Ernest, and Édouard) prospered in the tobacco business. Making use of his Creole identity to add luster to his products, Joseph attached his wife's surname to his own and presented himself as Don José Tinchant y Gonzales. This label for a cigar box shows Don José against a backdrop depicting the port of Havana. (Lithograph courtesy of Gérard van Eijk.)

Joseph Tinchant's granddaughter, Marie-José Tinchant, was born in Antwerp in 1916. In April of 1937, on her twenty-first birthday, she acquired a passport in order to rendezvous in London with her Belgian fiancé, in hopes that they could marry there despite the opposition of his parents. Her fiancé's father nonetheless intervened to block the issuance of a marriage license. The story was picked up by the London *Daily Mail,* and Marie-José explained to a reporter, "My mother is white, my grandmother is white, but I have colour, and André's parents will not hear of our match." (Photo courtesy of Michèle Kleijnen and her mother Liliane, who is the daughter of Marie-José Tinchant.)

7

"The Term Public Rights Should Be
Made to Mean Something"

It was hardly prudent for the twenty-three-year-old Édouard Tinchant to pick a fight with a distinguished literary figure in the pages of the newspaper read by their friends, neighbors, allies, and rivals. Armand Lanusse, now in his fifties, was the principal of the leading school for children of color and a frequent contributor to *L'Union*. For readers of this increasingly radical paper, Lanusse nonetheless carried the burden of having shown exceptional enthusiasm for the Confederate army in the early days of the war. Following the occupation of New Orleans by Federal forces, Lanusse felt obliged to draft a somewhat labored article under the title "Explication," in which he sought to justify his actions as a simple reflection of his loyalty to the state of Louisiana and to the honor of his fellow Creoles. He took care to endorse the subsequent decision of many men of color to join the Union army, though for his own part he declined to fight against Confederates whom he saw as his childhood friends.[1]

When in July 1864 Lanusse published his laudatory essay on Maximilian of Habsburg and the French bid for power in Mexico, Édouard Tinchant made an initial foray into print with a reply. Tinchant denounced the invasion of an American republic by the forces of Napoléon III and rebuked Lanusse for endorsing this imperialist adventure. The text of Tinchant's first letter to the editor is now lost, but the polemic was evidently off to a lively start.[2]

Within days, Lanusse responded to Édouard Tinchant's communiqué with a condescending letter of his own. He accused the youngest Tinchant of having misunderstood his original article, and of having responded simply out of an "itch" to write in order to impress his equally frivolous friends. Invoking Édouard's father Jacques' 1840 decision to move to France, Lanusse asserted (mistakenly) that the senior Tinchants still lived by choice in the country ruled by the monarch whom the son now denounced. He sought to put the knife in a bit further by accusing Édouard Tinchant of having with his letter also given great disrespect (an *énorme soufflet*) to his brother Joseph Tinchant—"to whom he owes everything"—just as Joseph was preparing to depart for Mexico with his family as a "pioneer of the class to which he belongs."[3]

Lanusse also argued that Édouard Tinchant's use of the term "fellow citizen" to refer to Lanusse was misplaced: the federally appointed state attorney general had recently ruled that "all negroes and persons of color in the State of Louisiana" were free, but had "not the right to become citizens of the United States under the Constitution as existing at present." As for equal rights under Federal authority, and the new ability to walk with one's head held high in the streets of New Orleans . . . well, what of the episode when Édouard Tinchant, in his Union uniform, had been expelled from a streetcar? Then, after complaining of his rival's poor command of the French language, Lanusse exhorted him sarcastically to take good care of his proofs of *French* nationality, papers he believed Édouard had saved so that they might serve as a "prophylactic" against conscription into the Union forces.[4]

This classic nineteenth-century epistolary polemic, filled with ad hominem jabs, was more than a quarrel among personal rivals. It reflected a major struggle over the meanings of citizenship, both in the tentatively reconstructed state of Louisiana and in what was emerging as a transformed United States. Édouard Tinchant now felt obliged to draft a reply—both as an exercise in political rhetoric, and as an effort to assert personal honor and standing in a rapidly shifting political environment. Written at a moment of great political tension in Louisiana, when access to the rights and privileges of state citizenship was in dispute in the ongoing constitutional convention and elsewhere, Tinchant's new letter contained a vivid expression of a particular vision of national citizenship. Bringing to bear both his understanding of French politics since the revolution of 1848, and of American politics in the midst of civil war, Tinchant crafted a claim to a U.S. citizenship of his own imagining. For this young man of the Atlantic, such a citizenship should carry with it not only the full political rights that were being refused by the 1864 Louisiana Constitutional Convention, but also a version of the "public rights" invoked by liberal constitutional theorists in Europe. These, in turn, could be transformed in the Americas into a weapon against state-sanctioned discrimination on the basis of color.

Édouard Tinchant's initial rhetorical goal was to refute Armand Lanusse's claim that Mexico under French occupation deserved the loyalty of Creoles of color. First, he denounced Napoléon III as the "assassin of December 4"—that is, the man who had ordered troops to fire on workers in the streets of Paris—and then he accused him of having gone on to occupy "the territory of Mexico by force of bayonets," "transforming this republic into a monarchy." Tinchant, who saw himself as French by birth and by language, implied that such violations of republicanism created a rupture between French nationality and its core principles. Then he pivoted to the perspective from the United States: Napoléon III's policy was also, he argued, a violation of the Monroe Doctrine. (Some later historians would observe that this was indeed precisely one of the goals of the imperial exercise.) The flag of the United States should be respected, Tinchant wrote, as the one under which the chains of "thousands of our brothers of African descent" had been broken.[5]

To those who might intimate that Édouard Tinchant was actually not a U.S. citizen at all, he countered by invoking his service in the Union army, when the Sixth Louisiana Volunteers had guarded New Orleans against a possible Confederate attack. He declared that although born French, he had won "American letters of naturalization on the ramparts of New Orleans, upright, my weapon in my hands, at the foot of the flag of the United States for which I was ready to spill the last drop of my blood." Ignoring the implicit question of whether he had followed up his military service with a formal legal procedure of naturalization, he wrote: "What human power can then deny me the title of American citizen?"[6]

If anyone should think to cite the U.S. Supreme Court's ruling in the case of *Dred Scott v. Sandford* to the effect that a man of his color had no possible claim to U.S. citizenship, Tinchant was quick to proffer the contrary opinion of federal attorney general Edward Bates, who had concluded in December 1862 that men of color could indeed claim citizenship in the United States. The Bates opinion, which asserted the possibility of such citizenship in part by distinguishing citizenship itself from the privilege of exercising political rights, had been discussed at the time in *L'Union*. The publishers of *L'Union* had even made available as a pamphlet (ten cents a copy) what they described as the attorney general's opinion on *le droit de citoyenneté* (the right to citizenship). For radical advocates of universal suffrage and full political rights, Attorney General Bates's distinctions among possible degrees of citizenship were not helpful, but his conclusion that citizenship itself was independent of color provided a new basis on which to advance further claims.[7]

In New Orleans in the summer of 1864, the all-white Unionist state constitutional convention, largely populated with lawyers and small-scale businessmen, was yielding repeated expressions of open racial hostility, and Union general Nathaniel Banks seemed willing to proceed with a Reconstruction that involved very few political rights for men of color. Under the circumstances, Lanusse could argue persuasively that the discriminatory practices still in force in Union-occupied New Orleans reflected a general hostility of the U.S. government to men of color. Tinchant countered that although the laws of the state of Louisiana were still stained with their origins in "aristocracy," once the roots of the Confederacy that "rotted deep in the earth" were extirpated, men of color would see their rights protected under federal law. National citizenship seemed to Tinchant a far more promising source of rights than state measures, though national citizenship in fact remained undefined, and federal policy uncertain.[8]

As for the incident the year before when Tinchant had been expelled from a streetcar by a fellow Union soldier, he insisted that he had been vindicated by a subsequent official rebuke by the provost marshal of Carrollton to the sergeant who had arrested him, and to the lieutenant who had taken him into custody. Tinchant added a dramatic touch: the provost marshal had threatened that if such an incident were repeated, he would tear up the streetcar line from New Orleans to Carrollton. "Can M. Armand Lanusse tell me under what flag one could have done more to redress a harm done to a simple soldier?" Although Édouard Tinchant's older brother Joseph, after having done his duty in the war, might justifiably choose to settle in Mexico in pursuit of peace and quiet for his family, Édouard asserted that he saw it as his own duty and that of other men of color in New Orleans to support the Union cause so that "a last and supreme effort of all of us together" could "defeat, reverse and obliterate this tyrannical aristocracy that forced our father to expatriate and which, ever since our earliest years, he has taught us to hate."[9]

In the course of their public exchange, Lanusse had revealed that Édouard Tinchant, Union veteran and self-declared citizen of the United States, kept his French citizenship papers carefully tucked away, in case of need. Tinchant acknowledged that he had kept those papers, as someone "indiscreet enough to go into the drawers of my armoire has reported to M. Lanusse." But he vehemently denied the implication that he might use them to avoid future conscription. By enrolling as a volunteer in the Union army, he wrote, he had lost his French nationality through an act of allegiance to the United States. Those French citizenship papers were nonetheless worth keeping, he noted, for they might enable him under other circumstances to render some additional service to "our cause."[10]

Thus were both citizenship and nationality severed from the usual anchors of parentage, birthplace, long-term residence, or official recognition. Instead, Édouard Tinchant proposed a kind of citizenship by adhesion: Wishing to serve what he saw as the underlying emancipationist and equal-rights values of the Union cause, he envisioned a United States citizenship that would conform to his ideals, and that would become accessible to him through the very change that a Union victory might bring. In the unstable political moment of 1864, with the outcome of the war still in doubt, Édouard Tinchant's gesture was an act of willpower, trying to imagine equal rights into existence through a combination of military service, political rhetoric, and strategic positioning.[11]

The debate would not be resolved through rhetoric, of course, for the success of men of color in claiming equal rights was entirely contingent on the outcome of the war. As the Union forces moved toward victory, a radical cross-racial Republican coalition in favor of universal manhood suffrage independent of color was emerging in New Orleans to rival the hesitant white Unionists, and to challenge unreconstructed Confederates. After the assassination of President Lincoln and the Confederate surrender, however, all was uncertain. Louisiana itself offered a preview of the struggles over the path of a postwar South. No one knew what President Andrew Johnson would insist upon, or what rearguard actions the more conservative Unionists might manage. Would the end of slavery carry with it full civil and political rights for those who had been enslaved and those who had been classed as free men of color, or would conservatives succeed in minimizing the challenge to the racial order?[12]

With Union victory, Édouard Tinchant's own star began to rise, and his political positions found further support among his neighbors. He became active in a local branch of the Grand Army of the Republic, convening meetings of this strong-willed veterans' association. And he hoped to marry a young woman, Louisa Debergue, daughter of a bricklayer from the Seventh Ward. It is not hard to imagine how they had met. The Tinchants were cigar manufacturers and merchants, and Louisa Debergue's neighborhood was full of cigar makers—including her brother and two men living in the other half of the same house. The most serious obstacle to their marriage, however, was the paucity of Édouard's resources, and perhaps also the general instability of life for those who were open proponents of equal rights and radical Republican policies.[13]

In the summer of 1866 a cross-racial group of radical Unionists sought to gather a new assembly of delegates and "reconvene" the Louisiana Constitutional Convention of 1864 at the Mechanics' Institute. Édouard Tinchant himself does not seem to have been among them (he may have been away selling cigars), but they were strongly supported by his fellow radicals at the *Tribune*. One of the goals for a convention was to find a way to create a legal basis for universal suffrage, independent of race, for the next elections. It was unclear, however, how much support they could count on for this move, which was based on the arcane procedure of reconvening a defunct wartime convention. It was quite clear that the mayor of New Orleans was dead set against it. As the proposed date of July 30 approached, white men opposed to black suffrage began to plan for an attack on the gathering. By July 27 rumors had reached even schoolchildren, one of whom apparently asked his father: "Why, Daddy, are they going to kill all the Union men and negroes in the city on Monday?"[14]

The pro-suffrage delegates and their supporters rallied on the night before the scheduled gathering and exhorted each other to stand firm. Mayor Monroe, however, was planning a direct police intervention to halt the proceedings. A witness later testified that one policeman had explained: "We're going to shoot all the damned Yankees," adding "I'm damned sorry for the niggers, but, by God, we have orders to shoot them too." At midday on July 30, the convention's deliberations had just begun when scuffles followed by shots were heard outside. The police began to move in, as planned, clubbing and shooting black men in the streets and on the sidewalk. Accompanied by white vigilantes, the police then proceeded to the meeting hall, where they attacked the unarmed delegates, as crowds of police and civilians in the surrounding streets went after those they perceived as supporters of the convention. Federal troops arrived too late to prevent what General Sheridan characterized as "an absolute massacre." The semiofficial death toll was between thirty-seven and forty-seven supporters of the convention, with only one death on the side of the opponents. Forty-eight supporters of the convention were severely wounded, none on the other side.[15]

Nationwide reaction to the unbridled action of the police in the massacre at Mechanics' Institute would, in the months that followed, reshape congressional policy on Reconstruction. For those who held to the view that Union victory should bring equal rights, Andrew Johnson's policy of placating conservative white southerners looked increasingly dangerous, as well as potentially suicidal for the Republican Party. Republicans in Congress took the lead, and the new Reconstruction Acts placed Louisiana under direct military administration and opened up voting to adult males independent of color. For the activists around the *Tribune*, the events at Mechanics' Institute had been absolutely traumatic, but congressional Reconstruction now opened doors they had been pushing against for a long time.[16]

In the fall of 1867, as the Reconstruction Acts began to reconfigure Louisiana politics in a radical direction, Édouard Tinchant became principal of a school in Faubourg Tremé funded by Post No. 4 of the Grand Army of the Republic. The school, which served some 250 boys, opened its doors in early September 1867, charging no tuition—and paying no salaries to its three teachers. Tinchant's equal-rights convictions were on display in his replies to questions posed by the conservative Orleans Parish School Board, which was surveying opinion among the teachers in the schools for children of color. The board hoped to persuade the teachers to cooperate with racial segregation in return for financial support. When they reached the school located at No. 280 St. Claude, between Ursulines and Bayou Road, however, the principal Édouard Tinchant replied categorically that he was in favor of "mixed schools."[17]

The school board's efforts reflected the apprehension of conservative Unionists about the possibility that the new constitutional convention that was soon to be seated, following elections carried out under military authority, might in fact mandate integrated education. The board hoped that by recruiting those who were teaching in schools for freed children to the project of separate public schools they might deflect the delegates from such an initiative. But they misjudged the depth of the commitment of men like Édouard Tinchant to the full range of what would soon be called equal "public rights."[18]

When the moment came to elect delegates to the new constitutional convention, this time through elections carried out with universal manhood suffrage, Édouard Tinchant presented his candidacy on the Republican ticket to represent the Sixth Ward of New Orleans. Under the new congressional rules on the franchise in areas under Union occupation, black and white voters now constituted what Jean-Charles Houzeau, editor of the *Tribune*, described as "a single political class." Houzeau wrote that the September 1867 election for delegates to the convention caught

Louisiana's conservatives off guard. Thinking that the folly of enfranchising men of color would soon pass, conservatives in some districts did not even present a slate of candidates.[19]

When the ballots were counted, Louisiana's electors were found to have endorsed a remarkable group of Republicans, most of them radical, and half of them men of color. Édouard Tinchant would now serve in the body convened to draft a constitution with which the state of Louisiana could reenter the Union. In addition to a respected family name and a good education in France, he brought to that meeting his own reputation as a Union soldier and a leader in the veterans' association, his experience as principal of a school for freed children, and his often-expressed loyalty to the Union. One of his first proposals on the floor of the convention was that "the Sergeant-at-Arms be instructed to cause the United States flag to be hoisted on top of this building from sunrise until sunset every day." This decision to fly the stars and stripes in the former Confederate city was a forthright gesture of defiance, a challenge to the unreconstructed among the citizenry.[20]

Édouard Tinchant soon had an opportunity to introduce a resolution on another matter of principle. He proposed that "this Convention shall provide, either by special enactment or by amendment to the Constitution, for the legal protection in this State of all women without distinction of race or color, or without reference to their previous condition, in their civil rights." It subsequently became clear that he was particularly concerned with the right of all women to sue for breach of promise of marriage. His proposal went on to the judiciary committee.[21]

Tinchant's political life was now on public view, as the local papers reported each day's proceedings. His private life took a back seat, but was not entirely neglected. On the tenth of December, he answered the roll call at the convention but left Mechanics' Hall to proceed to the office of a local justice of the peace to demonstrate his own commitment to the institution of marriage. He was accompanied by his fiancée Louisa Debergue, and by three men who would serve as their witnesses in the ceremony to follow: Lucien Mansion, a prosperous cigar maker, poet, and contributor to the *Tribune*; George Alcès, Mansion's nephew, who owned a substantial cigar factory in town; and the young Louis Albert de Tornos, born in Puerto Rico, whose father was a teacher. Mansion provided the financial guarantee required for Édouard to obtain the marriage license itself. By the end of the day, Édouard and Louisa had been "solemnly united in the bonds of matrimony" and had affixed their signatures to the marriage certificate.

The ceremony seems to have been carried out with dispatch, but the signatures on the accompanying documents provide a nice sense of Édouard and Louisa's social world. They had chosen a civil rather than a church ceremony, and as their public witnesses they selected men of the tobacco trade, themselves associated with the equal rights campaign, and one young Antillean who had recently taken on U.S. citizenship.[22]

Édouard Tinchant did not make it to the convention for roll call the next morning, but he did get there in time for the afternoon deliberations and votes. Over the next weeks, along with other members of the coalition of long-free men of color, northern and local white Unionists, and former slaves, Tinchant pushed to put strong equal-rights language into the state's new bill of rights. The text that they hammered out called for all citizens of the state to enjoy the same "civil, political, and public rights." The concepts of civil and political rights were very familiar, and were being debated in state conventions across the former Confederacy. But the phrase "public rights" seems to have been a Louisiana innovation, an echo of the language introduced in France decades earlier by the Italian émigré liberal and constitutional theorist Pellegrino Rossi. In Rossi's view, public rights—which could include the public "liberties" of freedom of assembly and freedom of the press—were due to all as a function of their membership in society. For Édouard Tinchant, who had weathered expulsion from public transportation in New Orleans, and for all those who recalled the 1866 attack on the assembly at Mechanics' Institute, an expansive interpretation of public rights would be a political demand of the greatest importance.[23]

One key value of the "public rights" formulation introduced in the convention was the way that it framed the rights of equal access to transport and accommodation. Rhetorically, the radical delegates had to resist the implication that they sought what white supremacists referred to ominously as "social equality." At the time of the 1848 abolition of slavery in France, the phrase *égalité sociale* had carried a positive valence, representing a refusal of caste distinctions. It had been evoked explicitly by Minister François Arago as he drafted rules for the implementation of abolition in the French colony of Martinique. In the United States, however, "social equality" was transformed into a loaded phrase, carrying implicit overtones of intimacy and sexuality. By attaching the label "social equality" to claims to equal access, white supremacists construed such policies as an impermissible intrusion into the private sphere. Those who adopted the phrase "public rights" tried to counter this by emphasizing that what was at stake was the right of all citizens to be treated with respect and dignity in the public sphere.[24]

The suggestion that an entitlement of all citizens to the same "public rights" be written into the state's bill of rights nevertheless created a great fracas on the floor of the convention. White conservatives could see the goal of the innovative category, and were infuriated. Even some men of color among the delegates hesitated at the prospect of confronting white hostility in public places. The report of deliberations published in the *Official Journal* was sparse, but it hinted at the drama of the debates.

Opponents of public rights argued that this was an issue of interest only to those formerly known as "free men of color" and that it would be of "no earthly use" to the freedmen. This line of attack aimed at associating the radicals with personal light-skin privilege, and with indifference to the real interests of former slaves. But in point of fact, many of the radicals pushing for equal public rights were also concerned with reforming the tax structure to make land more easily available for rent or purchase by the freedpeople, and with trying to assure physical protection for black voters in the face of violence. Everyone knew that some white supremacists in the state would use violence against former slaves who sought to vote, and that planters were resisting negotiations with workers over contracts for the year that would follow. As the December 27 session opened, C. C. Antoine of Caddo Parish urged that the convention express strong support for a renewal of the term of the federal Freedmen's Bureau, both in view of recent crop failures and floods, and because the "freedmen of the new reconstructed States are yet subject to much gross injustice and persecution at the hands of former rebels and slave-holders."[25]

Leaving the question of the Freedmen's Bureau for later, the delegates focused in on the core of their "unfinished business"—the language of the new state bill of rights. J. F. Taliaferro, of Catahoula, proposed that Article 2 should read "That citizens of this State owe allegiance to the United States; and that said allegiance is paramount to that which they owe to the state." Édouard Tinchant moved adoption of that sentence, whereupon the (frequently sarcastic) Judge W. H. Cooley of Pointe Coupée counterproposed an article declaring that "taxation without representation is tyranny." This particular piece of political theater—presumably designed to bring the drafting process to a halt—provoked a counter-counterproposal from the radical R. H. Isabelle: "That all men are born free and equal, and have certain inalienable rights; among these are life, liberty and the pursuit of happiness. To secure these rights, governments are instituted among men, deriving their just powers from the consent of the governed."[26]

The *New Orleans Times*, which was generally quite hostile to this cross-racial convention, provided a more vivid—if mocking—description of what followed. A cacophony of proposals apparently ensued, and eventually the chair ruled Isabelle out of order, while Taliaferro withdrew his "allegiance article." As the discussion turned to the guarantee to all citizens of the same "public rights and privileges," the split among the members became even clearer. The conservative Cooley, as was to be expected, insisted that "public places" were not "public property," and mounted the usual defense of owners' right to exclude whomever they might wish. P. B. S. Pinchback, a delegate of mixed African and European ancestry, pulled back from the charge that what was being sought was social equality. According to the report in the *Times*, Pinchback averred that "social equality, like water, must be left to find its own level," and that "any attempt to legislate for his social equality would, under present circumstances, be the death-blow of his people."[27]

At stake here were competing conceptions of honor and dignity. Pinchback would later explain that he declined to attempt to enter where he was not wanted; he, like Armand Lanusse, took the view that a man's honor was best defended by avoiding scenes of repudiation that would diminish his dignity. Édouard Tinchant and his fellow public rights proponents argued that, on the contrary, dignity *required* that one be assured the right to entry. Three years earlier, during the war, when Tinchant faced the violent imposition of segregation—the shove off the streetcar—he had held back from using his bayonet, but carried his protest up the Union army chain of command, and was vindicated. According to the *Times,* he now strongly defended the proposed constitutional language: "Mr. Tinchant, colored, said among other things that the term public rights should be made to mean something, and that everywhere a white man can go or travel the colored man should go." This position, initially portrayed by the *Times* as a ridiculous one, quickly built up support.[28]

Debate on the matter resumed the next day. By now, Judge Cooley was thoroughly exasperated and asked that a written explanation of his "nay" vote on the proposed language of public rights be "spread upon the minutes":

I. *Because*, I never heard the term "public rights" mentioned as a private one, and *because* I cannot understand the idea of a private individual exercising public rights.

II. *Because*, I do not wish to stultify myself by the use of such absurd terms in so important an instrument as the organic law of the state.

When the vote was taken, it became clear that one did not need to have gone to school in France, or to be identified as a radical Creole, in order to see the point of "public rights." The yeas were numerous—fifty-nine—and the nays were only sixteen. The bill of rights thus incorporated the radicalized version of language from the Declaration of Independence—"All men are created free and equal, and have certain inalienable rights"—and the words from the not-yet-ratified federal Fourteenth Amendment, recognizing birthright citizenship regardless of race. But it then went further than any other state constitution and declared that the citizens of the state "shall enjoy the same civil, political, and public rights and privileges, and be subject to the same pains and penalties."[29]

Lest anyone fail to recognize just what the term "public rights" "should be made to mean," Article 13 of the proposed new state constitution, suggested by the attorney Simeon Belden, and now supported by P. B. S. Pinchback, was blunt:

All persons shall enjoy equal rights and privileges upon any conveyances of a public character; and all places of business, or of public resort, or for which a license is required by either State, parish, or muncipal authority, shall be deemed places of a public character, and shall be opened to the accommodation and patronage of all persons, without distinction or discrimination on account of race or color.[30]

This language was adopted, and written into the final draft of the constitution.

There was a further matter that Édouard Tinchant wanted the convention to attend to. As a man of mixed ancestry, whose parents had been labeled free persons of color, Tinchant had already some years earlier identified himself in the pages of the *Tribune* as a "member of the population of color and a son of Africa." He was keenly aware that unions between women of color and white men had long been denied the status of marriage under Louisiana law, and that marriages between slaves had been denied civil effect. Tinchant now proposed that all women, independent of color, should have the right to sue for breach of promise of marriage. Moreover, he envisioned that the General Assembly that would be convened after ratification of the new constitution "shall also provide to compel to marriage upon application of one of the parties, such persons who may have lived together not less than one year consecutively."[31]

The statute that Tinchant was suggesting would have violated both sacramental and contractual understandings of the freely given consent necessary for a valid marriage, and he could not persuade his colleagues to follow him down this path. But it is not difficult to understand this desire to oblige men to marry the women with whom they lived and with whom they often had children. For a young man quite conscious of his own honor—and very recently married himself—the dishonor imposed on women of color by the various impediments to marriage was not an abstraction. Édouard's paternal grandfather, Joseph Tinchant, had apparently abandoned his grandmother, Marie Françoise Bayot. Édouard's French-born maternal grandfather, Michel Vincent, had died without marrying Édouard's other grandmother, Rosalie, though she had eventually taken on the surname Vincent. Édouard himself was the legitimate son of married parents, but he could see around him in New Orleans the consequences of the double juridical inequality imposed on women of color in unions with white men.[32]

Although there was no further talk of compelling men to marriage, the final text of the constitution did dismantle the legal barriers to marriages that crossed the color line. And along with guaranteeing "public rights" in matters of transportation, entertainment, and public accommodation, it prohibited the creation of public schools separated by race. When they had finished, the delegates had produced one of the most radical state constitutions in the post–Civil War period. Jean-Charles Houzeau described the document they had created as *magnifique par son libéralisme,* magnificent in its liberalism, and the next generation of activists would recall it with admiration.[33]

Affixing his signature to the Louisiana Constitution in March of 1868 may have been the high point of Édouard Tinchant's career as a public man. The registered voters of the state endorsed the work of the convention, and for the next eleven years all citizens of Louisiana could lay claim in the courts to the same "civil, political, and public rights." After Charles Sauvinet, who served as civil sheriff for the city, was refused service at a saloon in 1871, he filed suit in District Court and won damages of $1,000. Josephine Decuir, the eminently respectable widow of a landholder, was refused accommodation in the ladies' stateroom for an overnight journey by steamboat from New Orleans to Pointe Coupée to deal with her late husband's affairs. She successfully sued the captain who had tried to confine her to what the crew mockingly called "the Bureau"—a sarcastic reference to those served by the Freedmen's Bureau. By 1874, litigants from more humble backgrounds, supported by several combative attorneys, brought legal challenges in pursuit of modest damage awards after being refused service at soda shops and confectioneries.[34]

The gains made possible under the 1868 Louisiana Constitution would prove to be fragile. Louisiana's radicals had nonetheless created a constitutional and statutory space within which to press claims to respect, equal treatment, and access to resources. The concept of equal public rights even made its way into the Republican Party's national platform in 1872, and in 1876 the platform again called for "complete liberty and exact equality in the exercise of all civil, political and public rights." By the 1870s, however, the leaders of the Republican Party were wavering in their support for this dimension of citizens' rights. Following the compromises that resolved the contested elections of 1876, the term "public rights" disappeared from the lexicon of the Republican platform.[35]

The hostility of the federal Supreme Court to the public rights concept soon became clear. The heirs of the steamboat captain who had refused passage to Mme. Decuir challenged the damage award that had been granted to her and appealed to the U.S. Supreme Court. Citing the clause of the Constitution that reserved the regulation of interstate commerce to the federal government, the court overturned Decuir's victory. The court reasoned that the Louisiana law barring discrimination on steamboats was an inappropriate interference with interstate commerce, even if the passenger was making an intrastate journey, because the boat itself was continuing on to Mississippi. (Conveniently, the court would later forget this apparent limitation on state authority once conservatives were in power in Louisiana who chose to mandate forced segregation rather than the antidiscrimination advocated by their predecessors.)[36]

The phrase "public rights" would be remembered and revived by occasional writers in Louisiana, including George Washington Cable. In formal jurisprudence, however, the concept was largely abandoned after 1877. And in public debate, the aspirations that the concept had contained were ever more vigorously glossed by its enemies as pretensions to "social equality"—the inadmissible state of affairs so loudly denounced by white supremacists. That label seemed to stick, and even those rare white writers who professed to find something called "social equality" vaguely desirable often implied that it was unattainable through law. Within Louisiana, once the Democratic Party regained full power in 1877–1878, its leaders drafted a new constitution and expunged the public rights language of Article 1 and Article 13 that had been in the 1868 document.[37]

Long before the formal retreat from Reconstruction, radical activists like Édouard Tinchant were being edged out of power in Louisiana by pragmatic Republicans who sought to build a coalition with conservative white Unionists and a few Democrats. In the gubernatorial elections of 1868 the wily Henry Clay Warmoth, a Republican with very little commitment to equal rights, won handily. The records of the military government supervising the elections registered the receipt of a complaint from Édouard Tinchant about the balloting for local office at Poll 1, 13th Precinct, Second District. The complaint itself has not survived, and no action seems to have been taken. Indeed, it seems to have been Édouard Tinchant's last recorded political act in New Orleans.[38]

As Governor Warmoth's machine got into gear, the brief moment of prominence of the group associated with the *Tribune* was ending. With his radical colleagues in disarray, Édouard Tinchant's livelihood was at risk as well. Since September of 1867 the Orleans Parish School Board had been trying to block integration of the public schools and lock in a racially segregated educational system, in spite of the equal-access mandate of the new state constitution. One strategy attempted by the board was to try to take control of the various Freedmen's Schools and reopen them as racially segregated schools led by teachers of the board's own choosing, thus undercutting the long-term goals of equal-rights advocates like Édouard Tinchant. In October 1867 the board had conducted examinations for applicants for teaching positions and concluded that the great majority of those currently serving were not qualified to teach in the new schools. Unless the Grand Army of the Republic was prepared to provide an indefinite subvention to the school Édouard had directed on St. Claude Street, its days were probably numbered.[39]

With the reconfiguration of state politics, Édouard Tinchant had little claim on a patronage job in the city. Nor was he on good terms with the segregationists of the Orleans Parish School Board, whose blandishments he had refused a few months earlier. His career as a schoolteacher seemed likely to come to as abrupt an end as his career as a legislator. And all this just as he had become a married man, responsible for his wife and future family.

Édouard Tinchant's prospects in business in New Orleans were few and far between. The former Tinchant Brothers warehouse and cigar store in the city had closed down altogether during the war, and Édouard had not been invited to join in Joseph's move to work with their brother Jules in Mexico. Although Édouard had apparently inherited some of the Tinchant connections in the world of cigar making, Jules remained wary of him, warning Joseph that Édouard posed a risk to their reputation— perhaps because of his radicalism, perhaps because of his record of irresponsibility in Antwerp.[40]

As a practical matter, once the more experienced members of the family had given up their niche in the crowded New Orleans wholesale and retail cigar market, it was unlikely that the youngest brother could get it back. Having promised to make something of himself in the Americas, moreover, it would have been humiliating to turn around and flee back to Belgium. The stain of his embarrassing adventures in the port at Antwerp was hardly erased by a few months selling firewood in New Orleans, brief service in the Union army, and a turn as a teacher and radical spokesman in New Orleans. Indeed, he seems barely to have mentioned his political adventures to his parents at all, though he did brag a bit about his military service.[41]

It looked as though the public Édouard Tinchant, exuberant francophone radical, might soon have to give way to Edward A. Tinchant, an earnest young man living by his own labors. He and his wife now looked for a new place to start, and settled on the city of Mobile, located 140 miles away. This was Alabama's only port, opening out to the Gulf of Mexico, served by steamers from England, and historically second only to New Orleans in the volume of cotton that it had exported. Mobile's economy was reeling from the effects of the war, but for a beginner it might offer greater prospects than New Orleans.[42]

Édouard had learned the rudiments of the cigar business from his brothers, though he had generally worked alone, traveling upriver to Memphis with cases of cigars to sell. The Tinchant clan had some ties to Mobile from before the war, when Louis, Joseph, and Jules had traveled to Mobile for business and pleasure (including a bit of sea bathing), developing a friendship with a prosperous Creole grocer named Clément Joseph, whose son's education they later arranged in Belgium. The Tinchant and Joseph families seem to have been linked together in the minds of those who had known Édouard's older brother Louis, who was said to have visited Mobile every year and lodged with the Joseph family on Joachim

Street. So Édouard Tinchant had a bit of a base to build on, and Mobile had only a handful of cigar dealers, compared with the crowd in New Orleans. Perhaps there was room for a novice with a recognizable name.[43]

Shortly after they arrived, Édouard and Louisa found lodging in Mobile's Seventh Ward, inland and back from the river. In many ways, this ward in Mobile resembled the artisan and working-class neighborhoods in which each of them had lived in New Orleans. Their neighbors on one side included a white coppersmith, a white plumber, and a black laundress. On the other side was a man identified as mulatto who had a wood yard, and a short distance away was another man designated a mulatto who was a cigar maker. The Seventh Ward returned very large majorities for candidates designated "negro" who ran for secretary of state and for Congress in the 1870 elections.[44]

Édouard and Louisa may have used both English and French at home but otherwise could blend in with their neighbors. For some purposes—though not in the census—residents of Mobile had long used the term "Creole" to designate a subset of the population who traced their roots to long-settled immigrants from Spain and France. An element of African ancestry was acknowledged among Mobile Creoles but was generally treated as subordinate to what was described as the "Franco-Latin" colonial component. Allowed a separate identity in the years before the Civil War, but far less numerous than their counterparts in New Orleans, Mobile's Creoles played an open but relatively moderate role in Reconstruction-era politics in the city. One member of a Creole family, Phillip Joseph, was a well-known leader of a faction of the Republican Party.[45]

When the local census taker came to the dwelling of Édouard and Louisa in Mobile in July 1870, Édouard gave his age (accurately) as twenty-nine, his occupation as cigar manufacturer, and his name as Edward. He reported his birthplace as France, and both of his parents as foreign-born, but designated himself a U.S. citizen, thus conveying the impression that he was a naturalized foreigner. Taken together, these identifiers obscured his connections with long-free people of color in New Orleans. The enumerator put pen to paper and entered Edward and Louisa Tinchant as "White." It may well be that only Édouard himself appeared at the door to speak with the census taker and simply allowed the official to assume that his wife's color category matched what now appeared to be his own.[46]

Édouard Tinchant's newfound discretion on matters of politics and of color may have been a question both of business logic and of safety. The language of white supremacy used by Democrats in Mobile was even more direct than anything he was likely to have heard during his time as an elected official in New Orleans. The *Mobile Daily Register,* for example, described the great issue of the 1870 election as "whether Alabama is a WHITE MAN'S STATE and is to have a WHITE MAN'S GOVERNMENT or not." If that were not clear enough, the paper went on to declare that "The FIFTY YEARS of the REGISTER'S devotion to the true interests of the South, Democracy, and the WHITE MAN, leaves no need now for promises as to its course and position during the Campaign." The paper opposed the Fifteenth Amendment, which barred racial restrictions on the right to vote. The tone of these articles suggested something of the peril for a man like Édouard Tinchant: "Who is not for us is against us. It is white or black—true Southern man or scalawag—self-government against usurped government."[47]

Mobile did in the end turn out to offer Édouard Tinchant the possibility of establishing himself in the world of commerce. But it was going to be a politically lonely spot for a man who, just two years earlier, had proudly announced a principled commitment to color-blind universal manhood suffrage, equal rights for women, racially integrated public education, and an expansive understanding of republicanism.

8

Horizons of Commerce

Although Édouard Tinchant exalted the rights and duties of United States citizenship, his brothers' responses to the changing political and commercial scene would soon add another potential nationality to the family's repertoire. Joseph Tinchant had been willing to wait out the tense early months of the U.S. Civil War in New Orleans, and Édouard had relished the opportunity to make his political voice heard in the midst of the struggle over slavery, but Pierre and Jules Tinchant decided quite quickly that the conflict triggered by secession was not their fight. Although born in Louisiana, Pierre and Jules had spent the majority of their lives in Europe, and their connection to the United States was a conditional one. When war arrived, they looked to another shore. After the firing on Fort Sumter in April 1861, Jules headed south to explore the possibilities for commerce in Mexico, and Pierre joined him to try his luck working on small coastal vessels. Together, they began the process of shifting the center of the American branch of the family trading network away from the blockaded city of New Orleans and toward Veracruz, the port that was the Atlantic gateway to Mexico. Veracruz, however, would prove to be as much a vortex of imperial competition as Jérémie or Santiago a generation earlier.[1]

An established trade route had long linked Louisiana with Mexico. The first boom in Louisiana tobacco production had come in the late eighteenth century, when both regions were under Spanish rule and Louisiana growers were encouraged to supply leaf to the Mexican monopoly. That boom had collapsed by 1800, but the New Orleans–Veracruz connection was a durable one, continually reinforced by the movement of people and commodities across the Gulf. By the 1850s, the possibility of settlement in Mexico had taken on a particular meaning for free families of color in New Orleans, who found themselves under assault at home by statutory limitations on their rights, compounded by open political hostility. With the secession of Louisiana from the Union, and the establishment of the Confederate States of America, the southward pull across the Gulf became stronger.[2]

In 1861 an idiosyncratic French settlement in the town of Jicaltepec, at the mouth of the Nautla River, provided Jules Tinchant with a first Mexican home. A band of peasant families from Burgundy and Franche-Comté had been persuaded by a former follower of the utopian Charles Fourier to establish a model colony in Mexico. Apparently burdened by mismanagement, the collectivist experiment quickly failed in the hot, low-lying lands of the Gulf Coast. The surviving families began to farm on their own, and French newcomers came to join them, a few of them from the Tinchants' former home base of the Béarn in the Basses-Pyrénées, including members of the Sempé family, with whom the Tinchant brothers had gone to school in Pau. Eventually the colony in Jicaltepec, along with an adjacent one in San Rafael, came to be known for the export of vanilla, a luxury product with an expanding market in Europe.[3]

In the autumn of 1861, Jules Tinchant wrote letters back to Antwerp from Jicaltepec, full of enthusiasm for the economic prospects of Mexico. He was glib about what he took to be the failings of Mexicans, but he found Jicaltepec itself to be quite "civilized." In letters to his brother Ernest, Jules marveled at the quality of Mexican tobacco, and also predicted that European gin would find a ready market in the state. More of a trader than an agriculturalist by temperament, Jules soon moved on to the city of Veracruz and began to make his way into commerce by taking a job in a store run by a man named Bonnemaison. He thus dodged the floods and the epidemic of yellow fever that ravaged Jicaltepec a few months later.[4]

Jules seems to have been a charmer and an entrepreneur, eager to recruit other migrants to the enterprise of settlement in Veracruz. His immediate ambition was to lure fellow Creoles from Louisiana, particularly his brother Joseph, who had substantial experience in the Tinchant tobacco business in New Orleans. Two wars would intervene, however, before Jules successfully persuaded Joseph to move his family to Mexico.[5]

During the last days of 1861, military forces from Spain, joined by others from England and France, seized the port of Veracruz in order to control the revenue passing through the customs house, and thus extract payment for what they took to be the Mexican government's European debts—including loans contracted by the conservatives who had earlier waged war against the liberal Benito Juárez, now president of the republic. Napoléon

III of France was aiming to capture more than just revenue, however. When the magnitude of his imperial ambitions in Mexico became clear, Spain and Britain withdrew from the enterprise. French troops, supported by Mexican conservatives, moved inland and succeeded in forcing President Benito Juárez to withdraw from the capital itself. Confident in their military superiority, and in some cases believing themselves destined for triumph because of what they took to be their racial superiority, the French high command dramatically underestimated their vulnerability to guerrilla warfare. Combat would smolder and rage across Mexico for six years, pitting French and Austrian troops, along with some Mexicans, against forces loyal to Juárez.[6]

This was the European exercise in intervention that Édouard Tinchant would later denounce in the newspaper in New Orleans, and it certainly made it a bit delicate to be perceived as a Frenchman in Veracruz. Neither Jules nor the colonists in neighboring Jicaltepec, however, displayed any particular enthusiasm for the French expeditionary force, and among their Mexican colleagues they seem to have escaped direct association with the invaders. The primary concern of Pierre and Jules was to maintain their foothold in commerce as the region was engulfed in conflict. Following the lead established a decade earlier by their older brothers in New Orleans, they began to focus on tobacco as a possible option. Veracruz had long been a center both for the export of tobacco and for the production of cigars, and Jules set up his own retail tobacco, cigar, and dry goods business at Pescadería No. 580. From Belgium, brother Louis provided shipments of pipes, along with other European goods.[7]

The Civil War in the United States compounded the distance between the new enterprise in Veracruz and brother Joseph in Louisiana. After April 1862 and the Federal occupation of New Orleans, Joseph Tinchant had publicly committed himself to the Union cause and enlisted in the Federal forces. Following his demobilization from the Union army in the summer of 1863, however, he became increasingly embittered by the difficulty of earning durable respect from the high command, and by the continuing hostility of many white residents of the city to the men of color who were now pushing hard for equal rights. With interstate and international trade disrupted by war, moreover, the Tinchant Brothers cigar operation in New Orleans was cut off from clients in the Confederate states, making it difficult to collect monies owed to it.

The long-standing debate in Louisiana on the possibility of moving to Mexico remained open. Armand Lanusse and others suggested that the

French-supported ascent to power of the emperor Maximilian would bring prosperity, and that this was a monarchy pledged to respect rights and equality for all. Under the circumstances, Joseph could, if he wished, portray a decision to join his brother Jules as simply the pursuit of economic opportunity. He would not be obliged to make any open show of anger at the Union in order to explain his abandonment of the ongoing struggles in the city.[8]

Indeed, experienced tobacconists like Joseph Tinchant and his brother Louis back in Antwerp could see the logic of a move into Mexico. With careful attention to growing conditions, curing, and selection, the best Mexican tobacco might give Cuban leaf a run for its money. The demand for cigars was expanding in Europe, and the Tinchants' established transatlantic network promised them a potential head start. Seven years earlier Joseph Tinchant had installed the family's tobacco business in Antwerp in Belgium; perhaps now was the time to depart fractious New Orleans and formally expand their scope to Mexico.[9]

Proceeding cautiously, Joseph made a preliminary voyage to Mexico's Gulf Coast in early 1864, landing at Jicaltepec, the site of the French colony where brother Jules had been welcomed in 1861. He then returned to New Orleans on the schooner *Carisimo*, which carried a cargo of thirty-six bales of tobacco and eight bags of specie worth 4,000 Mexican dollars, consigned to a New Orleans merchant. The passenger list that the captain of the *Carisimo* presented on arrival in New Orleans contained just two names: F. H. Ollivier, a businessman operating out of Veracruz, and Joseph Tinchant, merchant. The voyage could presumably be counted a success.[10]

In June 1864, the very month that the emperor Maximilian arrived in Veracruz from Europe, Jules began to lobby Joseph again, hoping that he would now see the appeal of settling permanently in what promised to be a monarchy under a vaguely reformist Habsburg archduke. French forces had seemingly secured the country, and the outlook was for peace. Jules proposed that the three brothers establish a new business together, this one to be called Tinchant Hermanos. Jules knew Veracruz; brother Pierre knew the coasting trade; and Joseph knew cigars. Joseph had Louisiana friends capable of offering a loan to get them started. Jules made it sound very appealing.[11]

Joseph Tinchant's options in wartime New Orleans, moreover, were rapidly narrowing. He had closed his tobacco store on St. Charles Avenue in the summer of 1863 while he persuaded his neighbors to join him in the Sixth Louisiana Volunteers, and the overall financial situation of Tinchant Brothers was now disastrous. He later recalled that some $40,000 was tied up in apparently irrecoverable credits extended to their customers. The wisest course seemed to be to pay the firm's debts, maintaining Joseph's good name, and close up shop. From a commercial point of view, Mexico at peace now looked a good deal more promising than a Union-occupied territory adjoining the Confederacy at war.[12]

At the end of August 1864, Joseph Tinchant, his wife Stéphanie Gonzales, and their four-year-old son, Jacques, boarded the *Marie Douglas* in the port of New Orleans, headed for Veracruz. Their departure was announced with regret by the *Tribune*, the successor to the *Union*, whose writer took the occasion to highlight the hypocrisy of the Unionists in New Orleans who had failed to show proper respect to a man who had helped recruit a regiment to defend the city. This piece was likely penned by Armand Lanusse, as both a tribute to his former colleague and, perhaps, as a final jab at the presumptuous younger brother Édouard Tinchant, who was staying behind in New Orleans.[13]

As soon as Joseph Tinchant arrived in Veracruz, the three brothers set up a joint import-export enterprise, having persuaded Joseph's old friend and fellow Louisianan Zenon Decuir to stake them with a $4,000 loan. Pierre and Jules would be the active partners in the new Tinchant Hermanos, and Joseph would be a partner in *commandite*, co-signing the loan and sharing profits and losses, but leaving the management to Jules. Joseph later wrote bitterly that it was his own good name and credit in New Orleans that made it possible to begin the business, but that it seemed to be Jules who lived exceptionally well after the receipt of what was supposed to be a business loan.[14]

Joseph himself had bigger ambitions than running an import-export business down by the port in Veracruz. He planned to settle his family in the countryside and try his hand at serious commerce in the adjacent city and towns. Joseph and Stéphanie baptized their second son, Vincent, shortly after their arrival, and soon joined an agricultural colony recently established by various Louisiana migrants in the Tecolutla River basin, north of Veracruz and some miles in from the coast. This small community occupied rich land in and around a settlement called Cazonera, situated a few miles from the town of Papantla, at a bend in the Tecolutla River. Apparently employing laborers from among the surrounding Totonac Indian settlements, the farms at Cazonera included rich but dangerously low-lying land near the river.[15]

Joseph was undoubtedly aware from his early trading trip that in the upper reaches of the Tecolutla River basin planters were growing good tobacco that could be rolled into cigars or exported in leaf form to be made into cigars elsewhere. Here was a point in the "commodity chain" that promised profits, though the preparation would be laborious. The key was to develop close relations with planters in order to acquire the best leaf, then to make sure that the curing and selection were done well, then to pack it securely for shipment to Europe, and finally to establish among buyers a recognized brand that could command a premium on the market. Joseph's brother Louis, who knew the markets in Paris and London, insisted that if one were to develop and then introduce to European buyers a high-quality tobacco that could be distinguished from the ordinary Mexican leaf, there was lots of money to be made. Joseph seems to have identified "Tlapacoyan tobacco" (named after an inland growing region) as a category that might meet this standard. From Antwerp brother Louis pushed impatiently to get his hands on a sample. Louis was particularly eager to acquire what he described as *couvertures,* wrapper tobacco for cigars, which commanded an exceptionally high price.[16]

In pursuit of good cigar tobacco, Joseph was making his way into an agricultural activity that had a long history in the Tecolutla basin. Although the town of Papantla and the surrounding lowlands of the river valley were isolated—"not on the way to anywhere," as one writer puts it—the area provided good conditions for growing tobacco, particularly as one moved up from the tropical *tierra caliente* toward the foothills of the Sierra Madre Oriental. In 1854 the French vice-consul had appealed on behalf of the colonists of Jicaltepec for permission to plant tobacco for export. In 1856 the new Liberal regime had abolished the state's monopoly control over tobacco, expanding the areas in which the crop could now legally be grown. It seemed a promising moment for a man with know-how and access to markets.[17]

Following the lead of other Louisiana families of color who sought opportunity in Mexico, Joseph Tinchant's in-laws the Gonzaleses had apparently already arrived from New Orleans and acquired some land near Papantla. At least one *sitio y casa* (lot and house) in the neighborhood of Barriles and Cazonera, as well as an adjacent piece of property, was eventually owned by Stéphanie's family. Joseph seems to have established the industrial side of the enterprise, constructing buildings within which to roll cigars, purchasing tobacco from local growers, and working along with his extended family and additional artisans to produce the cigars.[18]

In the meanwhile, Jules continued to operate Tinchant Hermanos down in Veracruz, trying to cover costs and repay debts through the fruits of everyday commerce. From Antwerp, Ernest and Louis shipped out mixed lots of goods—including iron beds, tobacco pipes, and ribbon—which they envisioned that Tinchant Hermanos would offer for sale in Veracruz and beyond. The somewhat vague business records kept by Jules indicate that he did indeed develop a far-flung clientele, particularly among French settlers in the area; but expenses piled up far faster than income. Soon his brothers Louis and Joseph began to suspect the worst. Sending anything to Jules on consignment, Louis implied, was like throwing money into a bottomless pit. He asserted that some 12,000 francs worth of goods they had shipped to Jules from Belgium were more or less unaccounted for. Moreover, Louis feared that Jules would try to sell in Veracruz any tobacco acquired by Joseph, rather than shipping it on to Antwerp.[19]

The web of Tinchant financial commitments now extended far and wide. A school principal in Ghent had been clamoring for payment for tuition for the young Augustus Clément Joseph, for whom the Tinchants had arranged schooling in Belgium as a favor to family friends in Mobile, Alabama. Because of the war, the boy's parents had been unable to keep up payments, and the principal was dunning Jacques, who in turn tried to collect from Joseph in Mexico. A merchant in Paris who had provided credit to Jules and Joseph for their tobacco purchases reported that he had never received monies promised by Jules. Meanwhile, in Veracruz Jules kept signing bills of exchange *(traites)* left and right. Louis had his own creditors in Antwerp to deal with. His father Jacques had been the brothers' primary original financial backer, and by early 1867 Louis had to take on the repayment of Pierre and Joseph's portion of that loan, as well as his own. He reported angrily to Joseph that their aging parents were now living in *misère*.[20]

While waiting for the dreamed-of fine leaves of cigar tobacco—carefully chosen, impeccably cured, meticulously baled, safely shipped, and astutely placed on the international market—various members of the family looked back to New Orleans for some resources. Jacques Tinchant ordered his agent there to sell off the last properties still held in his name, while Pierre and Jules explored the possibility of collecting on credits due to the defunct Tinchant Brothers, New Orleans. After the end of the Civil War in the United States, Pierre made a trip to Louisiana, following up on old business and apparently collecting from some of their creditors. Jules and Joseph subsequently heard nothing more from him, however, and later learned that in December 1865 Pierre had boarded the schooner *Henriette Gentry,* bound from New Orleans to Veracruz, and been lost at sea.[21]

Shortly after the presumed death of their brother Pierre, the increasingly apprehensive Joseph proposed that Tinchant Hermanos be dissolved, so that each partner could go his own way. Jules refused, arguing that Mexican law required a two-year wait before the dissolution of an association if one of the associates had been lost at sea. Joseph had to stay in, like it or not. In April 1866, he made a first payment of $1,000 toward the balance of the advance that they had received from Zenon Decuir.[22]

It was not, however, an easy time to be a settler on the banks of the Tecolutla River. Although the region remained off the beaten path, the political and military struggle for control between forces loyal to Benito Juárez and those supporting the emperor Maximilian was intense. At this point, the war consisted of guerrilla and counterguerrilla maneuvers, including attacks on French-occupied territory in the state of Veracruz. By the summer of 1865 these attacks had reached Papantla, just a few miles from Cazonera.[23]

There is some mystery about Joseph Tinchant's possible involvement in the war itself. Despite speaking French as his first language, Joseph showed no attachment to the imperial enterprise of Napoléon III, and the families at Cazonera seem to have been generally perceived as *norteamericanos,* even if some had ties to the Francophiles within the Afro-Creole community of New Orleans. The U.S. government was hostile to the French intervention and increased its pressure along the border and at Veracruz as the end of the Civil War made such steps feasible. Moreover, to the extent that Joseph did identify with France, it was with the Republic, not the Empire. Having been in Paris in 1848, he knew that Napoléon III was the man who had ordered troops to fire on workers in the streets—"the assassin of the 4th of December," as his brother Édouard put it. Joseph's own sympathies in the ongoing struggle in Mexico almost certainly lay with Benito Juárez. It is even possible, though perhaps not likely, that Joseph had crossed paths with Juárez back in New Orleans in 1854, either through shared sociability in the cafés, or through the buying and selling of cigars.[24]

Did Joseph—the former Lieutenant Tinchant in the Sixth Louisiana Volunteers—go so far as to offer material or even armed support to those who were fighting for Juárez? The Juárez forces were quite happy to accept recruits from among Union veterans, and Juárez subsequently conferred Mexican citizenship on those who made this move. Several of the descendants of Joseph Tinchant later came to be convinced that their ancestor had indeed provided some kind of services to Juárez. The correspondence from Joseph at the time, however, shows no hint of any political or military engagement during his years in Mexico. Of course, it would hardly have been prudent to write openly about his loyalties or activities as long as the war continued and the outcome was uncertain. The mystery remains, however, for after the war Joseph emerged with a recognized claim to Mexican citizenship.[25]

Joseph's most urgent concerns, however, were commercial. Under pressure from his brother Louis in Belgium to expand into the export of high-quality leaf tobacco, Joseph had reluctantly promised to send him a sample from the region of Tlapacoyan, farther inland. In mid-1867 Joseph acquired three bales of the costly leaf and had Jules ship them from Veracruz to the Maison Américaine in Antwerp. After inspecting the bales, Louis sent Joseph a patronizing letter, criticizing several aspects of the selection, lecturing Joseph on procedures, and complaining that Joseph had entrusted the shipment to Jules, who was then slow to forward it from the port at Veracruz. In this business, time was of the essence, and baled tobacco was vulnerable to spoilage. The cranky oldest brother nonetheless predicted that if it were possible to follow up with thirty bales of what he bluntly referred to as this "imitation" product, it could easily be sold on the European market. From the vantage point of Antwerp, it looked as though the brothers were finally approaching the goal of shipping a Mexican leaf tobacco that could command a premium price. But the leaf did not come from the lowland fields cultivated by Joseph and his neighbors. Jules and Joseph had apparently acquired these three sample bales of Tlapacoyan tobacco with borrowed money. So instead of turning a profit, they had another uncovered expense.[26]

Louis sent his scolding letter to Joseph from Antwerp in June of 1867. Napoléon III's imperial adventure had by then collapsed in disgrace, and Maximilian could not possibly retain power in Mexico without French support. Forces loyal to Juárez had already taken the city of Querétaro, to which Maximilian had retreated. On June 19, 1867, Maximilian was executed on the orders of Benito Juárez. Juárez, the man who had rolled cigars for a living during his exile in New Orleans in 1854, would now resume the presidency of Mexico. Jules Tinchant in Veracruz was increasingly uneasy as the last of the European troops withdrew, but with the good news from Louis about the market for carefully selected wrapper tobacco, the Tinchant enterprise seemed on the verge of a commercial breakthrough.[27]

Instead, they faced a breakdown. Tinchant Hermanos in Veracruz had fallen drastically behind on the repayment of loans to a Mexican merchant, as well as to their Louisiana associate Zenon Decuir. Their trading ventures in Veracruz had brought in some revenue, but selling ribbon and iron beds imported from Antwerp, charging family expenses to the business account, and making promises of great cigars to come, all the while keeping sloppy records of debts and credits, was no way to make a fortune. The last stages of the siege of Veracruz had also caused a stagnation in business. Joseph had committed additional money to the purchase of the sample bales of tobacco, which Jules now referred to reproachfully as a "speculation" that had killed the company. A schooner of which they were part owners was leased to evacuate some of the defeated Austrian troops of the (late) emperor Maximilian, and may have brought them a profit. But overall their income did not come close to covering their expenses. By the last months of 1867, Jules realized that Tinchant Hermanos was headed toward bankruptcy. Antonio Gómez de la Serna, a merchant in Veracruz, was calling in a large bill of exchange, and they simply could not pay. In scenes reminiscent of a novel by Anthony Trollope or Gustave Flaubert, the creditors closed in as Jules tried desperately to find some solution.[28]

The fact that Joseph had co-signed for the original advances now loomed large, and although as a partner *en commandite* he did not share in the management of Tinchant Hermanos, he was on the hook for the firm's losses. In late October 1867, Joseph received a menacing letter from the businessman John Hart, criticizing him for having failed to pay the $1,200 due on the loan from Zenon Decuir. A few months earlier, Hart had journeyed north along the coast from Veracruz, and then traveled upriver to the farm at Cazonera to try to collect the debt directly from Joseph. Joseph had acknowledged that he owed the money, but had persuaded Hart to go back to Veracruz and collect instead from Tinchant Hermanos. But, as Hart now took pains to point out, Joseph's credit in Veracruz was "somewhat damaged," and his "associate" (brother Jules) was not in a position to make good on his commitments. The pending bankruptcy, moreover, promised to be a very painful one, since the business records were in disarray, and by implication unlikely to be accepted by a court as proof of their losses.[29]

148

Hart went on to make an entirely improper offer to Joseph: You have 60,000 cigars at Cazonera, ready to ship. Just send Decuir a batch of those cigars before the bankruptcy goes through. Draw up a receipt that says you have sold them to me at fifteen dollars per thousand, and we'll hold them for you or sell them, depending on what you decide and what the actual price turns out to be. You'll save your friend Decuir from ruin, and you'll keep the proceeds out of the hands of other creditors. Just be sure to include the false receipt; that will be the only way to keep the payment separate from the assets of Tinchant Hermanos when the bankruptcy goes through.[30]

Whatever Joseph did or did not do in response to this letter, he was making plans to leave the coast and move to the interior, closer to the centers of the tobacco trade. In December 1868, Tinchant Hermanos was on the ropes, though a formal liquidation was avoided. Despite the general financial insecurity that accompanied the resumption of power by President Benito Juárez and the Liberals, Jules continued to do business in Veracruz. Joseph was left with a burden of outstanding debt to their friends from Louisiana, and with the humiliation of being formally *protesté*—legally called to account—for nonpayment of his bills of exchange.[31]

By 1869, the farm at Cazonera was up for sale, and Joseph and Stéphanie had resettled in Tlapacoyan, farther inland near the foothills of the Sierra Madre Oriental. Growers in these upper reaches of the Tecolutla basin were producing high-quality tobacco, often shipped out through the port at Nautla. The move also brought the family closer to the hill town of Teziutlán, the base for many of the local tobacco merchants. By now, Joseph's relationship with brother Jules was fraught with quarrels over debts, and Joseph was apparently aiming to find his own place within the established tobacco trade of the region, either to continue with cigar manufacture or, as his brother Louis evidently hoped, to send some leaf tobacco to the export market through Antwerp. In one of the last more-or-less friendly letters addressed by Jules to Joseph, Jules sent along a treatise on tobacco growing—a gesture that was either a veiled insult, or a belated recognition that the brothers still had a great deal to learn on the subject.[32]

Years later, Joseph would assert that he had through his efforts developed the good reputation in Europe of tobacco from southern Mexico. Judging by the family correspondence that later ended up in the hands of his attorney, however, one would have to say that in the early 1870s

Joseph was still struggling. He seems to have acquired substantial skills and connections, but he did not pay off the debt to Zenon Decuir. Indeed, at one moment in 1871 Joseph wrote despairingly to his brother Ernest in Antwerp that in the "deplorable tobacco business" they had all been "blinded by ambition." Joseph seemed to want to come back to Belgium, but not as a failure, and so he persisted in his efforts in Mexico.[33]

By 1874, the reputation of the tobacco grown around Tlapacoyan was indeed well established. A visiting geographer, Antonio García Cubas, reported that tobacco was now the favored crop in the area, "both for the superior qualities of the plant and for its yield." He noted, however, that this tobacco was not well known in central Mexico, because it was exported directly to Europe. García Cubas believed that its destination was France; some, however, may well have passed through the hands of one or another Tinchant brother in Belgium.[34]

By the mid-1870s, Joseph Tinchant had begun to style himself Don José Tinchant, in keeping with local forms of address, and to present himself as a citizen of Mexico. Soon his claim was seen by local authorities as robust enough to commit to paper. On January 14, 1875, the commandant of the port of Veracruz issued a passport for Havana to the "Mexican citizen José Tinchant."[35]

Acquiring this passport, however, turned out to be a prelude to Joseph's definitive departure from Mexico. The trip to Havana was either a brief expedition to explore commercial possibilities, or a stopping point on what soon became a transatlantic journey—one in which he left unpaid debts behind. In late 1875 Joseph and Stéphanie, accompanied by their eldest son, Jacques, arrived in Antwerp and registered as foreigners with the local authorities. Their children Vincent, Pierre, and Eliza presumably followed shortly thereafter, perhaps accompanied by one of the Gonzales kin, or by a Belgian business associate of Joseph's.[36]

Upon arrival in Antwerp, Joseph found that the European side of the "deplorable tobacco affair" that had seemed such a burden back in Mexico in 1871 could indeed be the basis for a successful and profitable business. As planned, Joseph joined forces with his brother Ernest, and in 1875 they began to manufacture hand-rolled cigars. As he began to offer cigars for sale in Europe under the name Tinchant Frères, Joseph took another step to distance himself from their Louisiana past and to associate his family's image with Latin America. In a succession of letterheads and labels, he formalized his transformation from Joseph Tinchant into Don José Tinchant y Gonzales. He retained the courtesy title that had been used in Mexico—Don José—and now added his wife's surname to his own. By the 1890s, in an elegant lithograph prepared for the trade, his resplendent portrait stood out against a backdrop that seemed to be the port of Havana. The fusing of his decade in Mexico with his brief passage through Cuba was completed by the mention of a branch office in Havana.[37]

This appropriation of the Gonzales surname was further reinforced by the continuing connection of the Antwerp branch with Stéphanie Gonzales's Louisiana-born kin back in Mexico. Some remained in the area near Tecolutla, while her brothers Gustave and Damian moved farther south, into promising tobacco lands near San Andrés Tuxtla. Indeed, the Belgian-based Tinchants would eventually take out trademarks on cigars identified as being made by a firm called González, based in Tuxtla. Later histories of the tobacco industry around Tuxtla would take the brothers now called Damián and Gustavo González for Cuba émigrés, hence naturals in the task of producing fine cigars.[38]

When the Tinchant brothers had lived in Louisiana as French-speaking "free men of color," their Creole identity had necessarily linked their ancestry not only to France and the Caribbean, but also to Africans brought to the Americas as slaves. By virtue of his passage through the state of Veracruz, however, Joseph Tinchant now succeeded in transforming this Creole-ness into something associated with Mexico, and by extension with Cuba, reinforcing the air of quality surrounding Tinchant cigars. From the vantage point of Antwerp, each of these associations could be favorable, and few people were likely to inquire deeply about the particulars.

The Cuban connection implied by the lithographs prepared as part of the company's publicity made sense for a company selling high-end cigars they described as *havanes*. Not until the 1880s would the Belgian government begin to insist that to sell cigars under this name one had to be able to show that the merchandise actually came from Cuba. Throughout the late 1870s, the Tinchants showed themselves masters at the creation of *havanes* that were rolled in Antwerp workshops.[39]

When interviewed for a promotional article, a spokesperson for the firm of Tinchant Frères later explained that Don José had in 1873 introduced seeds from Cuba's famous Vuelta Abajo to "a neighboring Antillean island." This is somewhat puzzling, since in 1873 Joseph had lived in the inland town of Tlapacoyan, Mexico, and he seems never to have undertaken an agricultural enterprise elsewhere in the Caribbean. Some of the leaf tobacco used in Tinchant cigars rolled in Antwerp may well have been grown on farms near the Gulf of Mexico, and some of their cigars may have been authentic imports from Havana, but the unnamed island located near Cuba seems to have been an embellishment for the purposes of public relations. The main consignments of leaf tobacco to the factory were those made by Joseph Tinchant's brother-in-law Gustave/ Gustavo Gonzales, based in Tuxtla on Mexico's Gulf Coast. No matter; the brand was becoming well established, and the stories added to its luster.[40]

Ernest and Joseph Tinchant had found their way to a profitable formula. They hired Belgian workers to roll cigars in a three-story factory built on the grounds of the demolished city fortifications, near the railway station. They then packaged them in such a way as to invoke tropical seas and a Cuban landscape. With a good enough leaf to begin with, and appropriate skills among those who did the work, they could indeed produce fine cigars, and *havanes* by Tinchant commanded a high price in the market. Don José could now aspire to his own town house and to educating his children in style.[41]

Joseph and Ernest's youngest brother Édouard, by contrast, was trying to hold his own back in the United States by aiming at the bottom of the market. When the 1867–1868 Louisiana Constitutional Convention had begun its sessions, Édouard had been trying for some months to make a living by his earlier technique of buying cigars in New Orleans and then taking the steamer up the Mississippi to sell them. But this small-scale commerce, and his unpaid job as a school principal, could not possibly support a proper family. During the excitement of his months as a Republican delegate to the state constitutional convention he had married Louisa Debergue, and when the convention adjourned, they had resettled in Mobile, Alabama, to make a new start. Their first child, a girl, was born there in July 1870.[42]

This time, Édouard Tinchant's ambition was to become a manufacturer, not just a salesman. And so, beginning with nothing more than his own labor, he set up shop. Several of Mobile's cigar manufacturers were Cuban, and as Édouard accumulated a bit of capital he may have hired some recent immigrants as well as locals to work with him. At least two Cubans—Emilio and Fernando Pérez—appear in the 1871 naturalization records for Mobile, declaring that they had been residents for three years, which would put their arrival at just the moment of the wave of emigration driven by the 1868 Cuban war for independence. In the years

to come, other Cuban émigrés in Mobile would appear on lists of supporters of the separatist struggles. Édouard Tinchant would later write
that he had always been a supporter of the Cuban cause, and that he had
often "lent a helping hand" to Cuban émigrés. It seems quite possible
that he hired a few Cuban cigar makers for the "manufactory" that he
would soon be advertising to the public.[43]

Just as "Edward Tinchant, Cigar Manufacturer" was finding his foot-
ing, news came of the death of his father Jacques in Antwerp. In a lengthy
letter to his mother, Édouard reflected miserably on this loss, wishing
that God had prolonged his father's life long enough for him "to have
received news from me and to have given, before his death, the blessings
that I asked him to confer on my family." Édouard had never been able to
report the kind of business success that might have pleased his father,
and he seems not to have risked reporting on his political adventures.
Now there was the knowledge that he would never receive his father's
good wishes for his own new family of Louisa and their baby Antonine.
The drama brought back Édouard's old remorse at his misdeeds, and a
touch of his former grandiloquence: "I bow down nonetheless before the
will of God, for there is found the severe but, alas, justified punishment
for my culpable negligence toward my elderly parents."[44]

In collaboration with his cousins the Xaviers back in Louisiana, Édouard arranged for a small Mass to be celebrated in the Cathedral of
Saint Louis in New Orleans. This, he recalled, was the place where his
father had celebrated first communion, and had married. They apparently
invited just five guests, including John Duhart, Charles Lévêque (a close
friend of his brother Louis), and Paul Trévigne, "who loves Joseph like a
brother." This last name linked the ceremony to their common struggles
during Reconstruction—Trévigne had been a writer for the *Tribune*, and
was one of the long-standing radical Republican activists of New Orleans,
still committed to the legal campaign against segregation.[45]

Indeed, as Édouard Tinchant tried to resign himself to the fact of his
father's death—and of his own failure to please his father—he evoked
the war and revolution that he had lived through. The revolutions he had
seen in the "great nations" had persuaded him of the justice of a vengeful
God, he wrote. However absorbed he might be with the establishment of
his tobacco business, and with his new wife and their baby, his frame
of reference remained that of a believer in the Union cause, and in the
transcendent justice of the outcome of the Civil War. He offered his

mother some comfort by reporting on the activities of the baby, and explained that he had hoped to send a picture of her to the family in Antwerp, but could not afford to do so yet because of the purchase of mourning clothes and the expenses of the "little establishment" that he would be opening within the month. He nonetheless declared himself full of optimism for the future.[46]

That "little establishment" emerged into view in the 1872 city directory of Mobile, which carried an entry and an advertisement for "Ed. A. Tinchant. Cigar Manufacturer, 87 North Royal St., near cor. State. Trade and Consumers supplied with honest domestic Cigars at reasonable terms." His family had moved out of the modest Seventh Ward and into a building near the business district, a few blocks from the river, close to the Cotton Exchange. No color term was appended to his name in the directory.[47]

Over the next two years Édouard ran a similar advertisement, striking the theme of low cost and local production. Soon he had come up in the world sufficiently to earn a credit rating from R. G. Dun & Co. Initially the evaluator judged E. A. Tinchant not recommended for loans "unless for vy limit amts & within city limits." By November of 1874, however, the report suggested that he would be "safe" for a small line of credit, and that he paid his bills promptly.[48]

Édouard reported himself working long hours, and he stepped forward to help his brother Joseph track down some of the last creditors of the old Tinchant Brothers operation. His letters in mid-1874, however, were full of grief, consoling his wife for the loss of their first son to illness at the age of eight months, and wishing he had more news of his mother in Antwerp. The restless radical Édouard Tinchant—veteran, publicist, legislator, schoolteacher, and cosmopolitan proponent of equal rights—had for the moment been eclipsed by the burdened husband and father.[49]

In truth, it was not much of a moment to get involved in politics in Mobile. Murderous political competition and racist violence characterized the elections, and factionalism tore apart the Republican Party. A local Republican newspaper edited by the Creole activist Philip Joseph protested bitterly that "The white men in the Republican party fill all of the paying offices, and yet if a colored man dare part his lips on the subject he is charged with attempting to raise a black man's party." The political atmosphere was very different from that of Louisiana's Constitutional Convention, with its balance of delegates categorized as "white" and "colored."[50]

In late 1874, the political battles ended with a Democratic victory, followed by a congressional inquiry into allegations of fraud and intimidation. Curiously, Édouard Tinchant seems not even to have registered to vote, though he did pay the poll tax. Perhaps he was estranged from the particular factionalism of Mobile. Perhaps he feared being asked for documentation of his citizenship, or did not want to face the registrar's ledger, in which each voter was declared to be black, white, or creole. His maintenance of a racially unmarked identity for business purposes, after all, rested on avoiding direct inquiries.[51]

Édouard had experimented before with crossing boundaries, hiding his abolitionist sympathies from his brother Joseph's Confederate clients in wartime New Orleans, and apparently avoiding being labeled as "colored" on his business trips to Memphis during the Civil War. But when he was younger he had reported that he disliked being with his elite customers in Memphis, and that he wanted to settle back in to New Orleans to live "en vieux mulât"—literally, "like an old mulatto man"—a phrase, complete with Creole spelling, that evoked mixed ancestry and the ease of being among friends and family. In Mobile, Alabama, in the 1870s, however, there was no French-language newspaper in which to display his principles and his eloquence, nor a political base on which to build a career. Others already occupied the space of Republican politics, and they were under vicious attack from the Ku Klux Klan and its fellow vigilante organizations. Although the special role of those designated creole in Mobile may have created space for Édouard Tinchant as a businessman, there would be no ease in being seen as a political activist and a "mulatto man."[52]

The principles of respect and equal public rights had long been important to Édouard Tinchant. In Mobile, however, he had apparently been afforded a shortcut to public standing, for the stigmatizing term "colored' was absent from his entry in the census and the city directory. He could, of course, have grabbed the census enumerator's arm and said, "No, you've got it wrong. I *am* a colored man." But in its own way, a gesture like that would have been out of character for someone who had spent the first twenty-one years of his life in Europe, where such labels were not affixed to him. Moreover, he had always adapted to new circumstances, registering his French nationality with the French consul in New Orleans, but claiming U.S. citizenship two years later, after enlisting in the Union army. Now it was easier to be Edward than Édouard, and he could simply let the census taker assume that a man born in France was a white man. Louisa, as the wife of a foreign-born white man, apparently became a white woman by default, at least for the purposes of the federal census.

This adaptability carried over to the naming of his business: "Home Industry Cigar Manufactory." He was emphasizing that these were reasonably priced domestically produced cigars; he did not give his enterprise a French or Spanish name, and he did not vaunt his product as "Havana cigars," as did some of his competitors in Mobile and his older brothers in Antwerp. Instead, he emphasized his authenticity and low prices ("Bottom Prices to the Trade"). By 1875, the credit rater for R. G. Dun expanded the usual laconic notation and added that E. A. Tinchant had arrived "some 5 or 6 yrs ago with absolutely no means at all & has by hon indus & close atten worked up & now is wor[th] at least 4^M Cap." In a word of praise that stands in contrast to the modus operandi of the older Tinchant brothers in Mexico, the Dun representative added, "Would not order more than he could pay for."[53]

A fire insurance map of Mobile from this decade shows the rented space within which this "home industry" occurred. The front portion of a building on North Royal Street between State and St. Anthony was labeled "cigar factory," and the room behind it "warehouse." A narrow adjoining space was designated the store, with a shed in back. The neighboring property on one side was a carriage works, and on the other, a vacant lot. Édouard, Louisa and Antonine presumably lived upstairs from the workroom and warehouse.[54]

By 1876 Édouard Tinchant employed ten or twelve "hands," and in July of that year he was said to have opened a retail store in addition to his factory. The R. G. Dun inspector now believed his capital to be in the range of $5,000–$6,000, and his business practices to be exemplary. The report filed in May 1877 added that the business was "improving daily" and that E. A. Tinchant was very worthy and honorable. Everything looked good.[55]

And then, abruptly, Édouard Tinchant and his family disappeared from Mobile. The name Tinchant vanished from the city directory; his business dropped out of the R. G. Dun ledger books. The city tax collector estimated the value of Édouard Tinchant's furniture, machinery, and merchandise at $1,300 but marked this entry with a penciled note: "gone before the book was filed."[56]

The reasons may have been a mix of politics, business, and family. In Mobile, for all practical purposes, Reconstruction had already ended in

1874 with the statewide election of white-supremacist Democrats. But in 1877, power at the national level was shifting as well. The Hayes-Tilden compromise put a Republican in the presidency but created the conditions that allowed Democrats to dominate local offices in the South. Indeed, the compromise promised to undercut federal authority in the region. A new era of what Édouard Tinchant would later characterize as "infamous laws and stupid prejudices" lay ahead.[57]

The collapse of Reconstruction apparently forced Édouard to address the question of whether the United States was in fact the country whose citizen he wished to be. As Armand Lanusse had pointed out acidly over a decade earlier, Édouard kept his French citizenship papers tucked away in a drawer. In his own defense he had informed the readers of the *Tribune* that such papers might be useful to the struggle in another time and place. He knew from his family's long history that there would be other places.

To the extent that Édouard Tinchant explained his departure to colleagues in Mobile, he seems to have invoked the family business and to have said that his brother Louis needed him to come to Belgium to manage the Maison Américaine. Assuming that Louis, the eldest, did put out such a call to Édouard, the youngest, it was a sign of how much had changed. Five years of successful commerce in Mobile had eclipsed Édouard's earlier irresponsibilities, and his demanding older brother was ready to share the tasks of business with him.[58]

Before leaving the United States altogether, however, Édouard and Louisa and the children returned to New Orleans. There Louisa gave birth to a second daughter, whom they named Marie Louise Julie. The name may well have recalled Édouard's mother's sister Marie Louise, lost from view years earlier when the family had fled renewed warfare in Saint-Domingue, and about whom Édouard had perhaps heard stories. Indeed, in each succeeding generation of Édouard's descendants there would be a Marie-Louise, down to his great-granddaughter Marie-Louise Van Velsen, who today lives in Antwerp.[59]

When the baby was just a few months old, Édouard took out a passport for the family in New Orleans, signing the line that declared him to be "a loyal native citizen of the United States." Accompanied by a young servant to assist them, they boarded a ship for Europe. The restless Édouard Tinchant, long perceived as a troublemaker by his father and his brothers, was heading back to Antwerp, the city he had left in disgrace seventeen years earlier.[60]

Édouard's widowed mother, Élisabeth Vincent, was now getting very much on in years. Her Belgian identity papers said that she was only seventy years old, but judging by the baptismal certificate from 1799 in Saint-Domingue, and various statements of her age in intervening years, she would in fact turn eighty in 1879. Édouard had continued to send her tender letters during the years of his estrangement from his father. Perhaps he also thought it was time to bring his children back to settle near their grandmother.[61]

Arriving in Antwerp in July 1878, Edward Tinchant formally became Édouard again, and in the registration form required of foreigners he conveyed the details of his family history as he recalled them. He inscribed his wife as Louise Debergue, born in New Orleans on August 24, 1845. There were their three children: Marie Antonine Élisabeth Anne, born in Mobile in 1870; Arthur Jacques Antoine, born in Mobile in 1875; and Marie Louise Julie, born in New Orleans just a few months before their departure for Antwerp. Then Édouard entered information about his parents: Jacques, now deceased, had in Édouard's opinion been born in Baltimore (not the Halifax of a long-ago marriage record). The most intriguing item that he entered, however, was the birthplace for his mother. He apparently believed that she had been born in Santiago de Cuba. As of 1878, Édouard did not seem to be quite clear in his mind about the details of his mother's connection to Saint-Domingue, the birthplace that Élisabeth Vincent herself always acknowledged. But the mistake is a revealing one, for it suggests that at some point in Édouard's youth his mother conveyed one or another story about the time that she and her mother Rosalie had spent in exile in Cuba, and perhaps also the circumstances of her separation from her siblings.[62]

Shortly after Édouard and his family arrived in Antwerp, word came that the unpaid debts in Mexico, and the grudge carried by his brother Jules, had now yielded a lawsuit. Joseph Tinchant's quick success as a manufacturer when he returned to Europe only reminded others of the sums that he still owed to family friends back in Mexico. In 1879 Jules returned in person to Antwerp from Veracruz to find a lawyer, and to confront Joseph with a pile of old receipts and accounts. John Hart, of J. Ollivier and Co. in Mexico, sent another of his menacing letters directly to Joseph. Congratulating him on doing better in Belgium than in Mexico, Hart suggested "Don't you think that it is time for you finally to think about paying off the bills of exchange that I am still holding?" In response, Joseph deposited a sheaf of family correspondence and multiple memoranda with his own lawyer, the distinguished liberal attorney Jacques Cuylits, trying to establish that any outstanding debts were due to the profligacy and irresponsibility of his brother Jules.[63] Jules soon returned to Mexico, but the suit dragged on through 1887. In the end Joseph lost the court case and was obliged to pay off the old debts. He may have been justifiably exasperated with Jules, but even he knew that the unpaid debts of the Tinchant operation had left old family friends in the lurch.[64]

Despite the unpleasantness associated with those years in Mexico, the farm in Cazonera moved into the imagination of the next generations as a lost Garden of Eden. In 1894 Joseph and Stéphanie's son Vincent, who was being groomed to take over his father's business in Antwerp, took a trip to Mexico. He wrote home describing the network of kin and friends from along the Tecolutla River who turned out to greet him. To Vincent Tinchant, this was a true family in a place where he was welcomed and where Don José was warmly remembered. Among the Gonzaleses, he was particularly touched to see his maternal grandmother, whom he called Nénaine. From that date onward, Vincent Tinchant embraced a thoroughly Mexican version of the family's history.[65]

Over the years after 1875 each of the family tobacco enterprises based in Antwerp became a successful international business, bringing solid prosperity to the brothers, and then to their descendants. By the 1890s, the partnership of Joseph Tinchant and his brother Ernest, Tinchant Frères, counted clients and suppliers from Bucharest to Lisbon, and from Algiers to London. In 1895 Joseph established a new business titled "José Tinchant y Gonzales y Cie." with his son Vincent, whom he had long prepared for this role. [66]

As he moved into the management of the Tinchant y Gonzales operation, the exuberant and charming young Vincent Tinchant expanded the enterprise still further, made plenty of money, and bought himself a castle in the countryside. There he spun yarns of the family's once-fabulous Mexican estate he called Casoneras, and of the French aristocrats and Spanish grandees he imagined to number among the Tinchant ancestors. He sometimes spoke to his Belgian-born children in Spanish, and gave his horses names that evoked a deep Mexican past, including Quetzalcoatl and Tlaloc. (Vincent's great-granddaughter recalls that the Flemish-speaking groom on the estate found this linguistic whimsy particularly distressing.) All mention of exile, republicanism, and the struggle for equal rights in New Orleans fell away from this narrative of the family's ascent. A picture of cosmopolitan commercial success, enhanced by real manor houses in Belgium and imagined ones in Mexico, left no room for the question of color prejudice.[67]

9

Citizens beyond Nation

Purveyors of a high-status item in a time of expanding consumption, the Tinchant brothers flourished as cigar manufacturers in fin-de-siècle Antwerp. Their astute marketing campaigns evoked Mexico, Cuba, and the family's multiple links across the Atlantic, burnishing their products with a fitting touch of Creole expertise. Joseph Tinchant could arrange for his son Vincent to be educated by the Jesuits in Belgium, complemented by study in England and Germany, followed by a world tour of the cities in which Tinchant Frères did business. Yet the same cosmopolitan past that the brothers vaunted in their trademarks and cigar-box labels left their own precise nationality in some doubt. As they moved decisively into the urban bourgeoisie of a solidly European nation, such uncertainties required a resolution.[1]

In 1892, Ernest and Joseph, the proprietors of Tinchant Frères, began the process of seeking full citizenship rights as a Belgians. Joseph accompanied his formal request for *grande naturalisation* with a capsule autobiography that described a nice upward arc from birth in New Orleans to education in France, with an interval in Mexico, culminating in a flourishing career as a businessman in Belgium. At the time of the request, Joseph was said to own two pieces of real estate in the city and to be co-owner with Ernest of three cigar factories, one in Antwerp, one in St. Nicolas, and one in Eindhoven in the Netherlands. Joseph's narrative noted dramatically that Tinchant Frères had begun in Antwerp in 1875 with just ten workers but now kept some 2,000 workers occupied in the port and in the workshops. In 1891, he wrote, Tinchant Frères had exported more than fifty million cigars.[2]

Reassured by reports from authorities in Antwerp and Pau that there were no complaints against Joseph Tinchant, and presumably impressed by the scale and success of the brothers' business operations, the appointed *rapporteur* confirmed that Tinchant's "conduct and morality" were above reproach. On May 19, 1893, the Belgian Chambre de Représentants voted 71 to 16 to confer upon Joseph the requested *grande naturalisation,* which brought with it the full array of political and civil rights as a Belgian national and citizen, as well as eligibility for public office. The Chambre then promptly did the same for Ernest Tinchant.[3]

During a period of intense struggle over voting rights in Belgium, this *grande naturalisation* enabled two of the Tinchant brothers to move into a privileged category. Under the pressure of popular mobilization, the Belgian government was replacing highly restrictive property qualifications for the franchise with a nominally universal manhood suffrage. But under the system of "plural votes" introduced with the expanded suffrage law of 1893, recipients of *grande naturalisation* were given a greater political voice than the newly enfranchised workingmen.[4]

There was one oddity in Joseph's file, however. It was not clear what nationality or citizenship he might be thought to have held *prior* to his naturalization as a Belgian. Joseph Tinchant had been born a "free child of color" in New Orleans in 1827. Under the many restrictions that had emerged alongside the laws of slavery, his designation as a free person of color conferred no durable claim to national citizenship in the United States. If status as a slave implied absolute statelessness, status as a free person of color earned only a meager bundle of rights, and across the 1830s in Louisiana that bundle had been rapidly shrinking. Although the family's migration to France brought educational opportunities, Joseph was the foreign-born child of a non-French father. He could spend years at the *collège royal* in Pau without moving any closer to a credible claim to French nationality. Back in New Orleans as a young entrepreneur in the late 1840s and the 1850s, he had seen the prospect of a recognized citizenship in the United States close down with the 1857 Supreme Court decision in *Dred Scott v. Sandford,* and then open up in 1863, when he volunteered for service in the Union army and was commissioned as a lieutenant. But the hostility to officers of color shown by Union general Nathaniel P. Banks suggested the difficulty of giving substantive content to their claims of rights. As late as 1864 many white Unionists in Louisiana were still expressing strong opposition to full citizenship for men of color.

By the time that birthright U.S. citizenship independent of color was formally ratified with the Fourteenth Amendment to the Constitution in 1868, Joseph Tinchant was no longer a resident of Louisiana. Bitter at the affronts he had suffered in New Orleans, and pulled by the hope for opportunity on the other side of the Gulf, he had left for Mexico in August 1864. A decade later, when he decided to return to Belgium, Joseph—by that time styled as José Tinchant—was inscribed as a Mexican citizen on his passport, though the path by which he had successfully validated that claim is unclear. In the documents he later filed with the Belgian government, he did not mention Mexican citizenship. When his request for *grande naturalisation* was reviewed in 1892, the Ministry of Justice in Belgium filed a routine query to make sure that he owed no military service, and assumed that any such obligation would be to the United States. The now sixty-five-year-old Joseph assured them that no militia service was required of him in the United States.[5]

Across their multiple Atlantic journeys, Joseph and his brothers had reached for various components of national citizenship, though often without the formal set of legal rights that might be conferred by birth, parentage, or official naturalization. Indeed, as the six brothers reached adulthood, they pushed and pulled against the boundaries of nationality, experimenting with a sequence of alternate affiliations. Although the label "man of color" had often been a burden in Louisiana, Joseph Tinchant developed a public persona in Antwerp—taking on the elaborated denomination Don José Tinchant y Gonzales—in which his apparent mixture of European and non-European ancestry was construed as Mexican or Antillean. He thus enhanced his self-presentation as a man knowledgeable about tobacco and about the Americas from which that tobacco came.[6]

In all of this, the question of color nonetheless remained delicate, and nearly always unspoken. The portraits that Joseph and his brother Ernest commissioned as part of their advertising campaigns conveyed a generalized Creole image—sunshine, palm trees, and a bronzed complexion for the Don José of their magnificent lithographs; Cuban business affiliates and wavy hair in the case of Ernest. During most of the time that the Tinchants lived in Antwerp, the color markers associated with their various official documents sometimes made reference to an unspecific "dark" complexion, but no more. Early on, an angry school principal trying to collect monies from them had grumbled about "sang-mêlé" (mixed blood), but he was talking mainly about the child of their Mobile acquaintances who had been put in school in Ghent.[7]

As respectable businessmen, the Tinchant brothers were generally spared the old colonial and slaveholding label of *mulâtre,* which had been familiar to refugees of color from Saint-Domingue. But the term was still available in the local lexicon, and imposed when the occasion seemed to warrant a stigmatizing descriptor. In 1883 Louis Tinchant's feckless son Charles got into trouble with the Belgian police in Antwerp, and the word surfaced on the arrest record, where his complexion was described as "teint mulâtre." Charles, whom the police observed with some care because of his dubious financial dealings and suspicious associates, lacked Belgian nationality. He spent a good deal of time going back and forth between England, France, and Belgium, finally turning up in Louisiana. In contrast to the productive cosmopolitanism of his father and uncles, the young Charles seems to have slipped into the itinerant life of a dandy with few visible means of support, finally becoming the defendant in a suit for bigamy, though eventually acquitted. The Belgian policeman shadowing him in Antwerp reported that Charles spent an inordinate amount of time in cafés in the company of an alleged French mistress. From the point of view of the Belgian authorities, young Charles remained a suspicious foreigner, hence eligible for the descriptor *mulâtre*.[8]

Édouard Tinchant, in contrast to his older brothers, crafted a quite different strategy of national identification. By the 1890s he had been well established in Antwerp for more than a decade, but he did not see himself as Belgian. While Joseph Tinchant had quietly closed the book on his own years in Louisiana, in favor of his subsequent ventures in Mexico and Belgium, Édouard was initially pleased to identify himself as an American. As late as 1884, he had described himself as a "citizen of the United States" when filing an application to patent a cigar-making machine that he had developed.[9]

When it came to a public assertion of nationality, however, Édouard eventually opted for the one that he traced to his place of birth: France. Putting into action a combined commercial and familial strategy, Édouard made a move to resurrect the *qualité de français* that he had briefly claimed thirty-five years earlier, when he had been approaching the age of twenty-one. If successful, he would be able to pass this nationality on to his children.

As a matter of cultural affiliation, Édouard's life as a middle-aged businessman in Antwerp provided some support for identification as a Frenchman. His former classmates in Pau later recalled him as having been motivated across his life by a "vif sentiment de patriotisme, l'ardent désir de faire aimer la France"—a lively feeling of patriotism, a burning desire to bring others to love France. They evoked his associational activities in favor of French culture: establishing a *cercle français* in Antwerp, joining the French Chamber of Commerce in the city and participating in an initiative to bring the Comédie-Française to perform at the Théâtre des Variétés.[10]

Édouard's formal claim to French nationality faced some difficulties, however. He had initially arrived in Belgium in 1878 on a U.S. passport acquired by declaring himself to be a "native and loyal citizen of the United States," born of a father—whom he referred to as James Tinchant—who had "been born and resided in the United States." Édouard was well aware that he himself had served both in the Union army and as an elected official in Louisiana, acts that could certainly be seen as constituting a renunciation of any claim to French citizenship. He had acknowledged as much in his 1864 polemic with Armand Lanusse. So reaching back to his early years to vindicate his French nationality did pose potential risks.[11]

As a matter of law, claiming French nationality by sole virtue of birth on French soil had not always been easy. By the late 1890s, however, it had become feasible because of changes in the definition of French nationality, aimed in part at expanding the pool of recruits and conscripts for a possible future war with Germany. An individual born in France of a foreign father who had himself been born in France could now claim French nationality. For Édouard to meet that criterion required a stretch all the same. Inconveniently, his father Jacques had indeed been born in the United States (and Jacques' tomb in Antwerp etched in stone the claim of birth in Baltimore). In contrast, it was Édouard's mother who had been born in the French colony of Saint-Domingue, and her baptismal certificate was filed with a notary in New Orleans. Claim to French parentage through the maternal line, however, was unlikely to prevail, given the general rule that married women took on the nationality of their husbands.[12]

Édouard may or may not have made his "revindication" of French nationality in written form, but one way or another his claim to be French came to the attention of the French Ministry of Justice. (The context may have been an effort on Édouard's part to gain authorization to import French tobacco, which was under the monopoly control of the French state.) On April 28, 1897, an attaché in the cabinet of the minister of justice in Paris wrote to the consul in New Orleans with some puzzlement to ask whether there was any record that one Édouard Tinchant had been inscribed on the Registre d'Immatriculation of French nationals compiled in New Orleans back in 1862. He also asked whether Édouard had been taken to be French during the time that he was in Louisiana.[13]

In effect, the French authorities wanted to know both about the 1862 inscription, and about what was sometimes called the de facto *possession d'état* (possession of status): Did Édouard act like a Frenchman, and was he known as a Frenchman? The man serving as consul in New Orleans thirty-five years later could hardly be expected to know the answer to that second question, so it came back to the simpler matter of registration—thus confirming the prescience of Édouard's youthful strategy of signing up at the New Orleans consulate. Sure enough, when in 1897 the consul looked back through the archives of his post, he found an entry inscribed in September 1862 for Édouard Tinchant, born in Gan, Basses-Pyrénées, in 1841. The consul evidently had no idea whether Édouard had consistently been taken to be a Frenchman in New Orleans in the 1860s, but he reported back to Paris that the name was indeed on the Registre d'Immatriculation.[14]

Importantly for Édouard, the French authorities knew nothing of his U.S. military service decades before. During the polemical exchange in the *Tribune* in 1864, Armand Lanusse had charged that although Édouard claimed U.S. citizenship, he was actually keeping his French identity papers tucked away in an armoire. Édouard had explained in reply that he retained these papers because they might later be useful in defense of "our cause." To the extent that the "cause" was the defense of Édouard's own French-ness, he turned out to be right. Although no formal document attesting to his French nationality seems to have survived, he was apparently henceforth treated as French by the authorities in both France and Belgium.[15]

In much the same way that a cultural Mexican-ness was helpful in branding the cigars of brother Joseph/José, a generalized French-ness was becoming commercially useful to Édouard. His tobacco operation was modest compared with that of Joseph and Ernest, but Édouard publicized his signature contribution: he was by 1905 the local agent of the Régie Française des Tabacs, the French state monopoly, hence authorized to sell French tobacco products in Belgium. By building his associational life around French language and culture, he further distinguished himself from the other Tinchant tobacconists: Louis the American pioneer, and Joseph and Ernest the naturalized Belgians with large factories and far-flung markets. It was only Édouard who was able to sell tobacco products labeled "French."[16]

As he approached his sixties, however, Édouard did not want to be remembered simply as a successful businessman (though he was proud of the honors thus gained), and certainly not as a Quixote who had failed in his own political goals of asserting the right to public respect and civil equality independent of color. Schooled in Plutarch's lives of great men during his years in Pau, Édouard had a nice sense of heroic narrative, but one that was rarely called upon in his everyday commercial life. When he sat down in his office in Antwerp to compose a letter to General Máximo Gómez in September 1899, he took the opportunity to recast a chronicle of his family's experiences as a stirring and highly political narrative. With the affirmation of his French nationality secure at home, he was now able to construct an inclusive transatlantic narrative arc of his own and his parents' lives.

This 1899 letter, today buried in a box of correspondence to Gómez in the National Archives of Cuba in Havana, provided a particular reflection of the long and complex journey of the extended Tinchant family. Equally important, it conveyed a specific interpretation of the meaning of that journey. Taking the form of a commercial request written in English, typed in purple ink and signed with a flourish, it was in truth a complex exercise in rhetorical composition and self-presentation, built on a subtle reworking of family memory.

True to his early training, Édouard knew to begin by selecting elements from that memory that would be appropriate to the task at hand. (This stage of composition was known in formal rhetoric as *inventio*.) The task was a difficult one, for he was addressing himself to someone he knew to be an *homme illustre*, a Great Man: "In early and ardent sympathy with the Cuban cause, I have been always and pride myself on being still one of your most sincere admirers." And the moment was a serious one, when the war against Spanish colonialism was over, but the island of Cuba was under U.S. military occupation. Édouard Tinchant avowed to Gómez his sympathy "for your cause, not yet won unfortunately, but for the success of which I devoutly pray, wishing with all my heart to live to see its ultimate and lasting triumph fitly crowning your noble existence."[17]

Édouard's express purpose in writing the letter was to persuade the general to let him launch a brand to be called "Máximo Gómez," and to adorn the cigars with portraits of the Great Man. It was not easy to connect something as glorious as the Cuban cause with something as banal as a Belgian cigar, however. Édouard couldn't promise that the tobacco itself would be Cuban, and we can be reasonably confident that the cigars were to be manufactured by Belgian workers in a factory in Antwerp. It was bold indeed to ask that the box be decorated with a portrait of a man who personified the independence struggle in Cuba, home of the world's best cigars. And so Édouard crafted the letter with care, aiming to avoid any pretense that he put his own family on the same plane as Gómez, but constructing a universe of shared references and images. He downplayed Europe, drawing instead on connections across the Gulf of Mexico, between New Orleans and Havana.

He discreetly invoked his own military and political service. He had been, of course, only a simple soldier in comparison with the great General Gómez, but at key moments he had been willing to fight and work in defense of republicanism and against slavery. He began modestly: "I may not be altogether unknown to some of the survivors of the last struggle," meaning the Cuban wars. Then he rattled off his credentials as a public man in Louisiana: service in Company C of the Sixth Louisiana Volunteers, Banks Division, and later a representative of the Sixth Ward of New Orleans at the 1867–1868 constitutional convention. He emphasized that throughout this time, he had supported the "Cuban cause" and that he had "lent a helping hand" to various Cubans.[18]

Édouard went on to place these struggles into a wider arc, and to suggest that the underlying values expressed in his family's history paralleled those of Gómez. Máximo Gómez had been born in the Dominican Republic, which shared the Caribbean island of Hispaniola with Haiti. Édouard placed his own family on that same island at the founding moment of Haiti's history: "Born in France in 1841 I am of Haïtian descent as both my father and mother were born at Gonaïves in the beginning of this century." As Édouard surely knew, the birthplace of his father Jacques was generally given as Baltimore, Maryland, though Jacques' parents were indeed refugees from Saint-Domingue. Édouard's mother had been baptized in a village near Jérémie, Saint-Domingue, though based on forms Édouard filled out in the 1870s, he may have believed that she had been born in Santiago, Cuba. The word Gonaïves nonetheless evoked an appropriate beginning point for a heroic family biography: it was the place where Haitian independence was proclaimed by Jean-Jacques Dessalines on January 1, 1804, hence "in the beginning of this century."[19]

Máximo Gómez had built a portion of his political identity on his resolute opposition to slavery and on his antiracism. Édouard evoked the struggle against color prejudice with a set of clear signals, but nothing that overstepped the bounds of discretion about racial identifications that characterized much of Caribbean political discourse: "my father, although in modest circumstances left Louisiana for France with the only object in view of raising his six sons in a country where no infamous laws or stupid prejudices could prevent them from become MEN." There was no mistaking the "stupid prejudices" that would drive a couple said to be born in Haiti out of antebellum Louisiana.[20]

Perhaps alert to national sensitivities about the superior quality of Cuba's cigars, Édouard did not brag about his Antwerp factory or his brothers' role in the cigar business in Belgium. And he certainly did not invoke the family's long history of selling cigars meant to compete with—or imitate—the famous *havanes*. Instead, he limited himself to a reference to his earlier years "as a cigar manufacturer in Mobile Alabama from 1869 till 1877," and to a promise that the cigars on which he hoped to place Gómez's portrait were "a brand of my best articles."[21]

Máximo Gómez had come to embody Cuban nationhood. Born in the Dominican Republic, Gómez had crossed boundaries and borders, insisting on sovereignty and independence for the nations of the Antilles, and doing so through campaigns that drew recruits from New Orleans, Key West, and Mobile, as well as New York, Veracruz, and Paris. Following this lead, Édouard claimed no specific nationality for himself. "Haïtian descent" brought his family into the Caribbean, and membership in the Louisiana Constitutional Convention put Édouard in New Orleans, a city where Máximo Gómez had lived in the 1880s. Édouard's list of shared references grew, reinforcing the implication of shared values.

In his closing phrases, Édouard gambled everything on the narrative he had constructed: "More than many well rounded sentences these simple facts of our family history will give a fair insight into my true sentiments, and show you how deep may be my sympathy for your cause." Avowing sincerity, but modestly putting family ahead of self, he hoped to persuade the Great Man to confer upon him a great favor.[22]

It wasn't quite enough. Máximo Gómez had a policy of declining all such commercial requests. After reading the letter, Gómez penciled a note to his secretary at the bottom, instructing him to refuse the authorization that had been requested, but to do so "with courteous phrases." The old general may or may not have been as touched as Édouard hoped by the letter, but he was going to hold to his policy.[23]

Once the request had been refused, Édouard Tinchant initially refrained from going forward with the plan to develop a cigar brand called Máximo Gómez. But General Gómez passed away in June 1905, and Édouard's sense of obligation to defer to the general's express instructions seems by then to have diminished. In preparation for the International Exposition scheduled to open in the Belgian city of Liège in July 1905, various tobacco

169

producers contributed self-promoting prose and photographs for a commemorative volume, the Livre d'or, to be published on the occasion. The profile of Édouard Tinchant emphasized his connections with the French tobacco monopoly, and his various honors and awards. It then listed his brands of cigars, including El Porvenir (The Future), La Excelencia Cubana (Cuban Excellence), and . . . Máximo Gómez.[24]

Édouard Tinchant was not alone in reworking family memory with an eye to commercial advantage. The Mexican associations of the firm of "José Tinchant y Gonzales" were built up from the eleven-year sojourn of Joseph, Stéphanie, and the children in and around Veracruz decades earlier. The Maison Américaine of Louis Tinchant retained that name forty years after Louis had left the Americas. Édouard and his brothers, in effect, were finding different ways to make the most of their good fortune in having been Atlantic survivors. Many of the captives who had accompanied their grandmother Rosalie through the Middle Passage, and many of the neighbors of their parents Élisabeth Vincent and Jacques Tinchant in New Orleans, had lived and died as slaves, achieving neither freedom nor security for themselves or their children.

Across three generations, as they faced the direct constraints of law and racial prejudice, the descendants of Rosalie benefited from good fortune, but also from their own ingenuity. At times they joined in warfare, at other times they fled. Sometimes they displayed, at other times they left hidden, the papers they had brought into being to attest to status or birthright. They spoke out or kept their own counsel in moments of political debate. They claimed various forms of citizenship and nationality in France, the United States, Mexico, Belgium, and perhaps Haiti. Rosalie and her children and grandchildren repeatedly found ways to achieve leverage from otherwise unpromising elements: a document that lacked the official approval of a governor, a freedom paper drawn up under false pretenses, a set of citizenship papers that had by rights expired but could still be retrieved.

The sheer effort contained in all of this provides a crucial measure of the external forces that they were trying to countervail, and thus of the magnitude of the leverage that Rosalie and her kin had to achieve. Like a pole-vaulter seeking to bend a pole in order to catapult across a bar that is taller than the pole itself, they had to use their own strength to create the energy that could help them attain their goals. In many instances the bar must have looked very high: securing legal freedom for an African-born woman in the Cuban city of Santiago; obtaining a surname for a child born out of wedlock, when the Louisiana Civil Code prohibited a person of color from claiming paternity from a white father; proving French nationality for the son of parents with no certain nationality of their own.

It took courage, discernment, ingenuity . . . and many pieces of paper. One final image is emblematic of the way that the family crafted ceremony and documents to confer status and shape identity. It comes from the moment back in New Orleans in the 1830s when Élisabeth Dieudonné presented a New Orleans notary with a copy of her 1799 baptismal record. Rosalie Vincent herself is almost certainly the one who in 1823— soon after Élisabeth's marriage—persuaded the civil authorities in Cap Dame-Marie in Haiti to dig out and copy the sacramental record that confirmed Michel Vincent's signature as father at the baptism. When the time came, Rosalie had apparently climbed aboard a ship with that paper on her person, in order to bring it to Élisabeth in New Orleans. Perhaps by 1835 the risk of Rosalie's own possible reenslavement in Louisiana looked small, and the potential gain to Élisabeth's public standing large. Once a cooperative public notary was persuaded to accept the copy as evidence enough for a change in her name, Élisabeth Dieudonné became, for the record, Élisabeth Dieudonné Vincent. The evidence of her birth out of wedlock could be revealed to the notary, in order to make it invisible to those who saw her newly official name on subsequent documents.[25]

Rosalie and Élisabeth had long known that a piece of paper could turn a human being into a person with a price, and that other pieces of paper could restore freedom and standing. Life involved much more than notarized papers, however. There were also all the rituals and reciprocities that embodied kinship and the recollection of absent kin. Ten months after proffering the copy of her own baptismal record to the notary, Élisabeth Vincent gave birth to another boy. She and Jacques chose to name the baby Juste.

The choice of a name was significant. The couple had named their first son Louis, after Jacques' stepfather Louis Duhart. Their second son was Joseph, the name of Jacques' biological father. A third son was Pierre, the name of Jacques' half-brother Pierre Duhart. Now for the fourth child they chose the name Juste, invoking Rosalie's eldest son, the brother whom Élisabeth had apparently never seen again after the chaotic evacuation of Jérémie in 1803. The baby would thus have the name of a maternal uncle, one who was perhaps now living in Haiti, or perhaps lost during the flight to Cuba. The family was again reworking memory to create a thread of continuity with kin who had come to rest elsewhere in their Atlantic world.

And so, on October 8, 1836, Jacques and Élisabeth took the baby Juste to be baptized in the Cathedral of Saint Louis. It is often thought that free persons of color in Louisiana invariably labored to distance themselves from slavery, from Africa, and from blackness. But on that day the woman whom Jacques and Élisabeth asked to stand as godmother at the baptismal font in New Orleans was someone who had once been enslaved, had been born in Africa, and was entered into colonial records as a *négresse*. The priest inscribed her name on the baptismal register: Rosalie Vincent.[26]

Across multiple generations, members of this family had taken the unavoidable stigmatizing labels *négresse,* "natural child," or "man of color" and brought into being paper that could surround these words with other signs of continuity and recognition. Élisabeth was a "natural child," but one acknowledged by a father whose surname she could adopt as her own. Joseph was a man of color, but he displayed a courtesy title and a double-barreled surname that evoked honorable status and Latin roots: Don José Tinchant y Gonzales. At the same time, as they pulled away from the stigmas and stereotypes attributed to African ancestry in general, they drew on their specific ancestry, repeating an uncle's or an aunt's name from generation to generation, naming Haiti as a birthplace, and, in the case of Édouard at his moment of political prominence, declaring himself to be a "son of Africa."

Epilogue:
"For a Racial Reason"

The coronation of George VI as king of England provided the ostensible motive for the Associated Negro Press to send the journalist Fay M. Jackson from Los Angeles to London in January 1937. Reports of the upcoming ceremony in Westminster Abbey might be expected to find eager readers among the papers that subscribed to the wire service, including the *New York Amsterdam News* and the *Atlanta Daily World*. An outspoken reporter with years of experience in California, Fay Jackson was also an activist and a woman of color, known for her earlier lobbying in favor of federal legislation against lynching. Her mandate in London included the reporting of "material of particular interest to American Negro readers." Indeed, the coronation itself could be said to have such a dimension, for George VI would govern an empire whose subjects included what Jackson characterized as 400 million "black people—essentially of the same race as the Republican-governed American Negro."[1]

On the music scene in London, swing and jazz were much appreciated, and Jackson's familiarity with American actors and musicians seems to have provided her with an entrée, beginning with the tenor Ivan Harold Browning, formerly of the Harmony Kings. Jackson reported back that "American Negro newspapers" were much sought after by London-based activists and entertainers: "Weekly sessions are held in the home of [the] Harold Brownings where the American and British race folk gather to 'run' the Defender or the Courier or one of the many papers that popular couple receive."[2]

London in the spring of 1937 was a center of political debate and discussion among men and women of color from Britain, its colonies, and the United States. In the weeks prior to the coronation Jackson filed stories on a mass meeting of the League of Colored Peoples to protest Mussolini's invasion of Ethiopia, alongside reports on Paul Robeson's

173

filming of *King Solomon's Mines* in London and Africa.[3] She also paid close attention to the issue of the "color bar," reporting that there would be no racial discrimination in the hiring of waiters in London restaurants during the coronation, but that only two "chieftains" of color would be invited to the ceremony itself.[4]

On April 9, 1937, the question of color momentarily attracted the attention of a mass-circulation London newspaper as well. Under the headline "Fled to Wed Secretly in England," the *Daily Mail* reported an interview with the twenty-one-year-old "tiny, cultured daughter of a prosperous cigar merchant of Antwerp." Mademoiselle Marie-José Tinchant explained the situation: "I am of honorable family, but I am not a white girl, so his parents are trying to stop our marriage." She went on: "My mother is white, my grandmother is white, but I have colour, and Andre's parents will not hear of our match." Her own family, she reported, had consented to the marriage: "I am a woman of honour, and I am proud of my father and my family."[5]

Events had unfolded with all the drama of a Hollywood movie—one that would be of particular interest to Jackson's readers. The parents of Marie-José's fiancé André V. had apparently taken steps to block the marriage in Belgium, so the couple made plans to marry secretly in London, where Marie-José had an aunt, an uncle, and some cousins. To establish residency, André traveled to London in late March and lodged at the Chelsea Royal Hospital, where Marie-José's uncle was a physician. Marie-José followed in early April, taking a room at the Premier Hotel in Russell Square. When the couple went to the register's office to obtain a marriage license, however, they were told that André's father's solicitor had been making inquiries with an eye to stopping the marriage. Suspense was thus established: Would or would not André and Marie-José be permitted to wed on Saturday, April 10?[6]

That Marie-José Tinchant would give an interview to the *Daily Mail* on the day before her scheduled "secret" marriage suggests considerable public-relations savvy. She was able to frame the initial discussion of her prospective father-in-law's opposition, and to guarantee that his legal maneuver—the filing of a "caveat" at the registrar's office to impede the ceremony—would be made embarrassingly public. By insisting that André's parents' opposition to the wedding was based on racial prejudice, and by appealing to English public sentiment in terms of the freedom to marry, Marie-José might make it more difficult for the caveat to be sustained.[7]

Another newspaper, the *Daily Express,* further set the stage with an article that appeared on the morning of April 10: "Wedding-Day Bid to Stop a Marriage." Alongside a full-length portrait of the handsome couple, a story breathlessly told the paper's readers that "a few minutes before a wedding is due to take place at Chelsea Register Office this morning an attempt will be made to stop the ceremony by the bridegroom's father." The article suggested the reasons that André's father would proffer for objecting to the wedding: "M. André [V.] is due to do military service. He has not yet completed his law studies."[8]

André himself also provided an interview, and gave the story a different twist, attributing his parents' objection to religious differences. Marie-José's father, Pierre Tinchant, seemed to prefer that interpretation as well. On the matter of Marie-José's family background, the report quoted Pierre as saying, "I am Mexican. My wife is American." (Pierre was a naturalized Belgian citizen, born in Mexico; his wife was a Belgian from Liège. Presumably "American" actually referred not to Pierre's wife but to his mother, Stéphanie Gonzales, born in New Orleans.) Marie-José's father insisted that André's parents "object to the marriage because we are all Roman Catholics, but the wedding *will* take place."[9]

With this buildup established, Marie-José and André proceeded to the office of the register in Chelsea on April 10. As Fay Jackson recounted the story for the Associated Negro Press, "Marie, a happy girl, awoke in a London hotel in Chelsea . . . and dressed herself for her wedding . . . a few hours later she was weeping at the register's office because her marriage to the man she loved had been banned. Order to stop the wedding had been entered at the court house." In this account, Marie-José, crying bitterly, proceeded to the register-general to appeal the refusal of a license, and then returned two hours later, "still weeping." Jackson's article framed the story in terms her American readers would recognize: "Behind these dramatic circumstances in what might otherwise have been a beautiful romance lies the tragedy of mixed blood and race prejudice." In the spring following the Ethiopian invasion and of Mussolini's ban on actors of color on the Italian stage, the marital drama of Marie-José and André evoked an image of American-style racism replicated in Europe.[10]

In the days that followed the tearful scene at the register's office in Chelsea, the couple gained ground. Although André's father had apparently obtained assistance from the Belgian consul in entering his caveat at the register-general's office at Somerset House, the request for a ban on the marriage did not hold up under challenge. The register-general ruled that the couple had complied with the English marriage regulations, and that there was no reason why the marriage should not be performed.[11]

Marie and André rescheduled the wedding, which took place on Tuesday, April 13. Both sets of parents had by then returned to Belgium. Two solicitors were nonetheless present at the ceremony, one representing the bridegroom, and one representing the bridegroom's father. For all the romantic drama and publicity concerning their struggle, it was not an auspicious way to begin a marriage. André's father still threatened to take "legal advice in Belgium to get his son's marriage annulled there," though nothing much seems to have come of this.[12]

The couple returned to Belgium, where André reported for military service but was quickly discharged. As his parents had presumably feared, he did not finish his legal studies and did not have a job. Marie-José gave birth to a daughter, Liliane, in 1938, and to a son, Michel, in 1939. In May 1939 the young couple moved in with André's parents in Brussels.[13]

They were living in this perhaps uncomfortable family environment when the war in Europe began. Several Tinchant brothers and cousins joined the Belgian army; Marie-José's twin brother José Pierre was called into active service in August 1939. Marie-José and André's marriage seems to have run into difficulty by this point, and at the beginning of 1940 she left the home of her in-laws and returned with the children to her parents' house at 22 rue St. Joseph, in Antwerp.[14]

Marie-José's father, Pierre Tinchant, had occupied one corner of the Creole niche that his own father, Joseph Tinchant—who did business under the name Don José Tinchant y Gonzales—had established within the world of prosperous francophone families in the city. With the beginning of war, however, Pierre Tinchant and his exuberant brother Vincent now faced the impending collapse of their cigar business. Trade was disrupted, and the company factories fell idle. In April 1940 Marie-José's father Pierre died, leaving his widow and four children: Marie-José, José Pierre, their sister Liliane, and their younger brother Pedro.[15]

On May 10, 1940, the German invasion of Belgium began. Within eighteen days, the Belgian army had been overrun, and Marie-José's brother José Pierre Tinchant became a prisoner of war, sent to Stalag XB-Sandbostel, near Bremen, in Germany. Marie-José's estranged husband André apparently fled to France. France, however, offered no secure refuge, and also crumbled under the German assault. André returned to Belgium.[16]

The country now came under German occupation, bringing a long period of fear, division, and penury. The Tinchant household at 22 rue St.

Joseph, in which Marie-José lived, became something of a hotbed of patriotic sentiments: her younger brother Pedro Tinchant would eventually join the armed Resistance, as did her sister Liliane's husband, Jean Rul.[17] In January 1941, however, Marie-José left this house in Antwerp and moved with her two children into an apartment in Brussels at 29 rue du Damier. According to her brother José Pierre, at this point she was beginning to work with the Resistance.[18]

Marie-José was a young, educated member of a bourgeois francophone family whose kin had served in the Belgian army in the Great War and in 1939. Both her own and her parents' weddings had taken place in London, and she had long-standing ties to and family in Britain. Her profile fits well with that of other Belgian recruits to the intelligence networks of the Resistance, and it seems likely that intelligence was indeed the sector of the movement in which she worked. At some point she adopted the nom de guerre of Anita.[19]

The precise Resistance activities of Marie-José Tinchant, however, are nearly impossible to reconstruct, though later files on her contain an unconfirmed reference to the Réseau Zéro, a noted intelligence network. Marie-José seems by all accounts to have been an exceptionally determined young woman, adored by her father, respected by her twin brother, and prepared to take on the world. Her boldness in her interviews with the press at the time of her marriage suggests a consciousness of her own ancestry that added a new note to her family's carefully constructed story of Mexican identity. The "colour" to which she referred in London brought her closer to the "Negro" identity invoked by the journalist Fay Jackson, and to the Jamaican or Barbadian migrants who might come to mind when her father was first described in the London press as a tobacco merchant from "the West Indies." In addition to the nationalist and antifascist sentiments that motivated many Belgian recruits to the Resistance, Marie-José had additional reasons to find Nazi ideology repugnant.[20]

In early 1941 Marie-José's brother José Pierre—who spoke Flemish, German, and English in addition to his native French—managed to persuade his German captors that he was in fact Flemish. As part of a larger strategy of rapprochement with the Belgian region of Flanders, the Germans had decided to treat Flemish prisoners of war as privileged vis-à-vis their francophone Belgian counterparts. The Flemish identification attributed to José Pierre thus conferred the right to be repatriated to Belgium along with other prisoners of war in the same category. He was dropped off at the train station in Antwerp at 5:00 a.m. on January 26, 1941.[21]

As he later recalled it, José Pierre made his way home and found his wife, who had been struggling in his absence and relying on her parents to help raise their daughter Michèle. Unemployed and unwelcome at his in-laws', José Pierre seems to have been uncertain where to turn next. He soon learned that Marie-José had moved to Brussels. Unable to reconcile with his wife, José Pierre followed his sister to the capital. Having been released from a German prison camp under false pretenses, he was presumably discreet about his precise identity once in the city. By his own account, he too now became involved with the Resistance.[22]

During the first year of the occupation, the German police received many unsolicited letters from Belgians who saw fit to denounce their neighbors for imagined subversive activity. It was perhaps not a propitious moment for Marie-José Tinchant to be living as a single mother in an apartment in central Brussels, presumably with furtive visits from her brother and others. Marie-José left the apartment at Rue du Damier after just five months and was next registered as living at 12 rue du Théâtre, about half a mile farther out, just beyond the city's ring of boulevards. This corner of the Quartier du Nord was lively and full of small stores, but its buildings had been slated for destruction for at least a decade, and the neighborhood had been losing population. After the German invasion, however, refugees from the countryside sought accommodation in its many empty apartments, seeking safety in numbers. Marie-José now did the same; perhaps it was not a bad place to find allies and avoid attention.[23]

Then, on November 30, 1941, the ax fell. Marie-José Tinchant was arrested by what her brother referred to as the Gestapo. (The precise administrative term in Belgium for the overarching unit of which the Gestapo was a part was the Sipo, short for Sicherheitspolizei, or security police.) Surviving records confirm that Marie-José was first held in the St. Gilles prison in Brussels, and then, on December 10, transferred to Antwerp.[24]

José Pierre, believing the police to be on his trail as well, escaped occupied Belgium through France to Barcelona and then Lisbon. After presenting himself to a sympathetic consul, he declared his intention to reenlist with the Belgian forces in exile. The consul advanced him some money to enable him to reach Gibraltar, and take a boat for Britain. Pierre José subsequently trained in England as a member of the Special Air Service and would be parachuted into the Ardennes in September 1944.[25]

In 1940–1941, mindful of experiences in World War I, the occupying Germans were somewhat reluctant to hold Belgian women as prisoners, for fear of creating martyrs. At some point after December 10, 1941, the police apparently released Marie-José, perhaps for lack of proof. She and the children were subsequently entered into the civil registry as residing at 27 rue Frère Orban, in Brussels. An inquiry after the war, however, turned up no recollection of her among the neighbors at Rue Frère Orban. It may be that the registration had been done by a complaisant local official, and that she was living clandestinely elsewhere. As of December 1942 there was no further trace of Marie-José in the civil registers anywhere in Brussels. Her children seem to have been cared for by her sister Liliane and by their paternal grandparents. She had presumably gone fully into hiding.[26]

In Marie-José's absence, her husband André V. filed for divorce, alleging improper personal behavior on her part; he made no mention of politics. He listed her residence as Rue Damier in Brussels, although she had long since left that address. On June 8, 1943, the court granted a divorce to André V., ending his marriage to Marie-José Tinchant, "whereabouts unknown," hence receiving no formal notice of the proceedings.[27]

Seven months later, on January 18, 1944, Marie-José was arrested a second time, apparently on orders of the Sipo. When she was registered at St. Gilles prison in Brussels on January 19, the prison officials confiscated the fifty francs that she had on her, and she signed the register acknowledging the amount taken. Presumably unaware of the divorce decree, she signed with her married name.[28]

The German security police in Belgium subsequently destroyed many of their records, and it is impossible to know what charges they may have intended to bring against Marie-José. Next to her name on a later document is the ambiguous notation "IV 3," which appears to be a reference to a department within the Sipo that took charge of her case. The view of several of her descendants is that she was suspected of involvement in the gathering and/or the transmission of intelligence *(renseignements)* to be sent to the Allies. After the war, her husband apparently suggested that she had worked with the network called the Réseau Zéro.[29]

It is at least possible that Marie-José's arrest was instead an arbitrary, collateral result of one or another German wave of repression. By January 1944 the Nazis were increasingly fearful of an Allied invasion of the Continent, and arrests in Belgium had become more sweeping. If a suspect whom they sought was not at home, they were increasingly likely to take a father, a son, or a sister instead. The memoir of one prisoner interned at St. Gilles in these months conveys a sense of the widespread arrests made for all kinds of noncompliance, indiscretion, criminality, or just bad luck. But subsequent events would show that Marie-José Tinchant was a prisoner whom the Germans themselves categorized as "political." They were, moreover, quite apprehensive about the consequences of keeping detainees like her in Brussels in the face of a probable Allied advance toward Belgium.[30]

On June 6, 1944, the anticipated Allied invasion began on the beaches of Normandy. For some days the Germans believed that this might be a diversion, and that the full invasion could come through the Pas-de-Calais. If the Allies were able rapidly to gain control of Brussels, the political prisoners held at St. Gilles might be freed to join them. To prevent this, the Germans ordered virtually all the male political prisoners from St. Gilles transported to Buchenwald, and the female political prisoners to Ravensbrück. On page 55 of the transport list compiled at St. Gilles on June 15, 1944, on orders of the Sipo, Marie-José Tinchant is listed under her married name as one of the Belgian women to be "transported to the Reich."[31]

The convoy, including 308 women designated as Belgian, Polish, French, Dutch, Italian, Rumanian, English, and "Volksdeutsche," arrived at Ravensbrück on June 19. Marie-José was entered in the camp lists and given the registration number 42,791. Like the other women in this convoy of evacuees from Brussels, she was listed as *polit.*, arrested for political reasons, rather than *asozial* (for those deemed to be antisocial elements, to be excluded from society) or *Rassenschande* (those implicated in the crime of "racial defilement" or "race mixing"). Whatever the initial circumstances of Marie-José's arrest, the German police in Belgium considered her to be a political prisoner, as did the administration of the Ravensbrück camp.[32]

Ravensbrück represented one small piece of the massive Nazi project to employ enslaved labor to replace the thousands of workers conscripted into the military effort, and to set the stage for what Hitler imagined would be a productive new empire built on the subjugation and partial or total extermination of inferior peoples. The term "slavery" here is neither rhetorical nor metaphorical. These were men, women, and children held under intense physical control and deprivation, forced to labor until their physical condition or one or another twist of Nazi ideology caused them to be moved into the category of those who were less than slaves, and hence on to their deaths. The terminology of slavery was employed by the Nazis themselves. Heinrich Himmler argued in 1942 that "if we do not fill our camps with slaves—in this room I mean to say things very firmly and very clearly—with worker slaves, who will build our cities, our villages, our farms without regard to any losses," then there would not be enough resources to settle "real Germanic people" in the lands acquired to the east.[33]

Those who were subjected to this treatment also recognized it as slavery. Germaine Tillion, a precise and disciplined ethnographer who had been active in the French Resistance, was deported to Ravensbrück in October 1943. Tillion survived, and wrote several detailed studies of the camp. She employed the term "slaves" to describe the inmates who labored in order to create carefully calculated profits for the "Ravensbrück enterprise" in which Himmler himself was a primary investor. Tillion's colleague Marie-Claude Vaillant-Couturier, who also had been interned at Ravensbrück, testified at the postwar Nuremberg trials of major war criminals, and described the process by which representatives of the industrialists using inmate labor inspected the bodies of those whom the camp rented out: "It felt like a slave market. They felt muscles, looked for signs of good health, and then made their choices. Then each woman passed undressed in front of the doctor, who decided whether or not she was able to go to work in the factories."[34]

Some of the prisoners were put to work directly within the camp, either in subsistence activities or in a private manufacturing enterprise located inside the walls. With food costs deducted from the revenue at the clothing factory, starvation was a constant menace. Survivors remembered that the pace of work was brutal in each of the twelve-hour shifts, with a piece of bread provided only after the daily quota of 200 jackets or pants was reached. The bread was later eliminated; beatings on the shop floor by the male and female SS supervisors continued. Other prisoners were rented out to Siemens electrical works and to additional nearby factories.[35]

Back in Brussels and Antwerp, Marie-José's family had no way of knowing what had become of her after her deportation. As soon as Brussels and Antwerp were liberated by the Allies in the autumn of 1944, one of her siblings—almost certainly Liliane, who had been caring for Marie-José's daughter—directed an inquiry to the Red Cross. She explained that her sister had been arrested and that the family had no news of her, and hoped for a response. But the Red Cross had nothing to report.[36]

Only the faintest glimpse of the specific experience of Marie-José in Ravensbrück survives. By coincidence, in the summer of 1944 a woman named Nadine Droubaix, married to Marie-José's cousin Marcel Droubaix, had been arrested, perhaps as a result of the betrayal by a double agent of the resistance network in Marseille of which Marcel was a member. On September 2, Nadine Droubaix was herself deported to Ravensbrück.[37]

For a few days the paths of Nadine and Marie-José crossed, and they spoke. That conversation, as later conveyed to a postwar commission, may be the only direct evidence we will ever have of Marie-José's time in the camp. Marie-José apparently gave Nadine some food, and Nadine noted that Marie-José had made scraps of fabric into a tricolor insignia, the symbol that Belgians had worn in a silent protest against the Germans on Armistice Day in the first year of the occupation. Within a matter of weeks, however, Nadine was sent on to another camp.[38]

By the end of 1944, the slave labor camp of Ravensbrück was being converted in order to enable the administration to carry out executions more rapidly. Some groups of women had already been ordered to be shot. Then, in January 1945, skilled construction workers from a nearby camp were brought to build a gas chamber, and the authorities at Ravensbrück began choosing the women to be killed there, in groups of approximately 150. On one fragmentary surviving list, these women were recorded as to be transferred to "Mittwerda," a nonexistent convalescent camp, said to be located in Silesia. Other lists would use other language to hide the mass killing that was now under way.[39]

On March 28, 1945, Marie-José Tinchant was sent to what was referred to on the registers as the "sanatorium" ("san." on the available transcription). The term was another covering euphemism for the gas chamber that was by then in operation in a wooden building adjacent to the crematorium. A second list, now held by the International Tracing Service based in Bad Arolsen, provides information on 250 women from Block 7 in the camp who were apparently sent to the gas chamber on or before March 31. Her name is there as well, with the surname slightly misspelled and the first name rendered as Maria, but nonetheless unmistakable.[40]

As Allied troops drew closer, the administrators of the camp accelerated the executions and forced-march evacuations. They also burned the card file containing the names of the prisoners, along with a list of the dead that the detainees themselves had assembled and tried to conceal. The camp was finally liberated by the Red Army on April 30, 1945.[41]

With the liberation of Nadine Droubaix from another camp in May 1945, and her repatriation, the Tinchant family apparently learned that Marie-José had been seen in Ravensbrück months earlier. In hopes of obtaining further information and the return of her daughter, Marie-José's mother, Eugénie Tinchant, filled out a missing-person form, noting that Nadine Droubaix had reported Marie-José's presence in Ravensbrück in January 1945. (Nadine Droubaix had in fact passed through the camp in September 1944, not January 1945; the later date may have been based on a retransmission by Droubaix of more-recent information received from another prisoner.) Marie-José's mother described her daughter as a political prisoner with the *nom d'emprunt* (assumed name) "Anita." She provided a physical description: *type créole, cheveux crépus* (Creole appearance, tightly curled hair). The typist preparing the information for the files designated Marie-José Tinchant with the abbreviation PP for political prisoner.[42]

In early October 1945, a man named Milcamps, living in Ghent, also inquired about Marie-José. Milcamps too believed that she had operated under the assumed name "Anita," that she was a political prisoner, and that she had still been at Ravensbrück on January 5, 1945. He conveyed a slightly different physical description, but used similar terminology: her coloring was said to be *bazané*, which might be translated roughly as "swarthy." Her hair was tightly curled *(cheveux crépus)*. Perhaps to explain the physical description, he added that she had been born of a father who was Mexican, but who had been naturalized Belgian. The officials in charge of the locating of displaced persons and prisoners added these documents to her file, but still had no information on what had happened to her.[43]

Although the authorities at Ravensbrück had burned many of the camp records as they retreated, survivors began immediately after the war to assemble and analyze documents that had been smuggled out of the camp. It was almost certainly from a list compiled by the French Resistance member Marie-Claude Vaillant-Couturier, and provided by the association of survivors of Ravensbrück, that word eventually reached the family that Marie-José had perished on or around March 28, 1945. By 1947–1948, the Belgian Ministry of Reconstruction, which handled searches and documentation concerning prisoners and deportees, had updated its file on Marie-José, noting that she had been gassed on March 28, 1945. The source was given as the list of 299 Belgian women who had died in Germany, a list furnished by the French "Amicale de Ravensbrück." Further updates in 1949 and 1951 would add detail, including evidence on the date of her arrival at St. Gilles prison, and that of her subsequent deportation to Ravensbrück.[44]

In the complex political world of postwar Belgium, with the repatriation of tens of thousands of displaced persons and the ensuing struggles over the memory of the war, bureaucratic procedures were being established to create a formally definitive record of individual fates. In the case of Marie-José, the family could request legal proof of her disappearance, certified by a court, which would be followed by the issuance of a document that would function in lieu of a death certificate. The government was also developing—through highly political bargaining—a typology of statuses that could be officially attributed based on wartime experiences.[45]

There were several alternatives, each aimed at creating a fixed category encompassing what were, in practice, complicated and overlapping kinds of wartime activity. A man or woman could be declared to have been a participant in the armed resistance, with accompanying credit for the equivalent military service, or could be recognized as having engaged in the gathering of intelligence for the government in exile and the Allied forces. Others were judged to have participated in the "civil resistance"—a concept that was open to an almost infinitely malleable description, and to limitless debate. Based on the circumstances of arrest and the duration of incarceration, a Belgian who had been held by the Germans could be declared to have been a political prisoner. There were also recognized *déportés du travail*—involuntary forced laborers, who were entitled to special consideration in postwar employment. Finally, one could be declared simply a victim, the category that included those arrested under Nazi racial laws.[46]

To seek retrospective designation as political prisoner was to tumble into a bureaucratic process of huge dimensions. Eventually some 59,000 requests for attribution of this status would be made, 41,000 of which were granted. André V., Marie-José's former husband, seems to have viewed this as a possible avenue for obtaining financial support for their children. In December 1953 his attorney wrote to the Service Général de Renseignements et Action (SGRA). At this point the family knew the exact date of Marie-José's death at Ravensbrück, and the attorney suggested that Marie-José had been involved in activities in the Resistance, particularly the group the attorney referred to as "Ligne Zéro." The attorney then provided a list of names of the presumed associates of Marie-José Tinchant, known as "Anita." The list began with "Monsieur Albert, qui aurait plusieurs fois changé de nom" (Mr. Albert, who is said to have changed names several times) and concluded with M. Max Milcamps and M. Jotrand. In between were persons with the code names "Lapin" (Rabbit) and "Dolly." The attorney explained that the case was a tangled one, and that she had only limited information; hence her inquiry.[47]

There was a brisk reply six weeks later from an adjunct administrator of the service, claiming to have no information on a M. Albert associated with the group called Zéro, or on any of the other persons named as Marie-José's contacts. The specialists at the SGRA knew perfectly well that one of the founders of the Réseau Zéro was a man named Albert Hachez. But they seem not to have been inclined to inquire very deeply into the case of Marie-José Tinchant—and in truth, clues like "codename Rabbit" were not the kind of hint that could easily be followed. For the moment, the inquiry reached a dead end.[48]

Undeterred, André had his attorney proceed with the formalities for a declaration in lieu of a death certificate, and he filled out the forms requesting the posthumous grant of the status of political prisoner for Marie-José. They filed the petition for recognition of status just before the last date for such requests.[49]

The commission undertook the usual process of checking Marie-José's addresses, assembling copies of the prior written inquiries that had been made about her, including those of her sister, her mother, and of Milcamps, and verifying several technical requirements for eligibility. By December 1954, the documentation from the Amicale de Ravensbrück confirming Marie-José's internment and death there had also been reviewed.[50]

It was in the final deliberations of the commission on the attribution of status that her story took a curious twist. Under the law, the title of political prisoner could be granted based on arrest for "patriotic and disinterested action" or for political or philosophical beliefs. It could also be conferred based on evidence showing the prisoner to have been "animated by a spirit of resistance to the enemy" during incarceration. The arrest records were gone, and the man assigned to represent the Belgian state in the proceedings, W. Bonne, initially concluded that the reason for Marie-José's arrest was simply *inconnu* (unknown). He recommended that the commission attribute to her children the financial benefits due to heirs of a political prisoner, including compensation for the months that she had been incarcerated. However, in the place on the typed recommendation form where eligibility for the title of political prisoner was to be indicated, Bonne crossed out the word *titre* (title) and penciled in the word *qualité*, meaning attribute or civil condition. He thus recommended that the commission attribute the status and the *qualité* of political prisoner to her, triggering the payment of benefits to the children, but that it not accord to her the posthumous right to the title of political prisoner.[51]

The distinction that Bonne proposed to draw between being a beneficiary of the *status* of a political prisoner, hence due reparations, and the right to hold the *title* of political prisoner, hence due some additional form of recognition, was not particular to Marie-José's case. It reflected the continuing effects of a last-minute amendment proposed in 1947 by several

185

members of the Belgian Senate affiliated with the Catholic parties, during the debate over compensation and recognition for political prisoners. The stakes in this debate were high, because the results would help to create the public record of the relative role of communists, royalists, Catholic networks, and various individual public figures, all of which could shape postwar images and voting. The Chamber of Deputies had unanimously approved a version of the statute on status that would rely upon the *critère de la souffrance* (the criterion of suffering) to define the category of those who would be recognized and compensated, thus including victims of the deportations carried out under the Nazi racial laws. The amendment introduced in the Senate, however, proposed to confine the category of political prisoner to those clearly arrested for acts of "patriotic" resistance, and aimed to exclude from recognition many antifascists, Freemasons, and anticlerical activists who had been taken hostage or placed in preventive detention, as well as Jews who had been deported from Belgium.[52]

In the final text of the law, developed in a negotiated compromise, Belgians taken hostage or arrested for their political views were brought back in as eligible for the status of political prisoner, in addition to those who had engaged in explicitly "patriotic" resistance. Those arrested for "a racial reason," however, were ruled out. The status to be attributed to Jews deported from Belgium to Germany had in the end served as a bargaining chip—and been forfeited—in this Belgian domestic political negotiation. At the same time, conferral of the *title* of political prisoner (with the attendant right to display specific insignia) would be subjected to a more exigent set of criteria than conferral of the *status*.[53]

Bonne's recommendations in the case of Marie-José Tinchant, however, were not final. The commission, which included several representatives of associations of political prisoners, had convened a hearing on the case, at which they now took sworn testimony from Nadine Droubaix, who had crossed paths with Marie-José Tinchant in the Ravensbrück camp. Droubaix said that she had not had occasion to ask Marie-José about the circumstances of her arrest, but she evoked the telling detail that Marie-José had attached a tricolor *insigne* to her prison uniform. The tricolor *insigne*, Droubaix reported, had earned Marie-José difficulties with the German guards.[54]

Even though the Belgian legislature had decided that political prisoner status should not be granted based on the *critère de la souffrance*—the criterion of suffering—it was impossible to deny that Marie-José was a Belgian woman deported on orders of the Gestapo and incarcerated for many months at Ravensbrück. By 1954, the horrors of Ravensbrück were well established. Nadine Droubaix's testimony, moreover, could provide evidence to meet the criterion that Marie-José had been "animated by a spirit of resistance to the enemy" during her incarceration—hence eligible for both the status and the posthumous title of political prisoner. The commission, however, remained preoccupied with the question of the motive for her arrest.[55]

In a peculiar compromise, the commission finally ruled that the request on behalf of Marie-José's son and daughter was admissible and "partially" well founded. Marie-José Tinchant had indeed been arrested by the enemy and incarcerated for the specified length of time. Indeed, the commission modified the length of time acknowledged in the preliminary recommendation, extending it up to the March 28, 1945, date of death that the family had provided and that the available lists of Ravensbrück detainees confirmed. The children would therefore receive the allocation of funds and benefits appropriate to the heirs of one holding the status of political prisoner. But Marie-José Tinchant, the commission concluded, had been arrested not for political reasons, but for a *motif racial*—a "racial reason." She could not, therefore, presume to the posthumous title of political prisoner.[56]

The commission's last-minute introduction of the phrase "motif racial" in regard to Marie-José Tinchant is puzzling. Inside Germany, the Nazis had indeed arrested persons they perceived as having African ancestry, and they had been murderously contemptuous of the children of mixed unions between "Aryans" and people of color. In Belgium, however, the question of African ancestry seems not to have arisen. The Germans carried out a roundup in Belgium of "Latin American nationals" whom they hoped to exchange for German prisoners, but there is no evidence that anyone took Marie-José for a Mexican. Arrests for "racial reasons" in Belgium were overwhelmingly arrests of Jews.[57]

We cannot know what gossip André's attorney, who appeared before the commission at their final meeting on the case, may have conveyed about the Tinchants' ancestry. The attorney's primary concern, after all, was the pension for the children, not Marie-José's posthumous credit for courage, patriotism, or antifascism. The commission—part of whose job it was to serve as gatekeepers restricting access to the honorific title of "political prisoner"—may have based their attribution on the descriptions supplied by those who had sought to find Marie-José during and after the war: *teint bazané* (swarthy color), *type créole,* and *cheveux crépus* (tightly curled hair). Although no evidence was explicitly adduced to support the motive for arrest inferred in Marie-José's case, the phrase "racial reason" was ready at hand, having been applied during the 1947 parliamentary debates to the situation of the few survivors from among the tens of thousands of Jews deported from Belgium by the Nazis.[58]

It is impossible to know, at this remove, what the overtones of the inscription of the words *motif racial* in the decision on Marie-José's case may have been. But the evidence suggests that in these years the phrase could imply a discrediting or diminishing of the standing of the person in question. During the debates over the policy of reparation, one representative in parliament had spoken of "Jews arrested solely for racial reasons and other persons arrested for non-patriotic reasons, like those who were selling on the black market." It would be hard to avoid the impression that putting "racial reasons" alongside "non-patriotic" reasons conveyed a desire to portray the victims as undeserving of national recognition.[59]

By positing a "racial reason" for her arrest, and therefore denying her the title of political prisoner, the commission implicitly assimilated the circumstances of Marie-José Tinchant's arrest to those of Jews seized on orders of Section IV-B-3 of the German secret police in Belgium, the Judenabteilung.[60] In terms of the hagiography of postwar Belgium, Marie-José Tinchant was formally designated a victim, but not a hero. Like the Jews, she suffered a retrospective denial of standing as a result of a calculation aimed at limiting membership in the pantheon of martyrs who had "died for Belgium." Inquiries from family members, filed before any statute on government benefits had been voted, had referred to Marie-José Tinchant as a "political prisoner" and been taken at face value. The Germans had written the word "political" next to her name on the transport list of women deported from Brussels to the Reich in June 1944. But the Belgian commission officially declined to credit her capacity for patriotism or politics.[61]

However painful the official posthumous denial of the title of political prisoner, the recollection of Marie-José was not, in the end, fully in the hands of the commission to whom André's lawyer had addressed a formal request. "National memory" as metaphor is not the same thing as family memory. For Marie-José's children, the circumstances of their mother's death were confusing, but associated with the defense of Belgium. And under certain circumstances, that recollection could be made more secure by putting it in writing. When Marie-José's daughter Liliane married in 1956, the registrar designated her as the child of André V. and Marie-José

Tinchant, *morte pour la Belgique*—Marie-José Tinchant, who died for Belgium. The marriage did not last, but the words *morte pour la Belgique* became part of another generation's perception of the woman they could never meet.[62]

It is unlikely that Marie-José, brought up in luxury at 22 rue St. Joseph in Antwerp, ever heard a reference to Rosalie Vincent, the once-enslaved mother of her great-grandmother Elizabeth Vincent. Although Marie-José's father Pierre was described in the British press as a West Indian cigar merchant, most references to the Americas made by that branch of the Tinchant family evoked Mexico, not the Caribbean. Joseph Tinchant's children generally began the story of their Creole identity with their father's time in Mexico, not his years as a "free man of color" in New Orleans. Marie-José's great-uncle Édouard, who had once willingly spoken of himself as a "son of Africa," died the year before she was born; she would never hear his version of the family's history.[63]

In Antwerp and London in 1937, and perhaps in 1941 and 1944 as she faced the Nazis, Marie-José Tinchant nonetheless knew that in the eyes of many people she had "colour." In 1937 she decided to say so loudly, and to claim this identification as her own, rather than turning away from its implications. Was she arrested seven years later for a "racial reason," as the commission, having read the card describing her as *type créole, cheveux crépus,* concluded? As the moment of the Allied victory had approached, the machinery of fascism self-consciously covered its tracks more efficiently than had the machinery of slavery, making it more difficult to find records concerning the circumstances of Marie-José's arrests in 1941 and 1944 than it is to find the documents confirming the sale and manumission of Rosalie of the Poulard nation 150 years earlier. The great crime of slavery in the Americas operated within a legality of its own making and left a voluminous paper trail, both of the transactions that turned human beings into persons held as property, and of the efforts of people like Rosalie to escape that status. The authors of the great crimes of fascism, however, generally operated in some awareness of its own exceptionalism. Legal fictions were created, and copious records were generated. But as the war came to a close, its perpetrators put such records to the torch, and assassinated many of those who could have borne witness to what had happened.[64]

The latter-day freedom papers of Marie-José Tinchant, memorializing her resistance to that crime, would thus have to be assembled and created at the initiative of her kin and of the Belgian state. In response to a request by Marie-José's daughter and granddaughter, the officials in Brussels who are charged with these matters recently returned to the file. In April 2010, they sent a letter to Marie-José's daughter reiterating her eligibility for survivor's benefits. They also issued her a new social security card, one that identifies her as the legally recognized beneficiary of Marie-José Tinchant. The printed form designates Marie-José as "prisonnier politique ou bénéficiaire du Statut" (political prisoner or beneficiary of the status). The distinction once made between status and title is no longer visible. The letter also informs Marie-José's daughter Liliane that she is now entitled to free passage on all public transportation in Belgium.[65]

As it happens, however, Marie-José's daughter no longer lives in Belgium. Some years ago she set out for Mexico, in hopes of finding her family's roots there. During the journey, she changed her mind and disembarked on an island in the Atlantic off the coast of Africa—an island where Europeans had centuries earlier carried out experiments in the growing of sugarcane using enslaved laborers. Liliane decided to stay, settling into a small, Spanish-speaking community. In a garden that she has planted to incorporate elements of her imagining of José Tinchant's long-ago Mexican farm in Cazonera, Liliane now pieces together a memory of her own of her mother, Rosalie Vincent's great-great-granddaughter, the bold young woman who declared to a journalist in London in 1937, "My mother is white, my grandmother is white, but I have colour."[66]

NOTES

ACKNOWLEDGMENTS AND COLLABORATIONS

INDEX

ABBREVIATIONS

Archives

AANO   Archives of the Archdiocese of New Orleans, New Orleans

ADPA   Archives départementales des Pyrénées-Atlantiques, Pau
           AC-Gan: Archives communales de Gan

AGI   Archivo General de Indias, Seville

AGR   Archives générales du Royaume, Brussels
           MJ: Ministère de la Justice

ANC   Archivo Nacional de Cuba
           AP: Asuntos Políticos
           CCG: Correspondencia de los Capitanes Generales
           FMG: Fondo Máximo Gómez

ANOM   Archives nationales d'outre-mer, Aix-en-Provence, France
           DPPC: Dépôt des papiers publics des colonies
           SDOM: Saint-Domingue
           SUPSDOM: Supplément Saint-Domingue

ANS   Archives nationales du Sénégal

ASVG   Direction générale Victimes de la Guerre, Service archives et
           documentation, Brussels

BL   Baker Library, Historical Collections, Harvard Business School
           R. G. Dun: R. G. Dun & Co. Collection

CADN   Centre des archives diplomatiques de Nantes

CARAN   Centre d'accueil et de recherche des Archives nationales, Paris
Mi: Microfilm from Archives nationales
SOM: Séries Outre-mer

CEGES-SOMA   Centre d'études et de documentation Guerre et sociétés contemporaines, Studie- en Documentatiecentrum Oorlog en Hedendaagse Maatschappij, Brussels
SRA: Services de renseignement et d'action

CO, NO   Conveyance Office, New Orleans
COB: Conveyance Office Books

FA   FelixArchief, Antwerp
MA: Modern Archief

MGR-SGB   Mahn- und Gedenkstätte Ravensbrück/Stiftung Brandenburgische Gedenkstätten, Ravensbrück

MMA   Mobile Municipal Archives, Mobile, Alabama

NAUK   National Archives of the United Kingdom, Kew
CO: Colonial Office Records
T: Treasury Records
WO: War Office Records

NONARC   New Orleans Notarial Archives Research Center

NOPL   New Orleans Public Library
CA: City Archives
LD: Louisiana Division

QRE   Archives of the Human Relations Department of the Belgian Army, Quartier Reine Élisabeth, Brussels

RA   Rijksarchief te Antwerpen, Antwerp

TFP   Tinchant Family Papers
FC: Courtesy of Françoise Cousin
II: Courtesy of Isabelle Ivens
MK: Courtesy of Michèle Kleijnen
MLVV: Courtesy of Marie-Louise Van Velsen
PS: Courtesy of Philippe Struyf

UFL   University of Florida George A. Smathers Libraries, Gainesville
JP: Jérémie Papers
SC: Special Collections

UNO   University of New Orleans, Earl K. Long Library
LSCD: Louisiana and Special Collections Department

USNA   United States National Archives

Other

AGH   Association de généalogie d'Haïti
exp.   *expediente* (file)
fol.   folio
leg.   *legajo* (bundle)
RG   Record Group
sig.   *signatura* (call number)

PROLOGUE

1. Édouard Tinchant to Máximo Gómez, 21 September 1899, sig. 3868/4161, leg. 30, Fondo Máximo Gómez, Archivo Nacional de Cuba.

2. See "Wedding-Day Bid to Stop a Marriage," *Daily Express* (London), 10 April 1937, 13; and "Fled to Wed Secretly in London," *Daily Mail* (London), 9 April 1937, 11.

1. "ROSALIE, BLACK WOMAN OF THE POULARD NATION"

1. He used the phrase "son of Africa" in Édouard Tinchant, Communiqué, *La Tribune de la Nouvelle-Orléans*, 21 July 1864.

2. See David Robinson, "The Islamic Revolution of Futa Toro," *International Journal of African Historical Studies* 8 (1975): 185–221.

3. The baptismal record is transcribed in "Rectification de noms d'épouse Tinchant dans son contrat de mariage," 16 November 1835, act 672, 1835, Notary Théodore Seghers, New Orleans Notarial Archives Research Center.

4. The manumission paper, drafted in Les Abricots, Saint-Domingue, in May 1803, is transcribed in "Enregistrement de liberté par. de Marie Françoise," 26 Ventôse, year XII [17 March 1804], folios 25v, 26r, Actes, déclarations & dépôts divers, 10 Pluviôse, year XII [31 January 1804]–10 Vendémiaire, year XIII [2 October 1804], document 3, série 6, Supplément Saint-Domingue (hereafter SUPSDOM, following convention for call numbers, e.g. 6SUPSDOM/3), Dépôt des papiers publics des colonies (hereafter DPPC), Archives nationales d'outre-mer, Aix-en-Provence (hereafter ANOM).

5. This is the phrase that appears, for example, in the document titled "Saisie Dixon, 31 January 1806," in carton 2, Fonds (or Sous-Série) 4Z2, Archives nationales du Sénégal (hereafter ANS).

6. The text is: "avec une belle cargaison de nègres de nations Yolof, Poulard, et Bambara." Cited in Jean Mettas, *Répertoire des expéditions négrières françaises au XVIIIe siècle,* vol. 1: *Nantes,* ed. Serge Daget (Paris: Société française d'histoire d'outre-mer, 1978), 676 (entry 1192).

7. Médéric Louis Élie Moreau de Saint-Méry, *Description topographique, physique, civile, politique et historique de la partie française de l'isle Saint-Domingue,* 2 vols. (Philadelphia: by the author, 1797), 1:26, 27.

8. "Les Foules, appellés vulgairement Poules ou Poulards, voisins des Sénégalais et des Yoloffes, mais plus intérieurement placés." Moreau de Saint-Méry, *Description topographique,* 1:27.

9. Moreau de Saint-Méry describes the Poulard as of a "reddish" *(rougeâtre)* color (*Description topographique,* 1:27). Already in the seventeenth century Alonso de Sandoval had declared that "Fulos are distinguished by their light skin coloring, although many are very dark-skinned." Alonso de Sandoval, SJ, *Treatise on Slavery,* ed. and trans. Nicole Von Germeten (Indianapolis: Hackett, 2008), 44.

10. Although Poulard is not precisely synonymous with the more familiar term Peul, see Roger Botte, Jean Boutrais, and Jean Schmitz, eds., *Figures peules* (Paris: Éditions Karthala, 1999); and Oumar Kane, *La Première Hégémonie peule: le Fuuta Tooro de Koli Tengella à Almaami Abdul* (Paris: Éditions Karthala, 2004), 40–53, 90–91. On the information that can be extracted from ethnonyms see Michael Gomez, *Exchanging Our Country Marks* (Chapel Hill: University of North Carolina Press, 1998), chaps. 1 and 3. Megan Vaughan nonetheless cautions that such terms cannot necessarily "be relied upon to lead us to an ethnic or cultural 'root'—they lead us, rather, to a process." Megan Vaughan, *Creating the Creole Island: Slavery in Eighteenth-Century Mauritius* (Durham, NC: Duke University Press, 2005), 114.

11. We are grateful to Boubacar Barry, Mamadou Diouf, Martin Klein, David Robinson, Mamoudou Sy, Ibrahima Thioub, and Rudolph Ware for their discussions of the affiliations that can be signaled by the term "Poulard."

12. See J. Ho, "Les esclaves dans la zone d'occupation anglaise de Saint-Domingue en 1796," *Population* 26 (January–February 1971): 152–157. Ho found just 48 slaves designated Poulard among a group of 3,296 inventoried, while 314 were called Bambara, and another 121 Sénégal. See also G. Debien, J. Houdaille, and R. Richard, "Les origines des esclaves des Antilles," *Bulletin de l'Institut français de l'Afrique noire* (published in volumes 23, 25, 26, 27, and 29 of series B, between 1961 and 1967); and David Geggus, "Sex Ratio, Age and Ethnicity in the Atlantic Slave Trade: Data from French Shipping and Plantation Records," *Journal of African History* 30 (1989): 23–44.

13. Thomas Clarkson, *Letters on the Slave-Trade, and the State of the Natives in Those Parts of Africa, Which are Contiguous to Fort St. Louis and Gorée* (London: Printed and sold by James Phillips, 1791), 31–33, 80–81.

14. M. Saugnier, *Relation de plusieurs voyages à la côte d'Afrique, à Maroc, au Sénégal, à Gorée, à Galam, etc.* (Paris: Gueffier jeune, 1791), writes of "les Poules." See 203–209, quotation on 207–208.

15. See Robinson, "Islamic Revolution of Futa Toro"; Robinson, "Abdul Qadir and Shaykh Umar: A Continuing Tradition of Islamic Leadership in Futa Toro," *International Journal of African Historical Studies* 6 (1973): 286–303; and Rudolph T. Ware III, "A Walking Qur'an: Islamic Education, Embodied Knowledge, and History in Senegambia" (unpublished manuscript), chap. 1.

16. The first quotation is from a record concerning the killing of a merchant in the river trade, 7 August 1806, act 1694, carton 2, Fonds 4Z2, ANS. The term

"Poules" appears routinely on the maps of the late eighteenth century, including the one drawn for Thomas Clarkson around 1789–1790 by M. de Villeneuve and held in the Clarkson Papers in the William R. Clements Library, University of Michigan, Ann Arbor.

17. Robinson, "Islamic Revolution" and "Abdul Qadir." The underlying theological questions of Qur'anic interpretation concerning slavery are exceptionally complex. See Rudolph T. Ware III, "Slavery in Islamic Africa, 1400–1800," in *The Cambridge World History of Slavery,* vol. 3, ed. David Eltis and Stanley Engerman (Cambridge: Cambridge University Press, 2011): 47–80.

18. Kane, *La Première Hégémonie,* 273. The presence of speakers of Pulaar outside the dominion of Almamy Abdulkaadir Kan complicates the picture. It is difficult to know whether the Almamy would refuse to allow the passage of such individuals as captives. Some Pulaar speakers from further upriver toward Galam could also be shipped out via other routes to the north or the south of the river.

19. Saugnier went on to note that "they are always bought, despite the treaty with the Almamy to refrain from buying anyone from his nation, doubtless because it is believed that this treaty only applies when one goes into his land by convoy to go upriver to Galam." See Saugnier, *Relation,* 266. On these rivalries see Abdoulaye Bathily, *Les Portes de l'or: le royaume de Galam (Sénégal) de l'ère musulmane au temps des négriers (VIIIᵉ–XVIIIe siècle)* (Paris: Éditions L'Harmattan, 1989), 319.

20. On schooling in Senegambia, see Ware, "Walking Qur'an." See also Abbé David Boilat, *Esquisses sénégalaises* (1853; repr. Paris: Éditions Karthala, 1984), 384–386, 388–413. Boilat emphasized the large number of schools in the country as well as the wide literacy in Arabic (390–391).

21. Boilat used the term "Toucouleur" for the residents of Fuuta Tooro, drawing on the older term "Tekrur," and wrote of them: "They will not suffer for one of their number to be made a slave, and if it occurs, they will make any sacrifice in order to pay the ransom." Boilat, *Esquisses,* 394.

22. Rosalie is described as "approximately twenty-eight years old" in "Affranchissement de la négresse Rosalie par Marthonne," 2 December 1795, Notary Dobignies, file 9-218, Jérémie Papers, Special Collections, University of Florida George A. Smathers Libraries, Gainesville. Her long-standing designation as Poulard reflects the ethnonym used by the French; hence our inference that she was probably transported on a French ship out of Saint-Louis. Some boats did make multiple subsequent stops in Gorée and at the mouth of the Gambia River, however, and an origin in the more southerly region called Fuuta Jalon is not impossible.

23. On the early period see Abdoulaye Ly, *La Compagnie du Sénégal* (Paris: Éditions Karthala, 1993), 281–292. For the later period see Ibrahima Thioub, "L'esclavage à Saint-Louis du Sénégal au XVIIIᵉ–XIXᵉ siècle," *Jahrbuch 2008/2009* (Wissenschaftskolleg zu Berlin, 2010): 334–356.

24. Abdoul Hadir Aïdara, *Saint-Louis de Sénégal d'hier à aujourd'hui* (Brinon-sur-Sauldre: Grandvaux, 2004), 9–11; James F. Searing, *West African Slavery and Atlantic Commerce: The Senegal River Valley, 1700–1860* (Cambridge: Cambridge University Press, 1993). Negotiations between the French and the Almamy appear in correspondence of Governor François Blanchot. See "Registre et correspondance du commandant du Sénégal," 28 December 1789, 2 March 1793–8 November

1808, Fonds 3B1, ANS; and Mamadou Diouf, *Le Kajoor au XIXe siècle: pouvoir ceddo et conquête coloniale* (Paris: Éditions Karthala, 1990).

25. Saugnier, *Relation,* 287–300. On Galam and the trade goods taken there see Bathily, *Les Portes de l'or.* For an account of the trip upriver in the 1780s see Antoine Edme Pruneau de Pommegorge, *Description de la Nigritie* (Paris: Maradan, 1789).

26. For the many transactions upon arrival of the convoy see the records in cartons 1 and 2, Fonds 4Z2, ANS.

27. For an overview see Michael David Marcson, "European-African Interaction in the Precolonial Period: Saint Louis, Senegal, 1758–1854" (PhD diss., Princeton University, 1976).

28. See Searing, *West African Slavery,* chaps. 4 and 5. For estimates of the number of *esclaves de case* see Silvain Meinrad de Golbéry, *Fragmens d'un voyage fait pendant les années 1785, 1786, et 1787,* vol. 2 (Paris: Treuttel et Würtz, 1802), 328–363. On a parallel phenomenon in the port city of Lagos, to the south, see Kristin Mann, *Slavery and the Birth of an African City: Lagos, 1760–1900* (Bloomington: Indiana University Press, 2007), chap. 2.

29. See Affranchissement, 22 February 1789, carton 1, Fonds 4Z2, ANS. For an example of a mass manumission of African slaves by an owner who was of mixed ancestry see the act of the widow Thévenot, act 430, carton 1, Fonds 4Z2, ANS. We thank Mamadou Diouf for his suggestions concerning the interpretation of these documents.

30. The discussion of the Damel's captive is in order 111, folio 27r, dated 14 Frimaire, year XI [5 December 1802], of the register of correspondence between Governor Blanchot and the mayor of Saint-Louis, in Fonds 3B1, ANS. Copies of these orders were sent to the Ministère de la Marine et des Colonies in Paris, and the same order appears on pages 29–30 of "Livre d'ordres depuis le mois de mai 1792, époque du retour du citoyen Blanchot, commandant en chef du Sénégal," registre 30, sous-série 6, série C, ANOM.

31. See "Les Arbitres appellés par les héritiers de Marianne Fleury . . ." in folder "Minutes & autres actes du Greffe an 14," carton 2, Fonds 4Z2, ANS. Thioub, "L'esclavage," emphasizes the role of the threat of sale into the Atlantic trade.

32. It is therefore unlikely that the baptism that declared Rosalie's Christian name to be Marie Françoise took place as early as her passage through Saint-Louis. Some free Muslims in Saint-Louis, however, did convert. See "Affranchissement par la S. Louise Couvat négresse chrétienne de la captive Marie Dimbalaye," 22 September 1789, act 467, carton 1, Fonds 4Z2, ANS.

33. Several documents on Paul Bénis are in carton 1, Fonds 4Z2, ANS. See also Saugnier, *Relation,* 176, for a description of Bénis as a former barrel-maker *(tonnelier)* for the Compagnie in Gorée, transplanted to Saint-Louis.

34. Several of these can be found in carton 2, Fonds 4Z2, ANS.

35. The story of the shipwreck comes from the transcription of the logbook of the *Speculation* and from the depositions of the captain, in the folder marked "1804" in carton 2, Fonds 4Z2, ANS.

36. The brig had left Mr. Crousleatt's quay in Philadelphia on 10 December 1804 and stopped at Praia in the Cape Verde Islands to take on water. See document no.

856 (formerly no. 985), "Protest Cap^e Stewars," and the document labeled "No. 966, Rapport Capt. Steward," in the folder marked "1805," both in carton 3, Fonds 4Z2, ANS.

37. Ibid.

38. Ibid.

39. On the slave ship as a prison and place of terror see Marcus Rediker, *The Slave Ship: A Human History* (New York: Viking Press, 2007). For a French voyage of an earlier period, see Robert Harms, *The Diligent: A Voyage through the Worlds of the Slave Trade* (New York: Basic Books, 2002).

40. Jean Mettas, *Répertoire des expéditions négrières françaises au XVIIIe siècle*, vol. 2, *Ports autre que Nantes*, ed. Serge Daget (Paris: Société française d'histoire d'outre-mer, 1978), 372.

41. Ibid., 372–373. As historians have pointed out, each death on board presented to the other captives the spectacle of death without a proper funeral, a soul cut off from ancestors and descendants. See Stephanie Smallwood, *Saltwater Slavery: A Middle Passage from Africa to American Diaspora* (Cambridge, MA: Harvard University Press, 2007).

42. Detailed information on individual voyages is in Mettas, *Répertoire*.

43. See, for example, the reference to such paper in the cargo list "État des marchandises livrées par la Cie du Sénégal au Sr Mandeau pour une livraison attendue de 25 captifs à remettre à M. Paul Benis lors de la prochaine descente de Galam," 25 July 1788, carton 1, Fonds 4Z2, ANS.

44. Boilat, *Esquisses*, Atlas, plate n° 20 titled "Thierno Grand Marabout," or in some editions "Homme et Femme Toucoulaure. Marabout faisant un Grigri."

2. "ROSALIE . . . MY SLAVE"

1. For a description of the general process of disembarkation and naming, see Médéric Louis Élie Moreau de Saint-Méry, *Description topographique, physique, civile, politique et historique de la partie française de l'isle Saint-Domingue*, 2 vols. (Philadelphia: by the author, 1797, 1798), 2:685.

2. The last two of these documents (dated 1799 and 1803) were drawn up in the presence of Michel Vincent and refer unequivocally to Marie Françoise, *dite* Rosalie, who later identified herself as Rosalie Vincent, and who was the mother of Élisabeth Vincent, hence the grandmother of Édouard Tinchant. The first three documents (two dated in 1793 and one in 1795) are linked to the other two by the overlapping use by Marthe Guillaume of variants of the phrase "Rosalie de nation Poulard." Jérémie was a small town whose population included very few enslaved Africans designated as Poulard; Michel Vincent apparently had direct financial dealings with Marthe Guillaume. It seems safe to infer that all five documents refer to the same woman.

3. Jérémie was one of the five *quartiers* of the Partie du Sud, along with Petit-Goave, Saint-Louis, Les Cayes, and Cap-Tiburon. Moreau de Saint-Méry, *Description topographique*, 2:532.

4. See Moreau de Saint-Méry, *Description topographique*, 2:762–815; and Keith Anthony Manuel, "Slavery, Coffee, and Family in a Frontier Society: Jérémie and Its Hinterland, 1780–1789" (master's thesis, University of Florida, Gainesville, 2005).

5. See Julius S. Scott, "'Negroes in Foreign Bottoms': Sailors, Slaves, and Communication," in *Origins of the Black Atlantic,* ed. Laurent Dubois and Julius S. Scott (New York: Routledge, 2010), 69–98, quotation on 78.

6. Moreau de Saint-Méry, *Description topographique,* 2:685.

7. See the records of voyages 1259, 1311, and 1366 in vol. 1 of Jean Mettas, *Répertoire des expéditions négrières françaises au XVIIIe siècle,* ed. Serge Daget, 2 vols. (Paris: Société française d'histoire d'outre-mer, 1978–1984).

8. Moreau de Saint-Méry, *Description topographique,* 2:805.

9. Moreau de Saint-Méry believed that thirty-seven years earlier there had been only 2,147 slaves in Jérémie and environs (ibid., 2:806).

10. Ibid., 2:782.

11. The 1776 purchase by Marthe Guillaume of her first shop is recorded in an act dated 10 November 1777, Notary Bosc, Saint-Domingue (hereafter SDOM) 204, Dépôt des papiers publics des colonies, Archives nationales d'outre-mer, Aix-en-Provence, France (hereafter DPPC, ANOM). The list of her debtors includes some descriptions of merchandise. See "Remise de créance par le S. Marsolas à Marthe Guillaume," 30 August 1794, File 6C-210, Notary Lépine, Jérémie Papers, Special Collections, University of Florida George A. Smathers Libraries, Gainesville (hereafter JP, SC, UFL).

12. The apprenticeship contract is "Brevet d'apprentissage de Pierre Aliés," 1 August 1777, Notary Lefrotter, SDOM 1208, DPPC, ANOM. For baptisms at which she served as godmother see the abstracts of records from the Archives nationales of Haiti with reference numbers 342478 (19 April 1781), 342482 (29 April 1781), and 343314 (5 March 1787), available from the Association de généalogie d'Haïti (AGH) at http://www.agh.qc.ca.

13. For a large sale of captives, many of them bearing this brand, see "Vente de divers nègres par Marthone Guillaume Aliés faveur du Sieur Nartigue," 7 December 1784, Notary Lépine, SDOM 1277, DPPC, ANOM. Marthe Guillaume's baptism in the parish of Sainte-Rose in Léogane on 12 March 1741 is recorded in Saint-Domingue, Registres de la paroisse de Léogane, microfilm from Archives nationales, Centre d'accueil et de recherche des Archives nationales, Paris (hereafter given in call number format, SOM 5Mi/62, CARAN). In it, her father is identified as a slave and her mother as a free black woman. Her father subsequently became free and her parents married. We thank Andrée-Luce Fourcand for having helped steer us to this document.

14. For the 28 February 1783 marriage of Marthe Guillaume's daughter Marie Anne [Aliés] to Jean Baptiste Azor dit Fortunat see SOM 5Mi/60, CARAN. Azor, designated a *quarteron,* had acquired his freedom only a year earlier. See the marriage contract of 26 February 1783, Notary Lépine, SDOM 1273, DPPC, ANOM.

15. On the Couët de Montarand family see Regnault de Beaucaron, *Souvenirs de famille: voyages, agriculture, précédés d'une Causerie sur le passé,* vol. 1 (Paris: Plon-Nourrit, 1912), 97. On Michel Vincent, and the location of his land, see Jean Hébrard, "Les deux vies de Michel Vincent, colon à Saint-Domingue (c. 1730–1804)," *Revue d'histoire moderne et contemporaine* 57 (April–June 2010): 50–77.

16. Hébrard, "Les deux vies."

17. See "Vente par le Sr Collet faveur de Magloire d'une négresse nommée Julie," 20 March 1787, in Notary Lépine, SDOM 1283, DPPC, ANOM.

18. See Dominique Rogers, "Les Libres de couleur dans les capitales de Saint-Domingue. Fortune, mentalités, et intégration à la fin de l'Ancien Régime (1776–1789)" (doctoral thesis, Université de Bordeaux III, 2001); and Stewart R. King, *Blue Coat or Powdered Wig: Free People of Color in Pre-Revolutionary Saint-Domingue* (Athens: University of Georgia Press, 2001).

19. See the death registered in Port-au-Prince on 9 October 1835 of an aged man with the surname Couba, born in Africa: document 501960, abstracted for the AGH, accessed at http://www.agh.qc.ca.

20. In an 1802 marriage record from Jérémie, Alexis Couba appears as a witness and is given the age of ninety, which would place his birth around 1712. See the 17 July 1802 marriage of Jean Meynard and Marie Lada Étienne, document 343012, AGH, http://www.agh.qc.ca. Couba's own marriage is recorded 9 January 1781, Registres de la paroisse de Jérémie, reproduced on microfilm SOM 5Mi/59, CARAN.

21. Purchases of slaves by free persons of color, and occasional marriages between owners and slaves, appear in the notarial records from Jérémie held in the ANOM. On the Code Noir and manumission, see Malick Ghachem, *The Old Regime and the Haitian Revolution* (New York: Cambridge University Press, forthcoming 2012), chap. 2.

22. "Liberté de Lisette," 26 October 1783, in Notary Robinet, SDOM 1563, DPPC, ANOM.

23. The evidence that Rosalie had previously been owned by Alexis Couba is in a draft of Martha Guillaume's will. See "Testament de Marthe Guillaume," 8 January 1793, Notary Lépine, Folder 6C-116, JP, SC, UFL.

24. See "Remise de créance . . . ," 30 August 1794, Notary Lépine, File 6C-210, JP, SC, UFL. On the role of loans in creating social webs across class lines in ancien-régime societies see Laurence Fontaine, *L'Économie morale: pauvreté, crédit et confiance dans l'Europe préindustrielle* (Paris: Gallimard, 2008).

25. Many of Marthe Guillaume's dealings with contractors, merchants, and her neighbors were recorded by the notary Lépine and can be found in DPPC, ANOM or in JP, SC, UFL. In a contract with a mason drawn up in 1787, the house of hers to be repaired is listed as being on the Place d'Armes. See "Marché entre le Sr. Piffet & Marthone Guillaume," 19 October 1787, Notary Lépine, SDOM 1285, DPPC, ANOM.

26. On the interplay of expansive readings of the Code Noir and the new declaration see Ghachem, *The Old Regime*, chaps. 5 and 6.

27. For a translation of the Assembly's instructions see Laurent Dubois and John D. Garrigus, *Slave Revolution in the Caribbean, 1789–1804: A Brief History with Documents* (Boston/New York: Bedford/St. Martin's, 2006), 70–72.

28. See Beaubrun Ardouin, *Études sur l'histoire d'Haïti suivies de la vie du général J.-M. Borgella,* 11 vols. (Paris: Dezobry et E. Magdeleine, 1853–1860), 1:131.

29. See John Garrigus, *Before Haiti: Race and Citizenship in French Saint-Domingue* (New York: Palgrave Macmillan, 2006), 247–280; and Garrigus, "'Thy coming fame, Ogé! Is sure': New Evidence on Ogé's 1790 Revolt and the Beginnings

of the Haitian Revolution," in *Assumed Identities: The Meanings of Race in the Atlantic World,* ed. Garrigus and Christopher Morris (College Station: Texas A&M University Press, 2010), 19–45; as well as Ardouin, *Études,* 1:133–163.

30. See Ardouin, *Études,* 1:162; and Garrigus, *Before Haiti,* 109, 123, 132–135, 244.

31. Garrigus, *Before Haiti;* King, *Blue Coat,* esp. 266–274; Dominique Rogers, "On the Road to Citizenship: The Complex Route to Integration of the Free People of Color in the Two Capitals of Saint-Domingue," in *The World of the Haitian Revolution,* ed. David Patrick Geggus and Norman Fiering (Bloomington: Indiana University Press, 2009), 65–78.

32. See also Ghachem, *Old Regime,* and Laurent Dubois, *Avengers of the New World: The Story of the Haitian Revolution* (Cambridge, MA: Harvard University Press, 2004), 5.

33. Laurent Dubois, *A Colony of Citizens: Revolution and Slave Emancipation in the French Caribbean, 1787–1804* (Chapel Hill: University of North Carolina Press, 2004), chap. 3; Garrigus, *Before Haiti,* 250–251.

34. See Garrigus, *Before Haiti,* 250–252; and Carolyn Fick, *The Making of Haiti: The Saint Domingue Revolution from Below* (Knoxville: University of Tennessee Press, 1990), 137–138 and appendix C; and Ardouin, *Études,* 1:216–236.

35. See Dubois, *Avengers,* chap. 4; David Patrick Geggus, *Haitian Revolutionary Studies* (Bloomington: Indiana University Press, 2002), chap. 6; and Ghachem, *Old Regime,* chaps. 4, 5, and 6.

36. On the arming of slaves in the Grand'Anse see Ardouin, *Études,* 2:136; and David Geggus, "Slave, Soldier, Rebel: The Strange Career of Jean Kina," in Geggus, *Haitian Revolutionary Studies,* chap. 9.

37. For the episode in Jérémie see file 13 in Missions des représentants du peuple et comités des assemblées, 1789-an IV (série D), Comité des colonies (sous-série XXV), dossier 65 (generally known by the call number D-XXV/65), CARAN. On the south see Fick, *Making of Haiti;* and Ardouin, *Études,* 2:135–136.

38. Ardouin, *Études,* 1:311–312. See below for a discussion of Pierre Aliés and the militia.

39. "Remise de créance à Marthe Guillaume par le S. Marsolas," dated 30 August 1794, reflects her activities over many previous years. See in Notary Lépine, File 6C-210, JP, SC, UFL. The smallpox story is recounted in Ardouin, *Études,* vol. 2: 139.

40. On the April 4 Decree and its reception see "Rapport de Philippe-Rose Roume sur sa mission à Saint-Domingue en qualité de commissaire national civil," *Archives parlementaires de 1787 à 1860: recueil complet des débats législatifs & politiques des chambres françaises,* 1st series (1787–1799), vol. 57 (Paris: Paul Dupont, 1900), 67–80, esp. 72.

41. *Débats entre les accusateurs et les accusés, dans l'affaire des colonies, imprimés en exécution de la Loi du 4 pluviôse,* 2 vols. (Paris: Imprimerie nationale, Pluviôse an III [January–February 1795]), 1:291.

42. The draft is dated 8 January 1793, and is in Notary Lépine, File 6C-116, JP, SC, UFL.

43. "Vente par Marthe Guillaume à Mongol de la N^sse Rosalie," 14 January 1793, Notary Lépine, File 6C-119, JP, SC, UFL. Jean Baptiste Mongol had been

freed in 1782, acquired a female slave named Lisette, and then married her. See his 3 November 1787 marriage record, in St. Domingue, Registres de la paroisse de Jérémie, 1783–1786, SOM 5Mi/60, CARAN.

44. The paragraphs that follow rest on a critical reading of the printed "Adresse à tous les citoyens chargés des autorités civiles & militaires, et à tous les citoyens de la Colonie," dated "Jérémie, maison commune, le 7 mars 1793," copy in file 895, D-XXV/113, CARAN.

45. "Adresse à tous les citoyens chargés des autorités civiles et militaires, 7 mars 1793."

46. Ibid., 9.

47. Ibid., 13–33; and Ardouin, *Études,* 2:55–58.

48. See "Adresse à tous les citoyens chargés des autorités civiles et militaires, 7 mars 1793," 8–32. On Atlas see also Fick, *Making of Haiti,* 235; and Berger to Rochambeau, 26 June 1803, File 1954, Rochambeau Papers, SC, UFL.

49. The taking of prisoners is described in Ardouin, *Études,* 2:55.

50. See "Adresse à tous les citoyens chargés des autorités civiles et militaires, 7 mars 1793," 31–32; and Ardouin, *Études,* 2:219.

51. The actions of the émigré planters can be followed in the voluminous correspondence in War Office Records (hereafter WO) 1/58, National Archives of the United Kingdom, Kew (hereafter NAUK), and are analyzed by David Patrick Geggus in *Slavery, War, and Revolution: The British Occupation of Saint Domingue, 1793–1798* (Oxford: Clarendon Press, 1982), chap. 3.

52. This is the translation provided by Jeremy D. Popkin in his vivid account of the events, *You Are All Free: The Haitian Revolution and the Abolition of Slavery* (New York: Cambridge University Press, 2010), 212.

53. See [Le G. G.], "Aux origines de l'abolition de l'esclavage. Proclamations de Polverel et de Sonthonax 1793–1794," *Revue d'histoire des colonies* 36 (first trimester, 1949): 24–55, and 36 (third and fourth trimesters, 1949): 348–423. The initial decree, applicable in the north, declared all those in slavery to be free and entitled to all the rights of French citizenship, though subject to a special work regime (351–352).

54. Ardouin, *Études,* 2:265–276. See Geggus, *Slavery, War, and Revolution,* 65.

55. Bérault Saint Maurice, quoted in Geggus, *Slavery, War, and Revolution,* 68.

56. These are the terms used in Colonel Whitelocke to Mr. Lewis, 22 January 1794, in WO 1/59, NAUK. On the encampments in the hills, see "Adresse à tous les citoyens chargés des autorités civiles et militaires, 7 mars 1793."

57. "Extract of a letter from Henry Shirley Esq. to his Brother, dated Kingston 20th July 1794," 425, WO 1/59, NAUK.

58. See "Letter on the State of St. Domingo," August 1794, written by de Charmilly, 497–506, WO 1/59, NAUK.

59. De Charmilly to M. King, dated Jérémie 29 January 1794; Letter from an officer in St. Domingue, dated 22 May 1794; both in WO 1/59, NAUK. See also Dubois, *Avengers,* 167.

60. "Procuration spéciale et générale par la n^{sse} marthe guillaume faveur de M. Paillette," 12 February 1794, Notary Lafuge Jeune, File 3-10, JP, SC, UFL.

61. The strongest evidence for a beginning date of her relationship with Michel Vincent is the birth of her children, discussed below. On the exercise of freedom in the areas of the south controlled by Rigaud, see Carolyn E. Fick, "The Haitian Revolution and the Limits of Freedom: Defining Citizenship in the Revolutionary Era," *Social History* 32 (2007): 394–414.

62. See "Copie des Procès Verbaux des Délibérations du Conseil Privé de Mr. Whyte," 18 July 1794 to 12 September 1794, 82–83, in Colonial Office Records (hereafter CO) 245/5, NAUK.

63. "Remise de créance par le S. Marsolas à Marthe Guillaume," 30 August 1794, Notary Lépine, File 6C-210, JP, SC, UFL.

64. See the fragment dated 1795, Baptêmes, in Papers of the Greffe, folder 12, box 15, JP, SC, UFL.

65. "Affranchissement de la négresse Rosalie par Marthonne," 2 December 1795, Notary Dobignies, File 9-218, JP, SC, UFL.

66. See the discussions in the papers of the Conseil privé in December 1795 and January 1796, Treasury Records (hereafter T) 81/7, NAUK.

67. See the letter from the Conseil privé to Commandant Murray on 12 September 1795; the section "Affranchissement," 69; and Williamson to Murray, 13 January 1796; all in "Copie des Lettres Écrites par Le Conseil Privé . . . Williamson," a volume dated 28 Août 1795 but including some later materials, T 81/15, NAUK.

68. On the decline and withdrawal of the British see Geggus, *Slavery, War, and Revolution,* 373–381. On the civil war between Louverture and Rigaud see Dubois, *Avengers,* chap. 11; and Fick, *Making of Haiti,* 196–203.

69. A copy of the baptismal act is in "Rectification de noms d'épouse Tinchant dans son contrat de mariage," 16 November 1835, Act 672, Notary Théodore Seghers, New Orleans Notarial Archives Research Center.

70. Baptismal certificate in "Rectification de noms."

71. The estimated values of the houses in Jérémie are drawn from folios 4r to 9r of the Cadastre de Jérémie, dated Pluviôse, year X [January 1802], Supplément Saint-Domingue (hereafter SUPSDOM), série 5, document 5 (5SUPSDOM/5), DPPC, ANOM.

72. See the sale document dated 13 Pluviôse, year VII [1 February 1799], Notary Joubert, File 4-13, JP, SC, UFL.

73. See folios 4r to 9r of the Cadastre de Jérémie, Pluviôse, year X [January 1802], 5SUPSDOM/5, DPPC, ANOM. On notarial activity more generally see the records of the notaries Lépine and Joubert in JP, SC, UFL.

74. On the context for the French expedition see Yves Benot, *La Démence coloniale sous Napoléon* (1992; repr., Paris: Éditions La Découverte, 2006) 57–98, 359.

75. On the legal situation in 1802, see Jean-François Niort and Jérémy Richard, "À propos de la découverte de l'arrêté consulaire du 16 juillet 1802 et du rétablissement de l'ancien ordre colonial (spécialement de l'esclavage) à la Guadeloupe," *Bulletin de la Société d'histoire de la Guadeloupe* 152 (2009): 31–59.

76. See Ardouin, *Études,* vol. 5, chap. 11.

77. Ibid., 5:385.

78. Michel's plan to leave for France is explicitly referred to in the manumission document analyzed below.

79. "Enregistrement de liberté par. de Marie Françoise," 26 Ventôse, year XII [17 March 1804], folio 25v, 26r, Actes déclarations & dépôts divers, 10 Pluviôse, year XII [31 January 1804]–10 Vendémiaire, year XIII [2 October 1804], 6SUPS-DOM/3, DPPC, ANOM.

80. Ibid. On Leclerc's policies in 1802 see Ardouin, *Études,* 5:307.

81. "Enregistrement de liberté par. de Marie Françoise."

82. Ibid.

83. "Déclaration constatant l'état civil de Marie Jeanne par Charles Daromon demeurant à la Grande Rivière," 8 Messidor, year XI [27 June 1803], Notary Joubert, File 4-143, JP, SC, UFL.

84. On the ways in which notaries poured declarants' intentions into the molds established for official documents see Kathryn Burns, *Into the Archive: Writing and Power in Colonial Peru* (Durham, NC: Duke University Press, 2010). On similar strategies for formalizing freedom see Dubois, *Colony of Citizens,* 374–378.

85. Ardouin, *Études,* vol. 5, chap. 11.

86. Peter S. Chazotte, *Historical Sketches of the Revolutions and the Foreign and Civil Wars in the Island of St. Domingo* (New York: Wm. Applegate, 1840), 32–34.

87. See Thomas Madiou, *Histoire d'Haïti,* vol. 3 (Port-au-Prince: Éditions Henri Deschamps, 1989), 66–68; Jan Pachoński and Ruel K. Wilson, *Poland's Caribbean Tragedy: A Study of Polish Legions in the Haitian War of Independence, 1802–1803* (Boulder, CO: East European Monographs, 1986), chaps. 4 and 5.

3. CITIZEN ROSALIE

1. See, for example, the report by a ship captain in "Copie du Rapport du Citoyen Pruniet Capitaine de la falouche la Doucereuse venant de Jérémie," item 2021, the Rochambeau Papers, Special Collections, University of Florida George A. Smathers Libraries, Gainesville, Florida.

2. On the goals of the Leclerc expedition see Yves Benot, *La Démence coloniale sous Napoléon* (Paris: La Découverte, 2006), 57–99.

3. See the report numbered 888, dated 30 June 1803, filed in leg. 1537A, Papeles de Cuba, Archivo General de Indias, Seville (hereafter AGI).

4. See the letter from Bouny to the Governor, July 1803, in exp. 7, leg. 63, Correspondencia de los Capitanes Generales (hereafter CCG), Archivo Nacional de Cuba (hereafter ANC), and other petitions from captains in the same bundle.

5. On the arrivals in Santiago see Gabriel Debien, "Les colons de Saint-Domingue réfugiés à Cuba (1793–1815)," *Revista de Indias* 13 (October–December 1953): 559–605, esp. 568–574; and Alain Yacou, "Esclaves et libres français à Cuba au lendemain de la Révolution de Saint-Domingue," *Jahrbuch für Geschichte von Staat, Wirtschaft und Gesellschaft Lateinamerikas* 28 (Köln: Böhlau Verlag, 1991): 163–197. On the alliance between Spain and France see Barbara H. Stein and Stanley J. Stein, *Edge of Crisis: War and Trade in the Spanish Atlantic, 1789–1808* (Baltimore: Johns Hopkins University Press, 2009), 48, 416–421.

6. See the "Relación qᵉ manifiesta el nᵒ de personas francesas . . . en la Goleta La Fiel [?]," apparently dated 25 July 1803, in "Relaciones, 1801–1803," exp. 3, leg. 445, CCG, ANC.

7. The refugee referred to as "José L^s Tine" declared bluntly to the Cuban authorities that the thirteen *negros* and eleven *negras* on the schooner *La Última Necesidad* were "the slaves of various subjects on board the boats anchored in the port of Juragua." See exp. 889, leg. 1537A, Papeles de Cuba, AGI.

8. See the communications of Someruelos to the Governor of [Santiago de] Cuba, including those dated 14 June 1803 and 11 July 1803 in exps. 6, 9, and 12, leg. 63, CCG, ANC, especially Someruelos to the Governor of Cuba, 2 August 1803, in exp. 12.

9. See José Luís Belmonte Postigo, "'Intentan sacudir el yugo de la servidumbre': El Cimarronaje en el Oriente Cubano, 1790–1815," *Historia Caribe* (Barranquilla, Colombia) 12 (2007): 7–21.

10. See the June 1803 testimony of Berquier, fol. 20ff, exp. 889, leg. 1537A, Papeles de Cuba, AGI. Enrique López Mesa, personal communication, February 2009, points out that this kind of maneuvering was a standard part of the craft of commerce in the Caribbean.

11. See Deposition of Nicolas Dauvergne Cap^n de la Goleta francesa nombrada la Esperanza [ca. July 1803], in exp. 7, leg. 63, CCG, ANC.

12. The forthcoming work of María de los Ángeles Meriño and Aisnara Perera argues that a number of rights and privileges—including access to marriage and the ability to work outside the master's home—had long been accorded to urban slaves in Santiago.

13. Belmonte, "'Intentan sacudir el yugo,' " 10. An entry for Pierre Aliés Pardo, lodging with a sergeant of the Cuban militia of *pardos* (men of color), appears as document 99 in the registry of refugees compiled in July 1803: "Documento sobre que se den razon del alojamiento de los Extrangeros," exp. 57, leg. 8, Asuntos Políticos (hereafter AP), ANC.

14. Élisabeth's passage through Cuba is implied in comments made by the widow Aubert in "Contrat de mariage, Jacques Tinchant et Marie Dieudonné," 26 September 1822, fol. 31r–32r, Notary Marc Lafitte, New Orleans Notarial Archives Research Center. The widow's own time in Cuba is confirmed in records of slave sales.

15. Their means for earning a livelihood can be inferred from the record of Michel's succession, discussed below. On the French refugees in Santiago see Olga Portuondo Zúñiga, *Entre esclavos y libres de Cuba colonial* (Santiago de Cuba: Editorial Oriente, 2003), 58–97; Agnès Renault, "La communauté française de Santiago de Cuba entre 1791 et 1825" (doctoral thesis, Université du Havre, 2007); and Laura Cruz Ríos, *Flujos inmigratorios franceses a Santiago de Cuba (1800–1868)* (Santiago de Cuba: Editorial Oriente, 2006).

16. The manumission paper, discussed in Chapter 2, was transcribed into a register kept by the French Agence des Prises de la Guadeloupe, established in Santiago. "Enregistrement de liberté par. de Marie Françoise," 26 ventôse year XII [17 March 1804], fol. 25v, 26 r, Actes, déclarations & dépôts divers, 10 Pluviôse, year XII [31 January 1804]–10 Vendémiaire, year XIII [2 October 1804], série 6, document 3, Supplément Saint-Domingue (hereafter SUPSDOM, following convention for call numbers, e.g. 6SUPSDOM/3), Dépôt des papiers publics des colonies (hereafter DPPC), Archives nationales d'outre-mer, Aix-en-Provence (hereafter ANOM).

17. Through 1804, the Agence reported to the captain general of Guadeloupe. After the French army in Saint-Domingue retreated to the former Spanish Santo Domingo, however, General Ferrand made a grab for the resources of the prize ships. See Ferrand to Kindelán, 13 July 1806, exp. 33, leg. 138, AP, ANC. See also Michel Rodigneaux, *La Guerre de course en Guadeloupe XVIIIe–XIXe siècles, ou Alger sous les tropiques* (Paris: Éditions L'Harmattan, 2006), esp. 63, 136–137, and 156–167.

18. Michel Vincent's documents were eventually handed over to Colonel Joseph Ruiz. The will and the bundles seem to have been lost, though an inventory survives in 6SUPSDOM/2, DPPC, ANOM. Graham Nessler has uncovered Ruiz's activities as an officer under General Ferrand in Hispaniola during the reimposition of slavery on that colony. See Graham T. Nessler, "A Failed Emancipation? The Struggle for Freedom in Hispaniola during the Haitian Revolution" (PhD diss., University of Michigan, 2011).

19. "Enregistrement de liberté . . .," 26 Ventôse, year XII, fol. 25v, 26r, 6SUPSDOM/3, DPPC, ANOM.

20. "Remise de Succⁿ par Vallée," 9 Floréal, year XII [29 April 1804], fol. 40v, 6SUPSDOM/3, DPPC, ANOM.

21. Ibid. Because of the coincidence of the names, we initially believed that the reference was to Rosalie's daughter Marie Louise. The document's key phrases concerning the disposition of Marie Louise nonetheless seem to imply prior ownership as property: "qu'il [Vallée] était prêt a faire remise de la négresse nommée Marie Louise Désir egallement leguée à la même, mais dont il n'a pas voulu faire delivrance, vu les dettes dont la succession est grevée." The verbs *faire remise de* (to deliver or hand over) and *léguée à* (left to, as in a will) imply a property relation and suggest that Marie Louise Désir had been treated as a slave in the will.

22. "Remise de Succⁿ par Vallée," 9 Floréal, year XII. No mention is made in the executor's report of any heirs-at-law in France. In 1827, when France agreed to recognize independent Haiti in exchange for a massive indemnity, Michel Vincent's collateral descendants living in France appealed to the French government for a portion of the indemnity. See V 141, Vincent (Michel Étienne Henry), 1390, Indemnités traités, in 7SUPSDOM/97, DPPC, ANOM. See Jean Hébrard, "Les deux vies de Michel Vincent, colon à Saint-Domingue (c. 1730–1804)," *Revue d'histoire moderne et contemporaine* 57 (2010): 50–77.

23. Someruelos to Rafael Gómez Roubaud, 30 July 1804, exp. 1, leg. 9, AP, ANC.

24. Ibid.

25. Ada Ferrer has added complexity to the picture of Cuban responses to the news from Saint-Domingue. See Ferrer, "Speaking of Haiti: Slavery, Revolution, and Freedom in Cuban Slave Testimony," in *The World of the Haitian Revolution,* ed. David Patrick Geggus and Norman Fiering (Bloomington: Indiana University Press, 2009), 223–247; and Ferrer, "Talk about Haiti: The Archive and the Atlantic's Haitian Revolution," in *Tree of Liberty: Cultural Legacies of the Haitian Revolution in the Atlantic World,* ed. Doris L. Garraway (Charlottesville: University of Virginia Press, 2008), 21–40.

26. For the case of Adélaïde Métayer, who successfully defended her freedom in the coastal community of Baracoa, see Rebecca J. Scott, "Paper Thin: Freedom and

Re-enslavement in the Diaspora of the Haitian Revolution," *Law and History Review* 29 (November 2011): 1061–1087.

27. We thank Ada Ferrer for first suggesting that large-scale deportations may not have occurred, and Michael Zeuske, Edgardo Pérez Morales, and Alejandro Gómez for having tried to find records of any such crossings. None of us has located records of the departure or the arrival of boats carrying such deportees in 1804–1807.

28. The pioneering study of that world is Julius S. Scott, "The Common Wind: Currents of Afro-American Communication in the Era of the Haitian Revolution" (PhD diss., Duke University, 1986). See also Laurent Dubois and Julius S. Scott, eds., *Origins of the Black Atlantic* (New York: Routledge, 2009), pt. 1.

29. See the letters exchanged between Someruelos and Kindelán during the summer of 1808 in leg. 209, AP, ANC. The phrase "noticias modernas sobre ciertas occurrencias de España" appears in Someruelos to Kindelán, 20 June 1808, in exp. 27, ibid.

30. The corsair that was renamed had belonged to M. Dupuy in Baracoa. See the letter of 27 December 1808 in exp. 132, leg. 209, AP, ANC.

31. The strolling Catalan is described in a draft letter from Kindelán to Someruelos, 27 December 1808, in exp. 132, leg. 209, AP, ANC. On this period in Santiago see Olga Portuondo Zúñiga, *Cuba: Constitución y liberalismo (1808–1841),* vol. 1 (Santiago de Cuba: Editorial Oriente, 2008), 25–75.

32. On the intrigues and politics surrounding these "riots" see Yacou, "Esclaves et libres"; Portuondo Zúñiga, *Entre esclavos y libres;* and the documents from March 1809 in exp. 4, leg. 210, AP, ANC.

33. See *An Act to Prohibit the Importation of Slaves into Any Port or Place within the Jurisdiction of the United States* 2 Stat. 426 (1807). The U.S. consul in Santiago reported that he had "apprized the French Inhabitants, who held Slaves, of the Law which prohibited their introduction into the Territories of the U. States," but that he hoped that the U.S. government "may have the power and the inclination to grant them some relief from the precise rigor of established Statutes." Dunbar Rowland, ed., *Official Letter Books of W. C. C. Claiborne, 1801–1816,* vol. 4 (Jackson, MS: State Department of Archives and History, 1917), 364.

34. For the list of embarkations see "Estado, que p^r orden del Sor Gob^{or} de esta Plaza, se forma en este Resg^{do} de las Embarcacion^s q^e han transportado Pasag^s Extrang^s desde el 10 de Ab^l hasta la fha," exp. 9, leg. 210, AP, ANC.

35. For the arrival of the *Louisa* at Plaquemine see Rowland, *Official Letter Books,* 4:355. On the lobbying effort see Chapter 4.

36. See "Contrat de mariage, Jacques Tinchant et Marie Dieudonné." The activities of the widow and her companion in Santiago can be inferred from details provided in notarized sale documents later drawn up in New Orleans, discussed in Chapter 4.

37. See Pétion to Kindelán, 14 January 1809, and a letter from Kindelán to Someruelos, 23 January 1809, both in exp. 144, leg. 209, AP, ANC. President Pétion addressed Kindelán as "Monsieur le Gouverneur de la ville & dépendance de St. Yago à l'Ile de Cuba." Kindelán addressed him in return simply as "Pétion en el Puerto de Princip[e]."

38. "Estado . . .," exp. 9, leg. 210, AP, ANC. Rosalie's presence in Haiti is evoked in the 1822 marriage contract of her daughter Élisabeth, cited above.

39. "Estado . . .," exp. 9, leg. 210, AP, ANC.

40. For this paragraph and the two below see the report dated 14 November 1817, apparently from the governor of Santiago to the governor of the island of Cuba; and the copy of a report of 15 November 1817, from the governor of Cuba to the Real Audiencia, both in Correspondencia, exp. 4, leg. 125, CCG, ANC. We thank Olga Portuondo Zúñiga, who first located this item, for advice concerning its interpretation.

41. Letter of Juan Ximenez to Sr Brig^r Gobernad^{or} D^n Eusebio Escudero, 13 November 1817, and the list of those to be arrested, dated 12 November 1817, both in exp. 4, leg. 125, CCG, ANC. A ship named *Caridad* transporting captives in 1820 from East Africa to Cuba appears in the Transatlantic Slave Trade Database, voyage number 49789. A captain Morales appears as commander of the slaving ship *Circasiana* arriving in Cuba in 1818, voyage 41333. Both voyages in http://www.slavevoyages.org/tast/database/search.faces.

42. The phrase is "siempre tienen disposicion ó trahen aparejados la accion o efecto de quemar," implying an incendiary tendency to any such organization.

43. On slaving ships from Havana that ended up in New Orleans, see exp. 2839, leg. 74, Fondo Junta de Fomento, ANC. Some refugees expelled from Santiago also later returned, as passport requests from New Orleans confirm. Ana Teodoro Cleaver, personal communication, February 2011.

44. For an example of an African woman who remained in Santiago, at least temporarily, see the petition of María Micaela casta Jolofa to the Junta de Vigilancia in Santiago, asking permission to remain in order to care for her aunt, dated 1 July 1809, in exp. 73, leg. 210, AP, ANC.

4. CROSSING THE GULF

1. Dunbar Rowland, ed., *Official Letter Books of W. C. C. Claiborne*, vol. 4 (Jackson, MS: State Department of Archives and History, 1917), 354–355.

2. *Acts Passed at the First Session of the First Legislature of the Territory of Orleans*, 126–131; and *Acts Passed at the Second Session of the First Legislature of the Territory of Orleans* (both New Orleans: Bradford & Anderson, 1807); and *An Act to Prohibit the Importation of Slaves into Any Port or Place within the Jurisdiction of the United States*, 2 Stat. 426 (1807).

3. Rowland, *Official Letter Books*, 4:351.

4. Ibid., 4:354, 363, 372. On the authorization see *An Act for the Remission of Certain Penalties and Forfeitures, and for Other Purposes*, 2 Stat. 549 (1809). On the political context see Ashli White, *Encountering Revolution: Haiti and the Making of the Early Republic* (Baltimore: Johns Hopkins University Press, 2010), chap. 5.

5. Rowland, *Official Letter Books*, 4:380, and vols. 5, 6. On the question of status see Rebecca J. Scott, "Paper Thin: Freedom and Reenslavement in the Diaspora of the Haitian Revolution," *Law and History Review* 29 (November 2011): 1061–1087.

6. On these numbers, see Paul Lachance, "The 1809 Immigration of Saint-Domingue Refugees to New Orleans: Reception, Integration, and Impact," *Louisiana History* 29 (1988): 109–141. The reports from the mayor of New Orleans are in Rowland, *Official Letter Books,* 4:381–382, 387–423; and the *Moniteur de la Louisiane,* 24 March 1810.

7. For an early property transaction by the widow Aubert in which she is so labeled see "Vente d'esclave par Pelon Vve Aubert à P[rre] Fourcand," 29 June 1813, Notary Broutin, New Orleans Notarial Archives Research Center (hereafter NONARC).

8. Robert A. Rutland et al., eds., *The Papers of James Madison: Presidential Series,* vol. 1, *1 March–30 September 1809* (Charlottesville: University Press of Virginia, 1984), 350, citing Smith to Grymes, 7 September 1809; *Moniteur de la Louisiane,* 21 March 2010.

9. See Rebecca J. Scott, "'She . . . refuses to deliver up herself as the slave of your Petitioner': Émigrés, Enslavement, and the 1808 Louisiana Digest of the Civil Laws," *Tulane European & Civil Law Forum* 24 (2009): 115–136.

10. Ibid.

11. *Acts Passed at the First Session of the First Legislature,* chap. 30, 128–130.

12. See the announcement of Marigny's subdivision in the *Moniteur de la Louisiane,* 3 June 1809. The land purchase document is "Vente de terrain par B[d] Marigny à Lambert Détry," 20 July 1809, Notary M. de Armas, NONARC. See also the eighth entry on Rue Moreau, in Faubourg Marigny, on the manuscript schedules of the Third Census of the United States, 1810, reproduced on roll 10, United States National Archives (hereafter USNA) Microcopy M252.

13. Article 8, chap. 2, title 4, book 1 of *A Digest of the Civil Laws Now in Force in the Territory of Orleans (1808)* (Baton Rouge: Claitor's Publishing Division: 2007) held marriages between free white persons and free persons of color to be void. Détry and the widow appear in adjacent records of slave purchases in the notarial acts of Philippe Pedesclaux, 8 and 10 March 1817, NONARC.

14. On *plaçage* see Shirley Elizabeth Thompson, *Exiles at Home: The Struggle to Become American in Creole New Orleans* (Cambridge, MA: Harvard University Press, 2009), 11–12; Kenneth Aslakson, "Making Race: The Role of Free Blacks in the Development of New Orleans' Three-Caste Society, 1791–1812" (PhD diss., University of Texas, 2007). The purchase of Trois-Sous by Lambert Détry, acting in the name of the widow, is "Vente d'esclave par Louis Seguin à Pelon Vve Aubert," 11 June 1813, Notary Narcisse Broutin, NONARC.

15. See "Liquidation & partage de la Succ[on] Lambert Détry, aux termes de la transaction judiciaire passée entre les héritiers & les légataires de feu Lambert Détry" in Succession and Probate Records; and "Inventory of the Estate of the late Lambert Détry," file D-1821, Inventories of Estates, both in Court of Probates, Orleans Parish, Louisiana, in City Archives (hereafter CA), Louisiana Division, New Orleans Public Library (hereafter LD, NOPL).

16. See "Liquidation & partage" and "Inventory," cited above.

17. The group presenting themselves as the "lawful heirs" hired P. Derbigny as their attorney and charged that the will was null and void. See Marie Louise Blanche, widow Aubert, fwc vs. Détry Jean (François X. Freyd, testamentary ex-

ecutor of) Year 1822, case number 206 in Court of Probates (Numbered Series), filed with the "flattened records" in CA, LD, NOPL.

18. Marriage contract, Jacques Tinchant and Marie Dieudonné, 26 September 1822, Notary M. Lafitte, NONARC. The sacramental record of the marriage—which appears to have been poorly transcribed by the attending priest, who confused the name of the bride with that of the groom's mother—is act 328, 28 September 1822, in Saint Louis Cathedral, Marriages of Slaves and Free Persons of Color, vol. 1, 1877–1830, pt. 2, in Archives of the Archdiocese of New Orleans (hereafter AANO). It lists "la expresada Madre de la contrayente" (the aforementioned mother of the female contracting party) as one of the witnesses. Rosalie Vincent could conceivably have arrived in New Orleans from Haiti in the intervening two days since the drawing up of the marriage contract. Given the other errors made by the priest in this case, it is more likely that he simply mistook the widow Aubert for the bride's mother.

19. The baptismal act of one Joseph Tinchant, from a family that sent several migrants to Saint-Domingue, appears with the date of 30 May 1766 in Registres paroissiaux, Bonvillet, État civil, Archives départementales des Vosges. A Joseph Tinchant then appears in Baltimore at the baptism of A. H. J. Denis, 7 September 1793, Register of Baptisms 1782, SC 2707, reproduced on microfilm 1510-2, Maryland State Archives. William Thompson, *The Baltimore Town and Fell's Point Directory* (Baltimore: printed for the proprietors, by Pechin & Co., 1796), lists a Tinchant on page 76. The Baltimore newspaper announcement by Joseph Tinchant appears in *American and Commercial Daily Advertiser,* 4 September 1805. These are very likely all the same man, father of Jacques Tinchant.

20. For the identification as Bayotte see "Vente d'esclave par Mr. Louis Duhart à Suzette Bayotte, f. de c. l. [femme de couleur libre]," dated 6 January 1820, in Notary Marc Lafitte, NONARC.

21. A Bijotte Bayotte, from Saint-Domingue, lived in Baltimore in 1796 and was identified as a widow. Bijotte Bayotte had inherited goods from one Pierre Barrère, who had held slaves in Saint-Marc in Saint-Domingue. See Thompson, *Baltimore Town,* 6; and Pierre Barrère's 19 July 1795 will and 27 July 1795 post-mortem inventory, both held by the Register of Wills, 182 City Hall, Philadelphia.

22. Martin Duhart, Louis' grandfather, had died while on what appears to have been a slave-trading voyage to West Africa. On Louis' mother's side, one finds Saint-Domingue planters and several judges from the Conseil Supérieur in the town of Cap Français (frequently called Le Cap). The lives of the various Duharts in Saint-Jean-de-Luz and Nantes can be reconstructed from records in the Fonds Freslon, Archives départementales, Loire-Atlantique, http://www.loire-atlantique.fr/jcms/cg_31241 /fonds-d-archives-numerises.

23. Pierre's baptism is recorded as Act 593, 16 August 1810, "St. Louis Cathedral. Baptisms Slaves and Free Persons of Color," AANO.

24. In 1811, Louis Duhart was among the Freemasons who founded the Grand Consistory of Louisiana in New Orleans. See Michael R. Poll, "A Foundational Study of the Grand Consistory of Louisiana," http://www.louisianalodgeofresearch .com/pdf/09foundationalstudy.pdf, and Fonds maçonniques (FM2), Manuscrits occidentaux, Bibliothèque nationale de France. See also Caryn Cossé Bell, *Revolution,*

Romanticism, and the Afro-Creole Protest Tradition in Louisiana, 1718–1868 (Baton Rouge: Louisiana State University Press, 1997), 70. On Duhart's efforts as a planter see "Dépôt de l'acte d'association," 21 March 1817; "Acte supplémentaire d'association," 28 February 1818 and "Enregistrement Louis Duhart et autres," 13 April 1818; and "Dissolution de société entre les Srs Louis Duhart, Frédéric Letanneur, Auguste Louis Destournelles et Antoine Alvarez Cruz," 30 April 1818; all in Notary Broutin, NONARC.

25. See, for example, the sale of slaves from Antoine Réné Marie Lamy Soulmon (a colleague of Duhart's and fellow member of the same Masonic lodge) to Marie Françoise Bayot dite Suzette, 5 October 1815, Notary Narcisse Broutin, NONARC. Article 10, chapter 2, title 2, book 3 of the 1808 *Digest of the Civil Laws* prohibited a donation by universal title between those living in concubinage. The 1825 Civil Code was even more restrictive. On legal restrictions on free people of color see also Thomas Ingersoll, "Free Blacks in a Slave Society: New Orleans, 1718–1812," *William and Mary Quarterly* 48 (1991): 173–200.

26. On this first generation see Lachance, "1809 Immigration"; and Nathalie Dessens, *From Saint-Domingue to New Orleans: Migration and Influences* (Gainesville: University Press of Florida, 2007). On the activities and movement of people of color in the region more generally, see Jane G. Landers, *Atlantic Creoles in the Age of Revolutions* (Cambridge, MA: Harvard University Press, 2010).

27. See Jacques Tinchant vs. Marie Blanche widow Aubert, docket #3920, Parish Court, CA, LD, NOPL. Her postmortem inventory is "Inventaire de la succession de feu M^{ie} B^{che} Pelon Vve J. B. Aubert," 24 January 1849, Notary Octave de Armas, NONARC.

28. Baptismal record of François Louis Tinchant, 1 January 1825, act 679, in St. Louis Cathedral, Baptisms Slaves–Free Persons of Color, 1823–1825, Part II, AANO.

29. Thompson, *Exiles,* 81; article 1468, chap. 1, title 2, book 3, *Civil Code of the State of Louisiana* (1825); and "An Act to prevent free persons of colour from entering into this State, and for other purposes," Approved 16 March 1830, in *Acts at the Second Session of the Ninth Legislature of the State of Louisiana* (Donaldsonville, LA: C. W. Duhy, State Printer, 1830), 90–95.

30. "An Act to punish the crimes therein mentioned, and for other purposes," Approved 16 March 1830, in *Acts at the Second Session of the Ninth Legislature,* 96–97. On their life in France, see Chapter 5.

31. See the marriage contract of Jacques Tinchant and Marie Dieudonné, 26 September 1822, Notary M. Lafitte, NONARC, and the manumission document "Affranchissement de la négresse Gertrude par Jacques Tinchant et son épouse," 23 January 1833, act 40, Notary Théodore Seghers, NONARC. On the rules governing manumissions see Judith Kelleher Schafer, *Slavery, the Civil Law, and the Supreme Court of Louisiana* (Baton Rouge: Louisiana State University Press, 1994), 180–181; and Schafer, *Becoming Free, Remaining Free: Manumission and Enslavement in New Orleans, 1846–1862* (Baton Rouge: Louisiana State University Press, 2003), 1–14.

32. "Vente d'esclave par Marianne Nabon f.c.l. [femme de couleur libre] à J. Tinchant & Pr Duhart," 25 April 1836, act 695, 1836, Notary Théodore Seghers, NONARC.

33. See "Vente de terrain par Tinchant & Duhart à Blaise Léger n.l. [nègre libre]," 7 October 1835, act 590, Notary Théodore Seghers, NONARC. See the petition for the emancipation of Blaise in Petitions for the emancipation of slaves, 1813–1843, Orleans Parish Court, CA, LD, NOPL. Lambert Détry had died in 1821, when Blaise was only ten years old, and his will called for Blaise to be manumitted when this became possible under Louisiana law. See the inventory of Lambert Détry, cited above, and his will, located on page 200, Will Book 3, CA, LD, NOPL.

34. Marriage contract of Jacques Tinchant and Marie Dieudonné, 26 September 1822, Notary M. Lafitte, NONARC.

35. See the marriage contract of 1822, and the baptismal record of François Louis Tinchant, both cited above.

36. "Vte de terre par Jacques Tinchant à Eulalie Desprès g.c.l. [gens de couleur libre]," 20 September 1834, act 442, Notary Octave de Armas, NONARC.

37. See "Rectification de noms d'épouse Tinchant dans son contrat de mariage," 16 November 1835, act 672, Notary Théodore Seghers, NONARC.

38. Ibid.

39. "List of all Passengers taken on board the Brig Ann whereof Charles Sutton is Master at the Port of Port Au Prince and bound for New-Orleans," arriving April 20, 1835, in Passenger Lists of Vessels Arriving at New Orleans, 1820–1902, reproduced on roll 12, USNA Microcopy 259.

40. See article 226, chap. 3, title 7, book 1, *Civil Code of the State of Louisiana* (1825).

41. Legitimation was difficult, and even the lesser act of acknowledgment was complex. See articles 217, 220, and 221 of chap. 3, title 7, book 1, of *Civil Code of the State of Louisiana* (1825).

42. Religious institutions did on occasion provide some training for children of color. See Emily Clark, *Masterless Mistresses: The New Orleans Ursulines and the Development of a New World Society, 1727–1834* (Chapel Hill: University of North Carolina Press, 2007), chap 1; and Roulhac Toledano and Marie Louise Christovic, *New Orleans Architecture*, vol. 6, *Faubourg Tremé and the Bayou Road* (Gretna, LA: Pelican Publishing Co., 2003), 99–100.

43. The list, titled "Mayor's Office. Register of Free Colored Persons. 1840–1863," is on microfilm in LD, NOPL. On the nativist meeting see Joseph G. Treagle Jr., *Louisiana in the Age of Jackson: A Clash of Cultures and Personalities* (Baton Rouge: Louisiana State University Press, 1999), 309–313.

44. Unlike his brother Pierre, Louis Alfred Duhart had not joined their parents in France. The power of attorney is "Procuration par Tinchant à Duhart," 12 May 1840, act 294, Notary Théodore Seghers, NONARC. The final transactions of the Tinchant/Vincent family are in the notarial volumes of Théodore Seghers for the years 1839 and 1840, NONARC.

45. See "Vente d'esclave des époux Tinchant à Gertrude négresse libre," 9 May 1840, act 288, Notary Théodore Seghers, NONARC.

46. Ibid.

47. On the complexities of citizenship and the right to travel see Martha S. Jones, "Leave of Court: African American Claims-Making in the Era of *Dred Scott v. Sandford*," in *Contested Democracy: Freedom, Race, and Power in American*

History, ed. M. Sinha and P. Von Eschen (New York: Columbia University Press, 2007), 54–74.

5. THE LAND OF THE RIGHTS OF MAN

1. The first quotation is from Édouard Tinchant, "Communiqué," *La Tribune de la Nouvelle-Orléans* (hereafter *La Tribune*), 21 July 1864. The second is from Édouard Tinchant to Máximo Gómez, 21 September 1899, sig. 3868/4161, leg. 30, Fondo Máximo Gómez (hereafter FMG), Archivo Nacional de Cuba (hereafter ANC).

2. See Jennifer Heuer, "One-Drop Rule in Reverse? Interracial Marriages in Napoleonic and Restoration France," *Law and History Review* 27 (2009): 515–548.

3. For the 1833 statute see Jean Baptiste Joseph Pailliet, *Manuel de droit français*, pt. 2 (Paris: Le Normant, 1837), 1915. The phrase concerning equality before the law occurs in both the Constitutional Charter of 1814 and that of 1830. On the colonial policy of the liberal regime of the 1830s see Denise Bouche, *Histoire de la colonisation française*, vol. 2, *Flux et reflux (1815–1962)* (Paris: Fayard, 1991), chap. 1.

4. See the marriage of Martin Duhart to the young widow of another sea captain on 28 November 1741, folio 118v, Registres de la paroisse Saint-Nicolas, Nantes, Archives départementales de la Loire-Atlantique. Martin Duhart appears as captain in two slaving voyages between the Gulf of Benin and Saint-Domingue. See records 475 and 522 in Jean Mettas, *Répertoire des expéditions négrières françaises au XVIIIe siècle* (Paris: Société française d'histoire d'outre-mer, 1984), vol. 1, 279, 303.

5. See chap. 2, art. 95, *Civil Code of the State of Louisiana* (Published by a citizen of Louisiana, 1825), 76. On the sequence of rules on immigration and marriage see Sue Peabody, *"There Are No Slaves in France": The Political Culture of Race and Slavery in the Ancien Régime* (New York: Oxford University Press, 1996), chap. 7; and Heuer, "One-Drop Rule." Marie Françoise Bayot is referred to as Suzette Duhart in "Vente d'esclaves, Françoise Bayot dite S. Duhart, fcl [femme de couleur libre], Joseph Jourdan" and the "Certificate du Conservateur des hypothèques" added to the same act calls her: "Françoise Bayot dite Bayotte alias Suzette Duhart." Both in Notary T. Seghers, 11 March 1831, act 82, New Orleans Notarial Archives Research Center.

6. Acte de mariage, 17 April 1832, État-Civil, Pau, Archives départementales des Pyrénées-Atlantiques (hereafter ADPA).

7. See the records of parcels 719 and 720, sheet A, 1833, Matrice cadastrale, ADPA.

8. On their situation, see the censuses of 1834, 1836, 1841, 1846, Recensement de la population, Section de Canfranc, Archives communales de Gan (hereafter AC-Gan), 1F4, and the purchases and sales of land in Registre des mutations de propriété (III P 3/2), Matrice cadastrale 1833, 1842, 1864, 1867, all in ADPA.

9. See the "Acte de mariage" dated 14 January 1840, act no. 2, 1840, Mariages, AC-Gan, 1821–1853, reproduced on roll 4, microfilm 5 Mi 230, ADPA.

10. Antoine Prost, *L'Enseignement en France (1800–1967)* (Paris: A. Colin, 1968), parts 1 and 2.

11. Heuer, "One-Drop Rule," 540.

12. For intermittent appearances of the name Duhart see the *Annuaire administratif, judiciaire et industriel du département des Basses-Pyrénées* for the years 1830 to 1848, under the heading "Liste électorale, Canton de Pau-Ouest, Gan."

13. See Paul Gonnet, "Esquisse de la crise économique en France de 1827 à 1832," *Revue d'histoire économique et sociale* 3 (1955): 249–292.

14. The contract is "Vente," 25 September 1840, act 904, 1840, Notary Pierre Sempé, ADPA.

15. For a population estimate for Gan, see "Dénombrement de la population," 1846, AC-Gan, 1F4, ADPA.

16. The death certificate of Marie Françoise Bayot (dated 8 November 1840, act n° 77) is in AC-Gan, Décès, 1821–1853, reproduced on microfilm roll 6, 5mi230, ADPA. The same microfilm includes the subsequent death certificate of Louis Duhart (16 February 1849).

17. See Patrick Weil, *Qu'est-ce qu'un Français? Histoire de la nationalité française depuis la Révolution* (Paris: Grasset, 2002), 42–47.

18. The index to naturalizations is described at http://www.archivesnationales. culture.gouv.fr/arn and can be consulted at the Centre d'accueil et de recherche des Archives nationales, Paris. On the complexities of women's citizenship see Jennifer Heuer, *The Family and the Nation: Gender and Citizenship in Revolutionary France, 1789–1830* (Ithaca, NY: Cornell University Press, 2005), chaps. 7 and 8.

19. See act 904, 25 September 1840, Notary Pierre Sempé, ADPA.

20. The property is described in the purchase document, cited above. *Le Mémorial des Pyrénées,* 31 October 1840, reported on the grape harvest in Gan and Jurançon.

21. See the 1841 census of Gan, Recensement de la population, Section de Bastarrous, AC-Gan, 1F4, ADPA; and Michel Demonet, *Tableau de l'agriculture française au milieu du XIXᵉ siècle: l'enquête de 1852* (Paris: Éditions de l'EHESS, 1990), 49. Nineteenth-century commentary on *métayage* includes Adrien de Gasparin, *Mémoire sur le métayage* (Lyon: Impr. de J.-M. Barret, 1832); and Lucien Rerolle, *Du colonage partiaire et spécialement du métayage* (Paris: Chevalier-Marescq et Co., 1888).

22. All three census reports are in Recensement de la population, Section de Bastarrous, AC-Gan, 1F4, ADPA.

23. "Jacques Tinchant[,] Américain, près du pont, Jurançon Basses-Pyrénées" appears as the address on a letter sent by Louis Alfred Duhart, 7 July 1854, cited in the typescript "Histoire des Tinchant," compiled by Xavier Tinchant in 1997 and revised by Philippe Struyf in 2002. We thank Philippe Struyf for sharing a copy of this family record with us.

24. Prost, *L'Enseignement en France,* 21–69.

25. The inspection report of the school is in the *Annuaire administratif, judiciaire et industriel des Basses-Pyrénées* (Pau: Vigancourt) for 1845, in the section titled "Éphéméride," for July. Gustave Flaubert, *Madame Bovary,* was serialized in *La Revue de Paris,* October through December 1856. Honoré de Balzac, *Louis Lambert* (Paris: Gosselin, 1832) and Alphonse Daudet, *Le Petit Chose* (Paris: Hetzel, 1868) also depicted this phenomenon.

26. See Joseph Delfour, *Histoire du lycée de Pau* (Pau: Garet, 1890). Joseph Tinchant appears in the appendix. Édouard Tinchant's name appears on the *palmarès,*

the list of prizewinners from the *lycée* of Pau published in *Le Mémorial des Pyrénées,* on 31 August 1852, when he was in *huitième* (at the age of 10); 25 August 1853, when he was in *septième*; and again on 26 August 1854, when he had reached *sixième.*

27. André Chervel, *Les Auteurs français, latins, et grecs au programme de l'enseignement secondaire de 1800 à nos jours* (Paris: Institut national de recherche pédagogique/Publications de la Sorbonne, 1986), 43–123.

28. On his graduation and move to Paris see the "notice biographique" in dossier 3788, Naturalisations, Ministère de la Justice, Archives générales du Royaume, Brussels. On the prize see Delfour, *Histoire,* 432.

29. See the writing of Jean-Charles Houzeau, who later met Joseph Tinchant in New Orleans, especially "Le journal noir, aux États-Unis, de 1863 à 1870 (1)," *Revue de Belgique* 11 (1872): 5–28, reference on 8.

30. For Rossi's published works see *Œuvres complètes de P. Rossi publiées sous les auspices du gouvernement italien. Cours de droit constitutionnel professé à la Faculté de droit de Paris,* vol. 1 (Paris: Librairie de Guillaumin et Cie, 1866), introduction, 1–12.

31. For transcripts of courses that Rossi delivered in Paris see P. Rossi, *Cours d'économie politique: année scolaire 1835–1836, semestre d'été* (Paris: Ébrard, 1836). Pages 57–58 deal with slavery.

32. On this period see the essays in Marcel Dorigny, ed., *Les Abolitions de l'esclavage: de L. F. Sonthonax à V. Schoelcher, 1793–1794–1848* (Saint-Denis and Paris: Presses universitaires de Vincennes and UNESCO, 1995).

33. The classic formulation of a language of rights, liberty, and dignity, published some years later, was Charles Renouvier, *Manuel républicain de l'homme et du citoyen. 1848* (Paris: Pagnerre, 1848; repr., Paris: Garnier Frères, 1981).

34. *Œuvres complètes de P. Rossi,* 1:9–10.

35. Lawrence C. Jennings, "Cyrille Bissette, Radical Black French Abolitionist," *French History* 9 (March 1995): 48–66.

36. See Blandine Kriegel, "Les droits de l'homme dans les déclarations de 1848 et de 1948," in *Les Droits de l'homme et le suffrage universel,* ed. Gérard Chianéa and Jean-Luc Chabot (Paris: Éditions L'Harmattan, 2000), 187–192; Jennings, "Cyrille Bissette," 63. On the ferment of 1848 see Maurice Agulhon, *1848 ou l'apprentissage de la République* (Paris: Éditions du Seuil, 1973), esp. chap. 1.

37. See Maurizio Gribaudi and Michèle Riot-Sarcey, *1848: la révolution oubliée* (Paris: La Découverte, 2009), prologue, chaps. 1 and 2.

38. On the dialogue between European ideals of 1848 and subsequent political thought in New Orleans, written at the moment of his friendship with Joseph Tinchant, see Jean-Charles Houzeau, *Lettres adressées des États-Unis à sa famille. 1857–1868,* ed. Hossam Elkhadem, Annette Félix, and Liliane Wellens–De Donder (Brussels: Centre national d'histoire des sciences, 1994), 303–314, 374–430.

39. Jean-François Soulet, *Les Pyrénées au XIXe siècle: l'éveil d'une société civile,* 2 vols. (Bordeaux: Éditions Sud Ouest, 2004), 332–333.

40. The phrase "Republic in the village" is from Maurice Agulhon, *La République au village* (Paris: Plon, 1979). On "aristocratic tyranny" see Édouard's letter to the editor of *La Tribune* (New Orleans), July 21, 1864.

41. See Jeanne Dauzié, ed., *La Vie politique dans les Basses-Pyrénées sous la Seconde République,* vol. 1 (Pau: Centre départemental de documentation péda-gogique, 1976), esp. documents 6, 9, 18, and 22.

42. Agulhon, *1848, 52–56.*

43. See the Circulaire ministérielle no. 358, in *Bulletin officiel de la Martinique,* 7 May 1848, 594; and *Le Moniteur universel* (Paris), 15 June 1848.

44. On Louis-Eugène Cavaignac and the repression of the June Days see Agul-hon, *1848, 68–75.* In the May 1849 elections in Pau, the Party of Order won the plurality with 27.4 percent of the vote, though the Moderate Republicans and the Democrat-Socialists, as they were known, polled 14 percent and 18.9 percent re-spectively. See Dauzié, *La Vie politique,* 2:27.

45. On Louisiana in the midcentury French popular imagination we thank our colleague François Weil, personal communications, 2008.

46. The quoted phrase is from Édouard Tinchant to Máximo Gómez, 21 Sep-tember 1899, sig. 3868/4161, leg. 30, FMG, ANC.

47. The census entry is household 4647, Fourth Ward, Third Municipality, New Orleans, Seventh Census of the United States, 1850, roll 238, United States National Archives (hereafter USNA) Microcopy M432.

48. "List of all Passengers taken on board the Mount Washington . . . at the Port of Bordeaux and bound for New-Orleans," from "Passenger Lists of Vessels Arriving at New Orleans, Louisiana, 1820–1902," RG 36, USNA, reproduced on roll 29, USNA Microcopy M259. Census entry for household 4647, cited above.

6. JOSEPH AND HIS BROTHERS

1. See the entries for household 4647, Fourth Ward, Third Municipality, New Orleans, Seventh Census of the United States, 1850, on roll 238, United States National Archives (hereafter USNA) Microcopy M432. The record of the marriage, dated 18 December 1849, is in St. Mary's Italian Church, Chartres St., Marriages, Persons of Color, vol. 1, Archives of the Archdiocese of New Orleans (hereafter AANO).

2. This letter from Joseph Tinchant to Élisabeth Vincent Tinchant, 19 March 1850, has remained in the hands of the family. A transcription was graciously pro-vided to us by Philippe Struyf, one of Joseph Tinchant's descendants. We thank the family warmly for their generosity in sharing these private papers and for giving us permission to quote from the letters. They will be cited as Tinchant Family Papers, in the possession of Philippe Struyf (TFP-PS).

3. See "Renonciation à droits d'usufruit par Marie Blanche Vve Aubert dans la Succsn Jean Détry," 28 January 1848, act 28, 1848; and "Inventaire de la succession de feu Mie Bch Pelon Vve J. B. Aubert," 24 & 25 January 1849, act 16, 1849, both in Notary Octave de Armas, New Orleans Notarial Archives Research Center (hereafter NONARC).

4. Joseph Tinchant to Élisabeth Vincent Tinchant, 19 March 1850, transcrip-tion in TFP-PS. For a discussion of unions that were seen as marriages by their participants, despite being denied that status by the Louisiana Civil Code, see Diana

Irene Williams, "'They Call It Marriage': The Louisiana Interracial Family and the Making of American Legitimacy" (PhD diss., Harvard University, 2007).

5. The manumission record is "Affranchiss^t par Marie-Blanche Peillon Vve Aubert à Sophie, Marie Antoinette & Frédéric Bruno, ses esclaves," 12 September 1832, act 457, Notary Octave de Armas, NONARC.

6. "Inventaire de la succession de feu M^{ie} B^{ch} Pelon Vve J. B. Aubert," 24 & 25 January 1849, act 16, Notary Octave de Armas, NONARC.

7. "Testament de M^{ie} Blanche Pelon Vve J^n B^{te} Aubert f.c.l. [femme de couleur libre]," 5 April 1848, act 102, 1848; and "Inventaire de la succession de feu M^{ie} B^{ch} Pelon Vve J. B. Aubert," 24 & 25 January 1849, act 16, 1849, both in Notary Octave de Armas, NONARC. The slave named Louis, alias Jean Godeaux or Jean Godo, aged about twenty-five, ended up being sold to [Marie] Antoinette [Lambert] De-Coud. See page 468 of Conveyance Office Book (hereafter COB) 52, Conveyance Office, New Orleans (hereafter CO, NO). Many of the widow's former slaves appear to have lived together. The 1850 census shows a household composed of the brick-layer Antoine Decoud, his wife A. [Marie-Antoinette] Lambert, their children, as well as Sophie Lambert, age forty-eight and born in Saint-Domingue, Frédéric Lambert, and one younger Lambert. See dwelling 644, Household 761, First Ward, Third Municipality, New Orleans, Seventh Census of the United States, 1850, roll 238, USNA Microcopy M432.

8. "Testament de M^{ie} Blanche Pelon Vve J^n B^{te} Aubert," 5 April 1848.

9. "La succession de Madame Lambert s'est vendue récemment. Parmi les esclaves vendues se trouvait Trois Sous qui est encore bien alerte. Nous l'avons achetée." Joseph Tinchant to Élisabeth Vincent Tinchant, 19 March 1850, transcription in TFP-PS. The sale of Trois-Sous for thirty-seven piastres, by act dated 18 March 1851, is recorded on page 466 of COB 54, CO, NO.

10. See *Cohen's New Orleans Directory for 1853* (New Orleans: printed at the office of the *Daily Delta*, 1852), 224. On tobacco see Lewis Cecil Gray, *History of Agriculture in the Southern United States to 1860,* vol. 2 (New York: Peter Smith, 1941), 774, 1037.

11. The power of attorney is enclosed within "Vente de propriété par Mons. Jacques Tinchant à Mons. Pierre Duhart," 12 March 1853, act 107, Notary Ducatel, NONARC. Jacques Tinchant had earlier relied on A. Soubie to handle his business affairs in New Orleans. See, for example, A. Soubie to Jacques Tinchant, 19 April 1849, folder 108, Mss. 472, Armand Soubie Papers, Historic New Orleans Collection, New Orleans, copy courtesy of Adriana Chira.

12. The purchase of "a certain negro man, slave for life, named Martin" is recorded in "Sale of Slave. Matias Martinez to Louis & Joseph Tinchant," 28 October 1854, Notary Alex Bienvenu, NONARC. Louis and Joseph paid $125 in "ready money." (Note: Surnames of Spanish origin, such as González or Martínez, often changed spelling in Louisiana, and the original accent marks were then dropped.) Martin Mitchel appears in household 1041, Seventh Ward, New Orleans, Ninth Census of the United States, 1870, roll 522, USNA Microcopy M593. On North Carolina as a point of departure, and New Orleans as a place of arrival, see Steven Deyle, *Carry Me Back: The Domestic Slave Trade in American Life* (New York: Oxford University Press, 2005), 44, 118.

13. On Juárez in New Orleans see Rafael de Zayas Enríquez, *Benito Juárez: Su vida—su obra* (Mexico: Tipografia de la Viuda de Francisco de Léon, 1906), 50. For a discussion of New Orleans cigar makers, focused in part on André Cailloux, see Stephen J. Ochs, *A Black Patriot and a White Priest: André Cailloux and Claude Paschal Maistre in Civil War New Orleans* (Baton Rouge: Louisiana State University Press, 2000), 27–28, 57–59.

14. For the new occupational listing see *Cohen's New Orleans Directory [. . .] for 1854* (New Orleans: printed at the office of the *Picayune*, 1854), 228. On the particularities of the commodity chain in tobacco, which can also be seen as a commodity web, see Barbara M. Hahn, *Making Tobacco Bright: Creating an American Commodity, 1617–1937* (Baltimore: Johns Hopkins University Press, 2011).

15. Jean Stubbs, *Tobacco on the Periphery: A Case Study in Cuban Labour History, 1860–1958* (Cambridge: Cambridge University Press, 1985). On Mexico see José González Sierra, *El monopolio del humo: Elementos para la historia del tabaco en México y algunos conflictos de tabaqueros veracruzanos: 1915–1930* (Xalapa: Universidad Veracruzana, 1987), 70–72.

16. On the attack of the fungus in the region of Jurançon see *Mémoires de l'Académie des sciences, inscriptions et belles-lettres de Toulouse* Series 4, vol. 2 (1852): 414–415.

17. For the sale of Pédemarie see "Vente," 1854, act 116, Notary Pierre Sempé, Archives départementales des Pyrénées-Atlantiques, Pau.

18. On agriculture and the economy see Jean-François Soulet, *Les Pyrénées au XIXᵉ siècle: l'éveil d'une société civile,* 2 vols. (Bordeaux: Éditions Sud Ouest, 2004), 321–385. A letter from Alfred Duhart on 7 July 1854 was addressed to "Monsieur Jacques Tinchant[,] Américain, près du pont, Jurançon-Basses-Pyrénées" (cited in "Histoire des Tinchant," compiled by Xavier Tinchant and revised by Philippe Struyf, TFP-PS). The 1856 power of attorney is in "Vente de propriété, Jacques Tinchant à Jean Ducoing," 21 February 1857, act 56, Notary Joseph Lisbony, NONARC.

19. See, for example, the Marine News column of the *Bee/L'Abeille* for 14 June 1856, announcing the arrival of the ship *Baden* from Antwerp, carrying among other things cigars. Joseph Tinchant later recalled that he saw Belgium as "in every way favorable for the establishment of a cigar factory," though he was then referring not to his 1856 journey, but to a return to Belgium from Mexico two decades later. See the "Notice biographique" submitted to the Belgian government along with his request for naturalization in 1893. File 3788, Naturalisations, Ministère de la Justice, Archives générales du Royaume, Brussels.

20. E. Witte, É. Gubin, J.-P. Nandrin, and G. Deneckere, *Nouvelle Histoire de Belgique,* vol. 1, *1830–1905* (Brussels: Éditions Complexe, 2005). On Antwerp's assets as a commercial center see Anne Winter, *Migrants and Urban Change: Newcomers to Antwerp, 1760–1860* (London: Pickering & Chatto, 2009), esp. chap. 4.

21. Reference to this passport appears in his file in the police registry of foreigners, drawn up when he arrived in Antwerp, cited below. Evidence of Jacques' loan to his older sons is found in the documents produced for a later lawsuit, Tinchant v. Tinchant (1881), file 2173, Fonds Cuylits, FelixArchief, Antwerp (hereafter FA).

22. See the police registration record of Joseph Tinchant, number 14046, dated 22 December 1856, and that of Edmond Dédé, number 14012, dated 24 December 1856, both in the microfilm collection of the Vreemdelingendossiers, 1856–1857, Modern Archief (hereafter MA), FA.

23. The purchaser in this 6 December 1856 transaction was Joseph Benito "of this city." See page 426, COB 70, CO, NO. A preliminary search of the conveyance books has not yielded any purchases or sales of slaves by the family after 1856.

24. See the entry for 188 Boeksteeg on the list of residents called the Burgerlijke Stand, Antwerpen, 1856–1866, in MA, FA. On Belgium in these years see Sophie de Schaepdrijver, *Elites for the Capital? Foreign Migration to Mid-Nineteenth-Century Brussels* (Amsterdam: Thesis Publishers, 1990), esp. 16–17; F. Suykens et al., eds., *Antwerp: A Port for All Seasons*, 2nd ed. (Antwerp: MIM Publishing Co., 1986), 354–418; and Winter, *Migrants and Urban Change*.

25. For a social history of Antwerp in these years see Catharina Lis, *Social Change and the Labouring Poor: Antwerp, 1770–1860* (New Haven, CT: Yale University Press, 1986). On pages 71–73 she discusses what she refers to as the "Boeksteeg ghetto." Salomon Benni appears on the list of residents of 188 Boeksteeg, cited above.

26. The arrivals can be dated based on the information in the 1856–1857 list of residents of 188 Boeksteeg, cited above. It is not quite clear where the third son, Pierre, was at this moment; he may have followed Joseph to New Orleans some years earlier.

27. See the entry for 188 Boeksteeg, cited above.

28. The sale of these lots to A. Brousseau, 5 March 1857, is recorded on page 590, COB 70, CO, NO. For the transatlantic crossing see the list of passengers on board the *Philadelphia,* in the *New York Times,* 14 May 1858.

29. On the residences and occupations of the three Tinchant brothers see the entries for dwelling 1152 and dwelling 1201, Sixth Ward, New Orleans, Eighth Census of the United States, 1860, roll 419, USNA Microcopy M653.

30. The marriage of Joseph and Stéphanie is recorded on page 128, Parish of St. Ann, Marriages, vol. 2, 1856–1859, AANO.

31. See Mary Niall Mitchell, *Raising Freedom's Child: Black Children and Visions of the Future after Slavery* (New York: NYU Press, 2008), 16–21. Many of the records of the school are in AANO. For the activities of Joseph Tinchant see "Journal des séances de la direction, 23 avril 1859 à 4 mai 1875," particularly the minutes of sessions of 2 May 1859 and 1 July 1860, in AANO.

32. See the entries in Louisiana, vol. 2, p. 324, R. G. Dun & Co. Collection, Baker Library, Historical Collections, Harvard Business School. For an example of these advertisements see page 6 of the *Daily Picayune,* 2 May 1857.

33. For the full household in Antwerp see the Vreemdelingendossiers and the entry in the Burgerlijke Stand, both cited above. The sending of Augustus Clément Joseph to Belgium is recounted in the papers of a subsequent lawsuit, Quanone v. Tinchant, file 1792, Fonds Cuylits, FA.

34. On the politics of secession and the early war years in New Orleans see Justin A. Nystrom, *New Orleans after the Civil War: Race, Politics, and a New Birth of Freedom* (Baltimore: Johns Hopkins University Press, 2010), chap. 1.

35. On Lanusse more generally see Caryn Cossé Bell, *Revolution, Romanticism, and the Afro-Creole Protest Tradition in Louisiana, 1718–1868* (Baton Rouge: Louisiana State University Press, 1997), 125, 232–233.

36. See James G. Hollandsworth Jr., *The Louisiana Native Guards: The Black Military Experience during the Civil War* (Baton Rouge: Louisiana State University Press, 1995), chap. 1; Shirley Elizabeth Thompson, *Exiles at Home: The Struggle to Become American in Creole New Orleans* (Cambridge, MA: Harvard University Press, 2009), chap. 5; and Ochs, *Black Patriot,* chap. 3. The quotation is from Nystrom, *New Orleans,* 21. References to the enlistments of Armand, Gustave, and Paul Gonzales appear in the online database maintained by the U.S. National Park Service, Civil War Soldiers & Sailors System, http://www.itd.nps.gov/cwss/.

37. Joseph's letter of resignation was accepted at the meeting on 3 January 1862. See "Journal de séances de la direction . . . 23 avril 1859 à 4 mai 1875," AANO.

38. See, for example, an article concerning rumors that the northern states would henceforth consider slaves who resisted their masters in the seceded states to be free. Later dispatches clarified that the rumors were an exaggeration, but the stock market in Paris was said to have wavered in the face of the apparent possibility of "un appel à l'insurrection servile" (an appeal for a slave uprising). *Le Précurseur* (Antwerp), 11 July 1861. The wrangle over tuition payment can be reconstructed from Quanone v. Tinchant, file 1792, Fonds Cuylits, FA.

39. For the family's street address see *Le Double Guide commercial ou Livre d'adresses de la ville et faubourgs d'Anvers* (Antwerp: Ratinckx Frères, [October] 1862), 154. On Jacques' view of Édouard's behavior see Édouard Tinchant to his mother, 1 October 1861; and Édouard Tinchant to his parents, 25 December 1861, transcriptions in TFP-PS.

40. See Édouard Tinchant to his mother, 1 October 1861, transcription in TFP-PS. The genealogy compiled by Xavier Tinchant, and revised by Philippe Struyf, notes the absence of an official record of Édouard's departure. See page 40, "Histoire des Tinchant," TFP-PS.

41. Édouard Tinchant to his parents, 25 December 1861, transcription in TFP-PS.

42. The literature on the European intervention is substantial, and interpretations of the motives of Napoléon III vary. For an overview of the historiography see Erika Pani, *El segundo imperio: Pasados de usos múltiples* (Mexico City: Centro de Investigación y Docencia Económicas, 2004). See also Jean Avenel, *La Campagne du Mexique (1862–1867): la fin de l'hégémonie européenne en Amérique du Nord* (Paris: Economica, 1996); and Brian Hamnett, *Juárez* (London: Longman, 1994), chaps. 4 and 8.

43. Édouard Tinchant to his parents, 25 December 1861, transcription in TFP-PS. On the details of the French expedition see Avenel, *La Campagne du Mexique,* chap. 3; and Jean-François Lecaillon, *La Campagne du Mexique: récits de soldats, 1862–1867* (Paris: Bernard Giovanangeli, 2006), 5–14.

44. See Édouard Tinchant to his parents, 25 December 1861, transcription in TFP-PS. The term *crapuleux* carries a strong intimation of illegality as well.

45. The address on Prieur Street is given in Édouard Tinchant's later file in Carton 127, Série D, Année 1897, Consulat, Nouvelle-Orléans, Ministère des Affaires

Étrangères, Centre des archives diplomatiques de Nantes, France (hereafter CADN). He reported on the Gonzaleses' hospitality in Édouard Tinchant to his parents, 28 October 1863, transcription in TFP-PS.

46. Édouard refers to himself as an abolitionist in a letter to his mother dated 28 October 1863, transcription in TFP-PS.

47. The registration document is copied in Édouard's file in Carton 127, Série D, Année 1897, Consulat, Nouvelle-Orléans, CADN.

48. As noted in Chapter 5, it is not clear that Élisabeth Vincent [Tinchant] could have made such a claim to French nationality on her own, given that she was married to a man who may have been seen as foreign. On the requirements for citizenship in this period see Patrick Weil, *Qu'est-ce qu'un français? Histoire de la nationalité française depuis la Révolution,* expanded ed. (Paris: Gallimard, 2004), 67–73.

49. On the role of the French consul in the earlier question of conscription in the Confederate forces see Farid Ameur, "'Au nom de la France, restons unis!' Les milices françaises de la Nouvelle-Orléans pendant la guerre de sécession," *Bulletin de l'Institut Pierre Renouvin* 28 (Fall 2008): 81–106.

50. See the letters from the consul during June 1863 in "Correspondance avec la légation puis l'ambassade de France à Washington, juin 1863–juin 1864," in the papers of the Consulat de France à la Nouvelle-Orléans, reproduced on microfilm 2mi2327, CADN.

51. The French consul saw these activities as a violation of U.S. neutrality in the war between France and Mexico and raised objections with Secretary of State William Seward. See the reports of the consul and excerpts from Seward's reply in the letter from the French Legation to the consul in New Orleans, 2 June 1864, reproduced on microfilm 2mi2327, CADN. For Édouard's later discussion of his views concerning Napoléon III, see Chapter 7.

52. Jean-Charles Houzeau, "Le journal noir, aux Etats-Unis, de 1863 à 1870 (1)," *Revue de Belgique* 11 (1872): 5–28, esp. 8. This series of essays has been translated as Jean-Charles Houzeau, *My Passage at the New Orleans Tribune,* edited and with an introduction by David C. Rankin (Baton Rouge: Louisiana State University Press, 1984).

53. On these "sixty-day volunteers" see Ochs, *Black Patriot,* 156 and 156n. Édouard's letters home gave a dramatic account of his declaration of Unionist sympathies. See Édouard Tinchant to his mother, 28 October 1863, transcription in TFP-PS. He quoted gloating racist pronouncements made by his business associates during the early phase of the attack on Port Hudson and wrote that he could no longer hold back from expressing his own abolitionist convictions.

54. *L'Union* (New Orleans), 30 June 1863. Joseph Tinchant's role in recruitment is also described in a later article titled "Émigration," in *La Tribune de la Nouvelle-Orléans* (hereafter *La Tribune*), 25 August 1864.

55. *L'Union,* 30 June 1863.

56. The original certificate of Joseph's commission from Governor Shepley is in TFP-PS. See also the summary record of Tenchant [*sic*], Joseph, in Civil War [Union], Compiled Service Records, entry 519A, RG 94, USNA, reproduced on USNA microcopy M1820.

57. See the entry for household 1854, Sixth Ward, New Orleans, Louisiana, Eighth Census of the United States, 1860, roll 419, USNA Microcopy M653. Excerpts from the Union service records of the three Gonzales brothers appear in USNA Microcopy M1820, compiled as part of the online database U.S. Colored Troops, Military Service Records, 1861–1865, accessed through Ancestry.com.

58. Édouard Tinchant's name does not appear in the Civil War [Union], Compiled Service Records, cited above, and there seem to be very few surviving records from this short-lived unit. Édouard discussed his military service in detail in "Communiqué" (*La Tribune*, 21 July 1864), however, and others were apparently familiar with it. A photograph of Edouard in his Union uniform is in the papers of his descendants; we have seen a copy held by Philippe Struyf in Antwerp, and another conveyed by the late Xavier Tinchant to historian Mary Gehman in Donaldsonville, Louisiana.

59. *Jean-Charles Houzeau. Lettres adressés des États-Unis à sa famille: 1857–1868*, ed. Hossam Elkhadem, Annette Félix, and Liliane Wellens–De Donder (Brussels: Centre national d'histoire des sciences, 1994), 86.

60. The reference to "nos créoles" is in Édouard Tinchant to his parents, 28 October 1863, transcription in TFP-PS. The funeral is described in Ochs, *Black Patriot*, 1–5.

61. See Édouard Tinchant to his parents, 28 October 1863, transcription in TFP-PS. In describing the behavior of Union soldiers Édouard wrote that the Yankees had begun to treat the officers and soldiers of color like *nègres*. Édouard had earlier used the term *nègres* as a translation for the epithet "niggers" used by boastful pro-Confederates, but in this context "comme des nègres" may have implied "like slaves."

62. See the description of the episode in Édouard Tinchant's 21 July 1864 "Communiqué" in *La Tribune*, discussed in Chapter 7.

63. On the "vexations and humiliations" to which Joseph was subjected see the article "Émigration," *La Tribune*, 25 August 1864. On Banks's policy vis-à-vis officers of color see Hollandsworth, *Louisiana Native Guards*, 43–44.

64. Jules Tinchant to Joseph Tinchant, 5 June 1864, included in the appendices to the lawyer's case file of a later suit, Tinchant v. Tinchant, 1881, file 2173, Fonds Cuylits, FA; and Édouard Tinchant to his parents, 28 October 1863, transcription in TFP-PS.

65. For the reference to his Xavier cousins, see Édouard Tinchant to Élisabeth Vincent Tinchant, 3 December 1864, transcription in TFP-PS.

66. See the careful discussion of *L'Union* in Thompson, *Exiles*, 216–221.

67. Lanusse's major article on this theme was titled "Maximilien au Mexique" and appeared in *L'Union*, 12 July 1864. See also the founding document for the Eureka colony, later published as a pamphlet in New Orleans with the title *Documents (traduits) relatifs à la colonie d'Eureka, dans l'état de Veracruz, République Mexicaine* (New Orleans: Impr. Méridier, 1857).

68. Alfred J. Hanna and Kathryn Abbey Hanna, "The Immigration Movement of the Intervention and Empire as Seen through the Mexican Press," *Hispanic American Historical Review* 27 (May 1947): 220–246.

69. See Hamnett, *Juárez,* 152–157. See also Hanna and Hanna, "Immigration Movement," and the discussion of this call in the newspaper *L'Estafette* (Mexico).

70. "Maximilien au Mexique," *L'Union,* 12 July 1864.

71. For a discussion of the ending of slavery in Louisiana see Rebecca J. Scott, *Degrees of Freedom: Louisiana and Cuba after Slavery* (Cambridge, MA: Harvard University Press, 2005), 30–36.

72. See Peyton McCrary, *Abraham Lincoln and Reconstruction: The Louisiana Experiment* (Princeton, NJ: Princeton University Press, 1978); "The Legal Status of the Colored People," from the *Era,* reprinted in the *New York Times,* 10 July 1864; and *Louisiana, Debates in the Convention for the Revision and Amendment of the Constitution of the State of Louisiana . . . April 6, 1864* (New Orleans: W. R. Fish, 1864). Discussion of the actions of Judge Handlin appears on, among others, pages 552–559. The abolition of slavery appeared as Article 1 of the 1864 constitution, and the rules for suffrage remained somewhat open-ended (631, 633).

73. See also Hollandsworth, *Louisiana Native Guards,* 2–7.

74. Édouard Tinchant's opening salvo in the exchange with Armand Lanusse seems to have come in a July 1864 issue of *L'Union* that has not survived. For the continuation of the exchange see Lanusse, "Communiqué," *L'Union,* 19 July 1864, and the discussion in Chapter 7.

7. "THE TERM PUBLIC RIGHTS SHOULD BE MADE TO MEAN SOMETHING"

1. Armand Lanusse, "Explication," 8 October 1862; and "Communiqué," 19 May 1863; both in *L'Union* (New Orleans).

2. See Armand Lanusse, "Maximilien au Mexique," *L'Union,* 12 July 1864; and "Communiqué," *L'Union,* 19 July 1864.

3. In these weeks, detailed news was reaching New Orleans of what the *New York World* reported to have been the triumphal entry into Mexico City of Maximilian and his wife. "Nouvelles du Mexique," and Lanusse, "Communiqué," both in *L'Union,* 19 July 1864.

4. Lanusse, "Communiqué," *L'Union,* 19 July 1864. The attorney general's ruling is discussed in "The Legal Status of the Colored People," *New York Times,* 10 July 1864.

5. See Édouard Tinchant, "Communiqué," *La Tribune de la Nouvelle-Orléans* (hereafter *La Tribune*), 21 July 1864. On the goals of the French expedition see Jean Avenel, *La Campagne du Mexique (1862–1867)* (Paris: Éditions L'Harmattan, 1994); Alain Gouttman, *La Guerre du Mexique (1862–1867): le Mirage américain de Napoléon III* (Paris: Perrin, 2008).

6. Tinchant, "Communiqué," *La Tribune,* 21 July 1864. Tinchant wrote throughout in the first person plural *(nous)* rather than the singular *(je)*—a convention taught to students in French *lycée,* meant to convey an appropriate humility.

7. *Opinion of Attorney General Bates on Citizenship* (Washington, DC: Government Printing Office, 1863). Discussed in *L'Union,* 25 December 1862; copies advertised for sale in *L'Union,* 19 May 1863.

8. On the complexities of federal policy in Louisiana see Peyton McCrary, *Abraham Lincoln and Reconstruction: The Louisiana Experiment* (Princeton, NJ: Princeton University Press, 1978). The convention was still in session in July, when this exchange took place. *Louisiana, Debates in the Convention for the Revision and Amendment of the Constitution of the State of Louisiana . . . April 6, 1864* (New Orleans: W. R. Fish, 1864). Tinchant, "Communiqué," *La Tribune,* 21 July 1864.

9. Tinchant, "Communiqué," *La Tribune,* 21 July 1864.

10. Ibid. The phrase Édouard used for nationality was "qualité de Français." The exact citizenship status of French nationals who joined local military forces in Louisiana was murky. These issues had been formally debated during the Confederate period but were less clear-cut after Union occupation. See Farid Ameur, "'Au nom de la France, restons unis!' Les milices françaises de la Nouvelle-Orléans pendant la guerre de sécession," *Bulletin de l'Institut Pierre Renouvin* 28 (Fall 2008): 81–106.

11. The effort to gain recognition as a citizen through military service had a long history in Louisiana. See Caryn Cossé Bell, *Revolution, Romanticism, and the Afro-Creole Protest Tradition in Louisiana, 1718–1868* (Baton Rouge: Louisiana State University Press, 1997), 11, 30–33.

12. On Thomas Durant and the Friends of Universal Suffrage see Justin Nystrom, *New Orleans after the Civil War: Race, Politics, and a New Birth of Freedom* (Baltimore: Johns Hopkins University Press, 2010), 70; and Jean-Charles Houzeau, "Le journal noir, aux États-Unis, de 1863 à 1870," *Revue de Belgique* 11 (May–June 1872): 5–28, 97–122.

13. Her father, Mortimer Debergue, a bricklayer listed as mulatto, and her mother, Louise, appear in household 2745, Second Ward, Third Municipality, New Orleans, Seventh Census of the United States,1850, reproduced on roll 238, United States National Archives (hereafter USNA) Microcopy M432; and households 1450 and 1451, Seventh Ward, New Orleans, Eighth Census of the United States, 1860, on roll 419, USNA Microcopy M653. Édouard Tinchant's role as Commandant of Post No. 4 of the GAR appears in *La Tribune,* 31 October 1867.

14. See James G. Hollandsworth Jr., *An Absolute Massacre: The New Orleans Race Riot of July 30, 1866* (Baton Rouge: Louisiana State University Press, 2001). The quotation is cited on page 44. See also Nystrom, *New Orleans,* chap. 2.

15. A vivid account of the police riot is provided in *Jean-Charles Houzeau. Lettres adressés des États-Unis à sa famille: 1857–1868,* ed. Hossam Elkhadem, Annette Félix, and Liliane Wellens–De Donder (Brussels: Centre national d'histoire des sciences, 1994), 396–400. Hollandsworth, *Absolute Massacre,* cites the quotation from the policeman on page 89. See his chaps. 9–12 for the events on the day of the convention; the quotation from Sheridan is on the page preceding the table of contents. The estimates of the death toll, made by Surgeon Hartsuff at the time, are on page 141.

16. On the reaction see Eric Foner, *Reconstruction: America's Unfinished Revolution, 1863–1877* (New York: Harper & Row, 1988), 263.

17. The three teachers were listed as "E. Tinchand, colored, educated in France, principal; Victor Garderre, colored; Eugène Lucie, colored." Minutes of the Orleans

Parish School Board, 16 September 1867, in Louisiana and Special Collections Department, Earl K. Long Library, University of New Orleans (hereafter LSCD, UNO).

18. Joseph Logsdon and Donald Devore, *Crescent City Schools: Public Education in New Orleans, 1841–1991* (Lafayette, LA: Center for Louisiana Studies, 1991), chap. 2, esp. 64–70.

19. Houzeau, "Le journal noir," 112–116.

20. The progress of the election can be followed in both the French and the English pages of the *Tribune*. Tinchant's proposal on the flag is in *Official Journal of the Proceedings of the Convention for Framing a Constitution for the State of Louisiana* (New Orleans: J. B. Roudanez, 1867–1868), 12.

21. *Official Journal of the Proceedings,* 35. In a subsequent session, Tinchant went on to speak explicitly about breach of promise. See *Official Journal of the Proceedings,* 192.

22. The license, dated 10 December 1867, is in Marriage Licenses 1848–1880, Third Justice of the Peace, vol. 6, page 345; the certificate, also dated 10 December 1867, is in Marriage Certificates, 1846–1880, Third Justice of the Peace, vol. 6, page 52; both on microfilm in the Louisiana Division, New Orleans Public Library. We are grateful to Greg Osborn, archivist at the New Orleans Public Library, and to Ana Julieta Teodoro Cleaver for having located these two documents. The naturalization of Louis A. De Tornos in October 1868 is indexed on roll 4 of "Card Index to Naturalizations in Louisiana," USNA Microcopy P2087.

23. *Official Journal of the Proceedings,* 58, 115–117.

24. See Rebecca J. Scott, "Public Rights, Social Equality, and the Conceptual Roots of the *Plessy* Challenge," *Michigan Law Review* 106 (March 2008): 777–804. Arago's instructions appear in the circular on the enforcement of the decree of 27 April 1848, Circulaire ministérielle No. 358 of 7 May 1848, in *Bulletin officiel de la Martinique,* 594.

25. *Official Journal of the Proceedings,* 115–117; Rebecca J. Scott, *Degrees of Freedom: Louisiana and Cuba after Slavery* (Cambridge, MA: Harvard University Press, 2005), chap. 2.

26. *Official Journal of the Proceedings,* 115–117.

27. *New Orleans Times,* 28 December 1867.

28. Pinchback's statements do not appear in the *Official Journal of the Proceedings* but are conveyed, along with the quotation (or paraphrase) from Tinchant, in the *New Orleans Times,* 28 December 1867. Beth Kressel has traced Pinchback's changing views on public rights in her study of the post-1868 public rights litigation in Louisiana. See "Creating 'what might have been a fuss': Litigating in Defense of Equal Public Rights in Reconstruction-era Louisiana," forthcoming, cited by permission of the author.

29. *Official Journal of the Proceedings,* 115–118, 293–294.

30. This is the final text. The votes on the near-final text, as proposed by Belden, are in *Official Journal of the Proceedings,* 123–125.

31. *Official Journal of the Proceedings,* 192.

32. For a discussion of such unions in Louisiana see Diana Irene Williams, "'They Call it Marriage': The Interracial Louisiana Family and the Making of American Legitimacy" (PhD diss., Harvard University, 2007).

33. See the recollections of Rodolphe Desdunes, *Nos Hommes et notre histoire* (Montreal: Arbour & Dupont, 1911), chap. 11. Houzeau discusses the election and the convention on pages 112–116 of Jean-Charles Houzeau, "Le journal noir," 97–122.

34. See Sauvinet v. Walker 25 La. Ann. 14 (1875); and the transcript of testimony in John G. Benson, Plaintiff in Error, v. Josephine Decuir, in error to the Supreme Court of Louisiana, filed October 6, 1875, in Louisiana Supreme Court Historical Archives, Earl K. Long Library, UNO. The major cases are discussed in Roger A. Fischer, *The Segregation Struggle in Louisiana, 1862–77* (Urbana: University of Illinois Press, 1974), 69–70, and 142–143. For an analysis of the full range of locally initiated civil actions see Kressel "Creating 'What might have been a fuss.'"

35. See Francis H. Smith, *Proceedings of the National Union Republican Convention Held at Philadelphia, June 5 and 6, 1872* (Washington, DC: Gibson Brothers, 1872), 51; and M. A. Clancy, *Proceedings of the Republican National Convention Held at Cincinnati, Ohio June 14, 15, and 16, 1876* (Concord, NH: Republican Press Association, 1876), 56.

36. Hall v. Decuir 95 US 485 (1878) at 488–91, reversing Decuir v. Benson, 27 La. Ann. 1. See also Fischer, *Segregation Struggle,* 142–143.

37. See the discussion in Scott, "Public Rights, Social Equality," 790–794; and *Degrees of Freedom,* 70–77. In an 1888 essay, George Washington Cable wrote: "I saw that while private society always must and can take care of itself and its own complete defense, the day must come when the Negro must share and enjoy in common with the white race the whole scale of *public* rights and advantages provided under American government." See Cable, "My Politics" (1888), in Arlin Turner, *The Negro Question: A Selection of Writings on Civil Rights in the South* (New York: Norton, 1958), 9, 10.

38. On Warmoth's rule see Lawrence Powell, "Centralization and Its Discontents in Reconstruction Louisiana," *Studies in American Political Development* 20 (Fall 2006): 105–131. Tinchant's complaint appears in Vol. 61, Pt. 1, Entry 4574, Records of Letters Received, Civil Affairs, Fifth Military District, RG 393, USNA.

39. See Donald Devore and Joseph Logsdon, *Crescent City Schools: Public Education in New Orleans, 1841–1991* (Lafayette: University of Southwestern Louisiana, 1991), chap. 2; and Report of Committee on Col. Schools, in Minutes, 2 October 1867, Orleans Parish School Board, LSCD, UNO.

40. See the letter from Jules Tinchant to Joseph Tinchant, 15 June 1864, Tinchant v. Tinchant, Fonds Cuylits, FA.

41. The closing of the Tinchant Brothers cigar business was recorded after the war in Louisiana, vol. II, p. 324, of the R. G. Dun & Co. Collection, Baker Library, Historical Collections, Harvard Business School. The actual closing occurred in 1864, with the departure of Joseph Tinchant for Veracruz.

42. The *Directory of the City of Mobile* (Matzenger, 1861) lists six cigar dealers. Additional cigar makers apparently arrived in the diaspora of Cuban refugees after 1868.

43. On sea bathing see Jules Tinchant to Mme. Jacques Tinchant, 4 September 1859, and 5 November 1859, transcription in Tinchant Family Papers, in the

possession of Philippe Struyf. A note appeared in the *Mobile Register* many years later: "Mr. Louis Tinchant ... made the foundation of his prosperity and fortune in New Orleans before the war, where he was recognized in business circles as among the foremost of the Creole citizens of the Crescent city." *Mobile Register,* 11 December 1887; citation courtesy of Martha S. Jones.

44. On the overall composition of the Seventh Ward, and the rapid postwar growth of a poor African American population in the city, see Michael Fitzgerald, *Urban Emancipation: Popular Politics in Reconstruction Mobile, 1860–1890* (Baton Rouge: Louisiana State University Press, 2002), 21–22. The entries for Edward and Louisa Tinchant are household 1405, Seventh Ward, Mobile, Alabama, Ninth Census of the United States, 1870, reproduced on roll 31, USNA Microcopy M593. For election results see the *Mobile Daily Register,* 10 November 1870.

45. See Fitzgerald, *Urban Emancipation,* 209.

46. Household 1405, Seventh Ward, Mobile, Alabama, Ninth Census of the United States, 1870, reproduced on roll 31, USNA Microcopy M593.

47. See the *Mobile Daily Register* for 1 July, 20 August, and 11 November, 1870.

8. HORIZONS OF COMMERCE

1. See Jules Tinchant to Ernest Tinchant, 20 October 1861, transcription, Tinchant Family Papers, in the possession of Philippe Struyf (hereafter TFP-PS).

2. See Brian Coutts, "Boom and Bust: The Rise and Fall of the Tobacco Industry in Spanish Louisiana, 1770–1790," *Americas* 42 (January 1986): 289–309. On the attractions of Mexico for free families of color in New Orleans see Mary Niall Mitchell, *Raising Freedom's Child: Black Children and Visions of the Future after Slavery* (New York: NYU Press, 2008), chap. 1.

3. See David Skerritt, "A Negotiated Ethnic Identity: San Rafael, a French Community on the Mexican Gulf Coast (1833)," *Cahiers des sciences humaines* 30 (1994): 455–474. On the vanilla trade see Emilio Kourí, *A Pueblo Divided: Business, Property, and Community in Papantla, Mexico* (Stanford, CA: Stanford University Press, 2004), 88, 101.

4. See Jules Tinchant to Ernest Tinchant, 20 October 1861; and Jules Tinchant to Jacques Tinchant, 16 August 1862, transcriptions, TFP-PS. On yellow fever at Jicaltepec see Antonio García Cubas, *Escritos diversos de 1870 a 1874* (México, Imprenta de Ignacio Escalante, 1874), esp. 203–210; Jean-Christophe Demard, *Jicaltepec: chronique d'un village français au Mexique* (Paris: Les éditions du porteglaive); and Simone Gache, "Une colonie française au Mexique (San Rafael Jicaltepec)," *Population* 4 (1949): 553–554.

5. Jules Tinchant to Ernest Tinchant, 20 October 1861, transcription, TFP-PS.

6. On the French intervention and the Mexican Second Empire see Chapter 7, note 5; Erika Pani, *El segundo imperio: Pasados de usos múltiples* (Mexico City: Centro de Investigación y Docencia Económicas and Fondo de Cultura Económica, 2004); and Jean-François Lecaillon, *La Campagne du Mexique* (Paris: Bernard Giovangeli Éditeur, 2006). French commander Charles Ferdinand Latrille declared: "We are so superior to the Mexicans in race, organization, morality and

devoted sentiments that I beg your excellency to inform the Emperor that as the head of 6,000 soldiers I am already master of Mexico." Quoted in Michael C. Meyer and William H. Beezley, *The Oxford History of Mexico* (New York: Oxford University Press, 2000), 381.

7. On the noncommittal position of the colonists in Jicaltepec see Skerritt, "Negotiated Ethnic Identity," 459. On tobacco see Carmen Blázquez Domínguez, *Veracruz Liberal (1858–1860)* (México, D. F.: El Colegio de México, A.C., 1986), 195–196. The store run by Jules is described in the French translation of the 8 April 1865 notarized document that later established Tinchant Hermanos, deposited in the case file of the lawsuit styled Tinchant v. Tinchant, now with file 2173, papers of the lawyer Cuylits, in the FelixArchief, Antwerp (hereafter Fonds Cuylits, FA).

8. See Armand Lanusse, "Maximilien au Mexique," *L'Union* (New Orleans), 12 July 1864.

9. See Blázquez Domínguez, *Veracruz Liberal*, 195–196.

10. See the passenger list of the *Carisimo*, arriving in March 1864, in Passenger Lists of Vessels Arriving at New Orleans, Louisiana, 1820–1902, RG 30, reproduced on roll 50, United States National Archives (hereafter USNA) Microcopy M259.

11. Jules was emphatic that Édouard not be included in the plan, however, apparently believing that his behavior could hurt the others' reputation. See Jules Tinchant to Joseph Tinchant, 5 June 1864, file 2173, Fonds Cuylits, FA.

12. See "Émigration," *La Tribune*, 25 August 1864, and "Mémoire de Joseph Tinchant sur son frère Pierre," undated, file 2173, Fonds Cuylits, FA.

13. "Émigration," *La Tribune*, 25 August 1864. The article quotes a couplet that was a favorite of Lanusse's and reiterates the theme of the respect of the Mexican government for equal rights.

14. See their 8 April 1865 founding document; the undated "Rectifications" submitted by Joseph Tinchant to his attorney; the letter from Joseph Tinchant to John Hart, 1879; and evidence of the partial repayment of their initial loan in a set of replies prepared by Jules Tinchant's lawyer C. G. Brack, dated 22 June 188[1?]; all in file 2173, Fonds Cuylits, FA.

15. For the date and place of baptism see the copy of the 1895 marriage certificate of Vincent Tinchant, TFP-PS. On Cazonera's location and landscape see Kourí, *Pueblo Divided*, chap. 2. On the hydrology of the area see Ricardo Javier Garnica Peña and Irasema Alcántara Ayala, "Riesgos por inundación asociados a eventos de precipitación extraordinaria en el curso bajo del río Tecolutla, Veracruz," *Investigaciones Geográficas, Boletín del Instituto de Geografía, UNAM* 55 (2004): 23–45.

16. We thank Barbara Hahn for clarifying the concept of the "commodity chain" in tobacco, and John Womack for generously sharing his unpublished work on tobacco in Veracruz. See Barbara M. Hahn, *Making Tobacco Bright: Creating an American Commodity, 1617–1937* (Baltimore: Johns Hopkins University Press, 2011).

17. On tobacco see Kourí, *Pueblo Divided*, 58–63; and José González Sierra, *Monopolio del humo: Elementos para la historia del tabaco en México y algunos conflictos de tabaqueros veracruzanos* (Xalapa: Centro de Investigaciones Históricas, Universidad Veracruzana, 1987), 70–76.

18. See the 1873 "Escritura de venta de un sitio y casa en la Congregación de 'Barriles,' otorgada por José Tenchant [*sic*]," act 36, registered 15 April 1890, in "Libro de Registro Público," Notary Isaac M. Fuentes, Registro Público de la Propiedad, Papantla, consulted by Bruno Renero-Hannan, January 2011.

19. See "Comptabilité de la société Tinchant Hermanos"; and Louis Tinchant to Joseph Tinchant, 10 April 1867, in file 2173, Fonds Cuylits, FA.

20. See the impatient letter from Louis Tinchant to Joseph Tinchant, 10 April 1867, file 2173, Fonds Cuylits, FA; and the typed copy of an 1867 *quittance* from Jacques to Louis, TFP-PS.

21. The journey to New Orleans of Pierre in July 1865, and one by Jules in 1866, as well as a recitation of financial woes by Louis Tinchant to Joseph Tinchant, 13 June 1867, are all recorded in file 2173, Fonds Cuylits, FA.

22. The accounts of these bitter disagreements spilled out in the 1881 lawsuit Tinchant v. Tinchant, file 2173, Fonds Cuylits, FA.

23. See Jasper Ridley, *Maximilian and Juárez* (London: Constable, 1993), 210; and Joseph E. Chance, *José María de Jesús Carvajal: The Life and Times of a Mexican Revolutionary* (San Antonio, TX: Trinity University Press, 2006), chap. 10.

24. For Jules' perspective on the Mexican conflict as of 1866 see Jules Tinchant to Joseph Tinchant, 5 December 1866, file 2173, Fonds Cuylits, FA.

25. The story of service to Juárez became part of the unofficial biographical sketch of José Tinchant prepared by some of his descendants. One version of this text is titled "Biographie de José Tinchant y Gonzales" and is held in family papers in the possession of Isabelle Ivens. Joseph's family retained one official document describing him as a Mexican citizen, though it was a passport for a specific journey, not a formal naturalization paper. See the 1875 passport for Havana issued to the *ciudadano mexicano* José Tinchant, in Tinchant Family Papers in the possession of Françoise Cousin (hereafter TFP-FC).

26. Louis Tinchant to Joseph Tinchant, 13 June 1867, file 2173, Fonds Cuylits, FA. A proper bale of Mexican cigar tobacco generally consisted of eighty tied sheaves *(tercios),* including both filler *(tripas)* and wrapper *(capa)* leaves. John Womack Jr., personal communication, 2008.

27. See Louis Tinchant to Joseph Tinchant, 13 June 1867, file 2173, Fonds Cuylits, FA.

28. See Jules Tinchant to Joseph Tinchant, 1 October 1867; and the copy of Jules Tinchant to John Hart (also apparently October 1867), enclosed with a letter marked #14, both in file 2173, Fonds Cuylits, FA.

29. Copy, John Hart to Joseph Tinchant, 27 October 1867, file 2173, Fonds Cuylits, FA.

30. John Hart to Joseph Tinchant, 27 October 1867, file 2173, Fonds Cuylits, FA.

31. See Jules Tinchant to Joseph Tinchant, 7 April 1868; and the document titled "Refutations par M. Joseph Tinchant," dated 22 June 1881, in file 2173, Fonds Cuylits, FA.

32. See Jules Tinchant to Joseph Tinchant, 7 April 1868, in file 2173, Fonds Cuylits, FA. Joseph and Stéphanie's sons Jules de los Angeles and Pierre were born in Tlapacoyan, according to the notarized document prepared by Joseph Tinchant,

17 March 1894, in Notary Emile Deckers, Rijksarchief te Antwerpen (hereafter RA), Antwerp. A baptismal record for their daughter Eliza, registered in Teziutlán, is in TFP-PS. On Tlapacoyan and Teziutlán see Kourí, *Pueblo Divided,* 124.

33. In this 1871 letter, Joseph reflected bitterly on the decision to take such risks in the tobacco trade, though he believed that their motive had been noble—to make money in order to insure the greatest happiness for their parents. José Tinchant to Ernest Tinchant, 22 August 1871, transcription, TFP-PS.

34. García Cubas, *Escritos diversos,* 178–190.

35. The passport is in TFP-FC.

36. The family's date of arrival in Belgium is given as "a year earlier" in the police registration record dated 8 December 1876, file 14046, Vreemdelingendossiers, reproduced on microfilm, Modern Archief (of the Stadsarchief), FelixArchief, Antwerp (hereafter MA, FA).

37. Several lithographs from Tinchant Frères and from the later firm of José Tinchant y Gonzales are owned by Philippe Struyf in Brussels, who has generously allowed us to view them.

38. Stéphanie's older brother Vincent Gustave Gonzales had been born in New Orleans in 1832. See Louisiana Birth Records Index, 1790–1890, vol. 6, 338, accessed through Ancestry.com. "Los hermanos Gustavo y Damián González" are referred to as Cuban in a chapter on Cuban immigration to San Andrés Tuxtla in Leon Medel y Alvarado, *Historia de San Andrés Tuxtla, 1532–1950,* vol. 1 (Tacubaya, Mexico: Editorial Citlatepetl, 1963), 280–281.

39. On the development of cigar manufacturing in Antwerp, and the role of the Tinchants in producing *havanes* see Guillaume Beetemé, *Anvers: métropole du commerce et des arts,* vol. 1 (Louvain: Imprimerie Lefever, 1887), 194, 419.

40. The quotation is from the laudatory article on Tinchant cigars published in *L'Encyclopédie contemporaine illustrée. Revue hebdomadaire universelle des sciences, des arts, et de l'industrie,* 140 (3 May 1891). On the role of Vincent Gustave Gonzales see article 9 of the notarized statutes of Tinchant Frères, based on Rue Breydel in Antwerp, in "Statuts," 12 March 1883, Notary F. A. Gheysens, RA.

41. Drawings of the factories on Rue Breydel can be found in file 71, year 1896, section Hinderlijke inrichtingen (dangerous enterprises), Provinciearchief Antwerpen, Antwerp.

42. This description builds on two letters by Édouard to his mother, dated 3 December 1864 (describing his trips to Memphis to sell cigars) and 16 August 1868 (announcing his engagement and his travels each month, presumably to sell cigars), both transcriptions in TFP-PS.

43. See Clinton P. King and Meriem A. Barlow, *Naturalization Records, Mobile, Alabama, 1833–1906* (Baltimore: Gateway Press, 1986). Since Cuba was a Spanish colony at the time, other Cuban-born residents of Mobile may have been categorized simply as being from Spain. Édouard's reference to his support for the Cuban cause is in Édouard Tinchant to Máximo Gómez, 21 September 1899, sig. 3868/4161, leg. 30, Fondo Máximo Gómez, Archivo Nacional de Cuba (hereafter FMG, ANC). Cuban activists from Mobile appear in Paul Estrade, *José Martí: Los fundamentos de la democracia en Latinoamérica* (Aranjuez: Ediciones Doce Calles, 2000), 902.

44. The precise phrases are "pour qu'il put recevoir de mes nouvelles et nous donner avant de mourir la bénédiction que je lui demandais pour ma famille" and "Je m'incline cependant devant la volonté de Dieu car c'est là la bien sévère, hélas, mais juste punition de ma coupable négligence envers mes vieux parents." Édouard Tinchant to Élisabeth Vincent, 12 February 1871, transcription, TFP-PS.

45. On the Mass see Édouard Tinchant to Élisabeth Vincent, 12 February 1871, transcription, TFP-PS. On Paul Trévigne's continuing campaign against school segregation in New Orleans see the article "Affairs in Louisiana," *New York Times,* 24 October 1877.

46. Édouard Tinchant to Élisabeth Vincent, 12 February 1871, transcription, TFP-PS.

47. See *Directory of the City of Mobile* for 1872 (Mobile: Henry Farrow & Co., n.d.), 212, 218, and 320.

48. See the *Directory of the City of Mobile* for 1873 and 1874 (both published by Henry Farrow & Co.), which contain variants of the advertisement. The credit reports are in vol. 17, Alabama, R. G. Dun & Co. Collection, Baker Library, Historical Collections, Harvard Business School (hereafter R. G. Dun, BL).

49. See Édouard Tinchant to Élisabeth Vincent, 31 May 1874, transcription, TFP-PS.

50. "'Don't Raise the Question of Color,'" *Mobile Watchman,* 30 August 1873.

51. On Reconstruction politics see Michael W. Fitzgerald, *Urban Emancipation: Popular Politics in Reconstruction Mobile, 1860–1890* (Baton Rouge: Louisiana State University Press, 2002); and Joseph Matt Brittain, "Negro Suffrage and Politics in Alabama since 1870" (PhD diss., Indiana University, 1958). A review of the voter registration lists in the two wards in which Édouard Tinchant lived and worked did not turn up his name. It is possible, though not likely, that he registered in some other ward for which records no longer exist. See "Register of Voters, 1874," Mobile Municipal Archives (hereafter MMA). The City Tax Books for 1873, also in MMA, record his payment of the poll tax.

52. See Fitzgerald, *Urban Emancipation,* 110–117; and the pages of the *Mobile Register* for these years.

53. *Mobile City Directory for the Year 1876* (Mobile: Henry Farrow & Co., 1875), ad on front flyleaf; and entry for E. A. Tinchant dated July 1875 in vol. 17, Alabama, R. G. Dun, BL.

54. See sheet 5 of the Sanborn map for Mobile, Alabama, published in May 1880, available at the Archives of the University of South Alabama. The property was rented, not owned, by Édouard Tinchant, who is listed without any real estate in the tax records, MMA.

55. See the Tinchant entries of January and July 1875, January and July 1876, and May 1877, in vol. 17, Alabama, R. G. Dun, BL.

56. See the City Tax Books for 1877, MMA.

57. Fitzgerald, *Urban Emancipation,* 227–245; Édouard Tinchant to Máximo Gómez, 21 September 1899, sig. 3868/4161, leg. 30, FMG, ANC.

58. This account of a call from brother Louis was the one conveyed in a newspaper article a decade later (*Mobile Register,* 11 December 1887).

59. The 3 July 1878 entry for the family of Édouard Tinchant with the Administration de la sureté publique No. 148 in Antwerp gives their youngest child as Marie Louise Julie, born in New Orleans on 14 March 1878. See file 38914, Vreemdelingendossiers 1878, reproduced on microfilm, MA, FA. Édouard's passport application in New Orleans shows her name as Emilie L. (Passport application of Édouard Tinchant, issue date 29 May 1878, New Orleans, in Passport Applications, 1795–1905, RG 59, reproduced on roll 224, USNA Microcopy M1372.) Her full name was Marie Louise Amélia Julie Tinchant. For detailed information on Édouard's daughters we thank Marie-Louise "Loulou" Van Velsen.

60. See the Édouard Tinchant passport application cited above.

61. For Élisabeth's Belgian records see file 14534, Vreemdelingendossiers 1857, reproduced on microfilm, MA, FA. She gave her age as fifty in 1857.

62. See the entry for the family of Édouard Tinchant, file 38914, Vreemdelingendossiers 1878, reproduced on microfilm, MA, FA. When Jacques and Élisabeth had themselves filled out a similar police registration form upon arrival in Antwerp twenty-one years earlier, the birthplace of Élisabeth (referred to as Elisa) was given as "l'Île St. Domingue." See file 14534, Vreemdelingendossiers 1857, reproduced on microfilm, MA, FA.

63. See the letter of J. Hart to J. Tinchant, 9 September 1880, and other documents in file 2173, Fonds Cuylits, FA.

64. See the onionskin copy of a letter from Joseph Tinchant to John Hart, probably late 1880, in file 2173, Fonds Cuylits, FA.

65. See Vincent Tinchant to his family, 12 December 1894, TFP-PS.

66. See "Société en nom collectif," 12 June 1895, Act 200, Notary Émile Decker, RA; "Liquidation & Partage," 9 March 1897, Act 80, Notary Émile Decker, RA.

67. The recollections about the use of Spanish and the naming of horses are from Françoise Cousin, personal communication, January 2011. Various Tinchant descendants take differing views on the plausibility of Vincent's picture of the family's history.

9. CITIZENS BEYOND NATION

1. Vincent Tinchant's school photos, and letters home from England, are in Tinchant family papers in the possession of Françoise Cousin (hereafter TFP-FC).

2. The request and accompanying reports are filed as dossier 3788, in the section Naturalisations, Ministère de la Justice, Archives générales du Royaume, Brussels (hereafter MJ, AGR).

3. Dossier 3788, Naturalisations, MJ, AGR.

4. See André Weiss, *Traité théorique et pratique de droit international privé*, vol. 1 (Paris: Larose & Tenin, 1907), 270–274. On suffrage, see Gita Deneckere, "Les turbulences de la Belle Époque, 1878–1905," in Michel de Dumoulin et al., *Nouvelle Histoire de la Belgique*, vol. 1 (Brussels: Éditions Complexe, 2005), 71–114.

5. Dossier 3788, Naturalisations, MJ, AGR. The original passport issued in Veracruz on 14 January 1875 is in TFP-FC.

6. Various lithographs that conveyed this persona, including one labeled "La Flor de Don José," have been collected by Philippe Struyf in Antwerp.

7. See Quanone v. Tinchant (1865), file 1792, Fonds Cuylits, FelixArchief, Antwerp (hereafter FA).

8. See the document headed Maison de sûreté, Anvers, in dossier 411951, Dossiers, Police des étrangers, MJ, AGR. On the bigamy charge see "Arrested for Bigamy. A Former New Orleans Man in Trouble in France," *New Orleans Daily Picayune,* 27 April 1900.

9. Edward Antoine Tinchant, Cigar-Machine, U.S. Patent 319,349, filed 25 November 1884 and issued 2 June 1885.

10. These activities are described in the obituary for Édouard Tinchant published in the bulletin of the alumni of the lycée in Pau, a photocopy of which was provided to us by Michèle Badaroux, née Tinchant.

11. The application for Édouard Tinchant, filed in New Orleans on a form marked "For Native Citizen," is dated 29 May 1878. It is from "Passport Applications, New Orleans," RG 59, United States National Archives, reproduced on roll 224, USNA Microcopy M1372.

12. Patrick Weil's history of French nationality discusses the tangle of interpretations emerging from an 1889 law and an 1893 ministerial circular. Patrick Weil, *How to Be French: Nationality in the Making since 1789* (Durham, NC: Duke University Press, 2008), chaps. 2 and 3.

13. See the letter of L. Ayrault to M. le consul de France à la N^lle-Orléans, 28 April 1897, file labeled "Tinchant, Édouard," in carton 127, Série D, Consulat de la Nouvelle-Orléans, Centre des archives diplomatiques de Nantes (hereafter CADN).

14. Draft of reply from the consul to Ayrault, 14 May 1897, file labeled "Tinchant, Édouard," carton 127, Série D, Consulat de la Nouvelle-Orléans, CADN.

15. Édouard's daughter Septima was the ultimate beneficiary of her father's bureaucratic maneuver, enabling her as the daughter of a Frenchman to make her own affirmative declaration of allegiance to France when she reached the age of twenty-one. Marie Louise Van Velsen, whose mother was Septima's niece, recalls having heard a story of Septima's trip to the town hall to register as French. Personal communication, Marie-Louise Van Velsen, June 2010. When Septima Tinchant returned to Antwerp after exile in Paris during World War I, her "foreigner registration record" listed her nationality as French. See file 38914, Vreemdelingendossiers 1878, reproduced on microfilm, Modern Archief (of the Stadsarchief), FA.

16. Édouard Tinchant's role as "Agent Spécial de la Régie Française" is discussed in Charles-L. Waitte and Remy Geerts, *Le Livre d'or du tabac et des industries qui s'y rattachent* (Brussels: Imprimerie L. Vogels, 1905), 54.

17. Édouard Tinchant to Máximo Gómez, 21 September 1899, sig. 3868/4161, leg. 30, Fondo Máximo Gómez, Archivo Nacional de Cuba (hereafter FMG, ANC).

18. The claim of support is a credible one. For letters written by Cuban activists describing their fund-raising in New Orleans see various files in the Fondo Donativos, ANC, including "Diez y siete comunicaciones firmadas por Francisco Guillen," exp. 48–41, caja 157.

19. Tinchant to Gómez, 21 September 1899.

20. Ibid.

21. Ibid.

22. Ibid.

23. Ibid. We thank Marial Iglesias for having discerned, deciphered, and interpreted the faintly penciled instructions by Gómez at the bottom of the letter.

24. We are grateful to Philippe Struyf for having spotted this reference in *Le Livre d'or*, 54.

25. See "Rectification de noms d'épouse Tinchant dans son contrat de mariage," 16 November 1835, act 672, 1835, Notary Théodore Seghers, New Orleans Notarial Archives Research Center.

26. See the baptism of "Juste Tinchant et Bayole enfant légitime," 8 October 1836, act 326, vol. 25, "St. Louis Cathedral, Baptisms—Slaves and Free People of Color," Archives of the Archdiocese of New Orleans, New Orleans. The marginal notation "Bayole" in the baby's name repeats the error concerning Elisabeth's surname that dates back to the garbling of the sacramental record of Jacques and Elisabeth's marriage by the priest or a subsequent copyist, who confused the name of Jacques' bride with that of his mother.

EPILOGUE

1. "Brilliant Newswoman to Cover European News for Colored Press," *Atlanta Daily World*, 5 January 1937, 1; and Fay M. Jackson, "Two Officially Represent Race at Coronation," *Pittsburgh Courier*, 8 May 1937, 24. On her earlier activities see "Churches Asked to Hit Lynching," *Los Angeles Sentinel*, 21 February 1935, 6.

2. See the item by Fay M. Jackson in the *California Eagle*, 5 March 1937, as well as Jackson, "Swing Music Craze Causes Furore in London," *Atlanta Daily World*, 1 March 1937; Jackson, "Wanted: American Papers!" *Atlanta Daily World*, 6 March 1937, 1.

3. Fay M. Jackson, "Trail of Blood, Vandalism in Wake of 'Rape of Ethiopia,' Britishers Told," *Pittsburgh Courier*, 17 April 1937, 21; Jackson, "Paul Robeson Picture Sets New Tempo," *New York Amsterdam News*, 13 March 1937, 10.

4. Fay M. Jackson, "No Color Bar for Waiters at Coronation," *Pittsburgh Courier*, 27 March 1936, 3; Jackson, "Color Line May Be Drawn at Coronation," *Atlanta Daily World*, 6 May 1937, 1.

5. Phyllis M. Davies, "Fled to Wed Secretly in England," *Daily Mail* (London), 9 April 1937, 11.

6. The narrative can be reconstructed from the articles in the *Daily Mail* (9 and 14 April 1937) and the *Daily Express* (10 and 14 April 1937), as well as the official "Entry of Marriage" from the Metropolitan Borough of Chelsea, dated 13 April 1937, a certified copy of which was obtained from the General Register Office, Great Britain. Out of respect for the privacy of the family of origin of the fiancé, with whom we have not been in contact, we have replaced André's surname with the initial *V.*

7. Davies, "Fled to Wed Secretly."

8. "Wedding-Day Bid to Stop a Marriage," *Daily Express* (London), 10 April 1937, 13.

9. Ibid.

10. Jackson seems to have written her story in the days that followed (referring to the events as having occurred "last Saturday"), but it was not published in the United States until a few weeks later. The *New York Amsterdam News* of 1 May 1937 published it on page 11 under the title "Father Halts Wedding. Mixed Blood Not So Good Even Abroad. Belgian Couple Can't Marry Because of Color."

11. The details of the legal proceedings are from the accounts in the *Daily Express* and the *Daily Mail,* as well as Jackson's story in the *New York Amsterdam News.*

12. The *Daily Mail* and the *Daily Express* each ran short follow-up articles. They reiterated the objections advanced by the fiancé's father—legal studies and military service—while dropping all reference to color. "Belgian Couple Wed," *Daily Mail,* 14 April 1937, 11; and "Father Fails to Stop His Son's Wedding," *Daily Express,* 14 April 1937.

13. Much of the detail on their lives is from the file on Marie-José Tinchant in the Dossiers des statuts de reconnaissance nationale de la guerre 1940–45 (hereafter Dossier Statut, Marie-José Tinchant), held in the archives of the Direction générale Victimes de la Guerre, Service archives et documentation, Brussels (hereafter ASVG), and consulted there with permission from Marie-José Tinchant's granddaughter Michèle Kleijnen.

14. Dossier Statut, Marie-José Tinchant, ASVG. Marie-José's brother José Pierre was apparently working as an administrator in the family company when he was called up for service. Letter of José Pierre Tinchant to Michèle Tinchant Ivens, 17 January 1996, in the papers of Isabelle Ivens (hereafter TFP-II).

15. A splendid full-length oil portrait of Vincent Tinchant, cigar in hand, gold watch chain at the waist, is owned by Philippe Struyf.

16. The information on André V.'s flight to France comes from a subsequent inquiry by a social worker concerned with the postwar situation of their daughter, Liliane. See "Dossiers concernant Liliane [V.] conservés par l'Institution publique de protection de la jeunesse et transmise à l'intéressée à sa demande le 20 janvier 2000," Tinchant Family Papers in the possession of Michèle Kleijnen (hereafter TFP-MK). José Pierre Tinchant's time in the Stalag is described in his letter to his daughter Michèle Tinchant Ivens, dated 17 January 1996, in TFP-II.

17. Marie-José's younger brother Pedro served as driver for Rul during the takeover of the Hotel de Ville in Antwerp as the Allies approached. See TFP-MK. Rul's service with the Réseau Bayard and later with the Royalist MNR is documented in his file with the Services de renseignement et d'action (SRA), currently held at the Centre d'études et de documentation Guerre et sociétés contemporaines, Brussels (hereafter CEGES-SOMA). On the Réseau Bayard see Fernand Strubbe, *Services secrets belges 1940–1945* (Brussels: Union des Services de renseignement et d'action, 1997), 383–389.

18. Marie-José's registration at 29 rue du Damier appears in her Dossier Statut, ASVG. The recollection that Marie-José was active in the Resistance in January 1941 comes from José Pierre Tinchant to Michèle Tinchant Ivens, 17 January 1996, TFP-II. Although postwar assertions of Resistance activity are always sub-

ject to a certain skepticism, José Pierre Tinchant had little reason to exaggerate his sister's activities. He himself ended the war as a decorated hero of a parachute regiment composed of Belgian forces in exile. See the published accounts of his service in TFP-II.

19. See Emmanuel Debruyne, *La Guerre secrète des espions belges, 1940–44* (Brussels: Éditions Racine, 2008), chap. 4, and Dossier Statut, Marie-José Tinchant, ASVG.

20. This description of her personality is based on the written records cited in this chapter, on personal communications from Françoise Cousin, and on a personal communication from Michèle Kleijnen, 27 June 2008, conveying comments made to her by her grandfather André V., Marie-José's former husband. The phrases concerning color and the "West Indies" are from Davies, "Fled to Wed."

21. See "Livret matricule et de punitions," in the Dossier matriculaire, José Pierre Tinchant, The Archives of the Human Relations Department of the Belgian Army, Quartier Reine Élisabeth, Brussels (hereafter QRE); and José Pierre Tinchant to Michèle Tinchant Ivens, 17 January 1996, TFP-II. On the divisive German policy concerning Belgian POWs see I. C. B. Dear, general ed., *The Oxford Companion to World War II* (New York: Oxford University Press), 120.

22. See José Pierre Tinchant to Michèle Tinchant Ivens, 17 January 1996, TFP-II.

23. The neighborhood around the rue du Théâtre, now razed, is in the commune of Molenbeek. We thank historian Sophie de Schaepdrijver for this description. See also Chantal Kesteloot, *Bruxelles sous l'occupation, 1940–1944* (Brussels: CEGES-SOMA, 2009).

24. The recollection of her arrest on November 30, 1941, is from José Pierre Tinchant to Michèle Tinchant Ivens, 17 January 1996, TFP-II Papers. Her transfer to Antwerp on December 10, 1941, is recorded in the volume titled "Saint-Gilles. Listes de transports du 17.9.40 au 23.7.42," labeled TR. 16.781, Rap. 497, and held in the ASVG. On the Gestapo in Belgium see Céline Préaux, *La Gestapo devant ses juges en Belgique* (Brussels: Éditions Racine, 2007), 16.

25. José Pierre's itinerary through Spain to Lisbon, his departure from Gibraltar, and his enlistment in the SAS are confirmed by his Dossier matriculaire, held at the QRE.

26. Information on her residences is in the judicial records filed with the Dossier Statut, Marie-José Tinchant, ASVG. Emmanuel Debruyne notes that the occupation government later overcame this reluctance to punish women harshly. Debruyne, *La Guerre secrète*, 32, 310. The wartime custody of the children is discussed in "Dossiers concernant Liliane [V.] conservés par l'Institution publique de protection de la jeunesse," TFP-MK.

27. A copy of the divorce decree is in the Dossier Statut, Marie-José Tinchant, ASVG.

28. The register of entries (Registre d'écrou) in St. Gilles prison for 1944 is now held in the ASVG.

29. See the Dossier SRA of Marie-José Tinchant, CEGES-SOMA, consulted with the permission of her granddaughter, Michèle Kleijnen.

30. Marie-José's designation as "polit." appears on an entry list held in the archives of the Ravensbrück Memorial: "Sondertransport v Brüssel, 19.6.44," KL/15-1, Mahn- und Gedenkstätte Ravensbrück/Stiftung Brandenburgische Gedenkstätten (hereafter MGR/SGB). The typescript memoir of a prisoner at St. Gilles, apparently referred to as "Lamfuss," is catalogued as "Mémoires [Prisonnier de St. Gilles]," AB 2259, CEGES-SOMA.

31. The record of Marie-José's departure is the typed "Transportliste" (with a subhead translated as *Femmes provisoirement arrêtées pour Ravensbrück*), dated at St. Gilles, 15 June 1944, copy held in file TR 6719/497, in ASVG. Her entry is number 304 on page 47, and her name is repeated on page 55, on a separate list headed IV-3. On the context of the German evacuation of the prisons see Pieter Lagrou, *Mémoires patriotiques et occupation nazie: résistants, requis et déportés en Europe occidentale, 1945–1965* (Bruxelles: Éditions Complexe; Paris: Institut d'histoire du temps présent, 2003), 206.

32. Her arrival at Ravensbrück is recorded on "Sondertransport v Brüssel, 19.6.44," KL/15-1, MGR/SGB. On this convoy see also Grit Philipp, *Kalendarium der Ereignisse im Frauen-Konzentrationslager Ravensbrück, 1939–1945* (Berlin: Metropol Verlag, 1999), 296.

33. This translation of the quotation from Himmler is in Seymour Drescher, *Abolition: A History of Slavery and Antislavery* (Cambridge: Cambridge University Press, 2009), 431.

34. See the chapter "Profit et extermination," with its subsection "L'entretien des esclaves," in Germaine Tillion, *Ravensbrück* (Paris: Éditions du Seuil, 1988), 214–248. The description of the inspections is on the third (unnumbered) page of the typescript "Procès des grands criminels de guerre. Nuremberg. Débats. 22 janvier–4 février 1946. Ravensbrück. Déposition de Madame Claude [*sic*] Vaillant-Couturier," in the file numbered 1163, T25/58, CEGES-SOMA.

35. Tillion, *Ravensbrück*; Bernhard Strebel, *Ravensbrück: un complexe concentrationnaire,* (Paris: Fayard, 1966), 186–214; and the fourth page of the "Déposition de Madame Claude Vaillant-Couturier," cited above.

36. In this undated postcard, apparently sent on October 18, 1944, the sender is listed as living at 34 avenue Van den Nest in Antwerp. The card is now in the Dossier Statut, Marie-José Tinchant, ASVG, along with a copy of the reply from the Red Cross, dated 17 November 1944.

37. See the entry for Droubaix in the transport list of 11 August 1944, indexed in *Livre-mémorial des déportés de France arrêtés par mesure de répression et dans certains cas par mesure de persécution, 1940–1945*, vol. 3 (Paris: Éditions Tirésias, 2004), available online at http://www.bddm.org/liv/details.php?id=I.262.#DEROU BAIX. Her place in the family genealogy was determined with the help of Philippe Struyf, supplemented by the marriage record of Lawrence Quinlivan Bulger and Marie-Christine Droubaix, formerly Tinchant, dated 30 October 1901, copy obtained from the General Register Office, Great Britain. The betrayal by a German double-agent of the Resistance network in Marseille of which her husband, Marcel Droubaix, was a member, "Mithridate," is recounted in Nigel West, *Historical Dictionary of World War II Intelligence* (Lanham, MD: Scarecrow Press, 2008), 100–102.

38. On Nadine's exchanges with Marie-José see the testimony of Nadine Droubaix, née Crabbe, given before the Commission d'agréation pour prisonniers politiques et ayants-droit, 6 January 1955, manuscript copy in Dossier Statut, Marie-José Tinchant, ASVG. On the tricolor insignias in 1940 see Paul Delandsheere and Alphonse Ooms, *La Belgique sous les nazis: 1940-1941* (Brussels: L'Édition universelle, 1946), 399. The memoir by Geneviève de Gaulle, *La Traversée de la nuit* (Paris: Éditions du Seuil, 1998), is also evocative of various gestures of solidarity and resistance. In solitary confinement for much of the time, she apparently did not cross paths with Marie-José Tinchant. See Geneviève de Gaulle Anthonioz to Michèle Kleijnen, 8 March 2000, in TFP-MK.

39. See Strebel, *Ravensbrück,* 454-455 on the shootings, and 455-464 on the gas chambers. The Mittwerda List, a fragmentary record signed by the director of the camp, was presented as evidence in subsequent war crimes prosecutions. We thank Alyn Bessmann of the Museum and Archives at Ravensbrück for her assistance in understanding the nature of this list, and its use in the 1946 British Military Trial on Ravensbrück.

40. Marie-José also appears with her camp identification number 42,791 on a document prepared in France from the list retrieved from Ravensbrück by the French Resistance leader Marie-Claude Vaillant-Couturier, and made available by the French Amicale de Ravensbrück. The document was forwarded to the Belgian Ministry of Reconstruction by Mlle. Dorlodot, an emissary in Paris. "Noms de Belges relevés *textuellement* sur les *listes allemandes* du Camp de Ravensbrück. Document rapporté de Ravensbrück par Mme Vaillant-Couturier et remis à l'Amicale de ce Camp, 10, rue Leroux. Paris," now filed as 1163, T25/17, CEGES-SOMA. A similar list is in 1163, T25/20 CEGES-SOMA. On the use of the term "sana" see Annexe 1 in Tillion, *Ravensbrück,* 339. The contents of the list dated 31 March 1945 and held by the Tracing Service were conveyed to us by Alyn Bessmann.

41. On the burning of the files see Annexe 1 in Tillion, *Ravensbrück,* 339. On the last days of the camp, and the circumstances of its liberation, see also Tillion, "Réflexions sur l'étude de la déportation," *Revue d'histoire de la Deuxième Guerre mondiale* 15-16 (July–December 1954): 3–38.

42. See the form filled out by Madame Eugénie Tinchant, in the Dossier Statut, Marie-José Tinchant, ASVG.

43. In 1944 the Belgian government in exile had formed the Service de documents et recherche (SDR) in anticipation of the repatriation of those who had been deported to Germany, and other organizations also compiled files of missing persons. Milcamps sent a request for information that included the descriptive terms cited, as well as information that presumably came in part from Nadine Droubaix: "[Marie-José Tinchant] a été au camp de Ravensbrück raisons politiques, y était encore le 5 janvier 1945. Elle servait les pommes de terres aux autres détenues." A portion of his information was transferred to a "Fiche de recherche de disparu" for the Commissariat belge au rapatriement. This inquiry, along with the one from Marie-José's mother, is in the Dossier Statut, Marie-José Tinchant, ASVG. Milcamps, who listed himself as living in Ghent, is also mentioned as one of Marie-José's Resistance contacts, given as "Max Milcamps,"

in the attorney's letter of 1953, in the SRA file of Marie-José Tinchant, CEGES-SOMA.

44. See Dossier Statut, Marie-José Tinchant, ASVG, and the copy of the list compiled by Marie-Claude Vaillant-Couturier, now held at CEGES-SOMA, cited above. On the history of records concerning Ravensbrück see Tillion, "Réflexions."

45. See Lagrou, *Mémoires*. We thank the researchers and archivists at CEGES-SOMA and ASVG for ongoing discussions of this process.

46. Lagrou, *Mémoires*, 95–106, 189–196. One could also be refused any of these statuses, on the grounds either of improper *(incivil)* behavior, or of having volunteered to perform labor in Germany.

47. Lagrou, *Mémoires*, 194–196. Letter from the attorney J. P. to the Chef du S.G.R.A., 26 December 1953, in the Dossier SRA of Tinchant, Marie-José, CEGES-SOMA. We have consulted this document with the permission of Michèle Kleijnen.

48. Letter from A. Hauzeur, 15 February 1954, in the Dossier SRA of Tinchant, Marie-José, CEGES-SOMA.

49. Correspondence in the Dossier Statut, Marie-José Tinchant, ASVG.

50. The logs in her Dossier Statut include the entry "2/12/54 Amicale de Ravensbrück," which appears to correspond to the arrival from France of a copy of the list compiled by Marie-Claude Vaillant-Couturier.

51. The task of reconstructing her Resistance activities was made more difficult by the fact that Marie-José's parents were now dead, her youngest brother had emigrated to Brazil along with her brother-in-law Jean Rul, and her twin brother was embroiled in difficulties of his own. André V., who filed the request for recognition on behalf of the children, had been estranged from Marie-José during the war. See the Dossier Statut, Marie-José Tinchant, ASVG; and the Dossier matriculaire, J. P. Tinchant, QRE. We are also grateful to Michèle Kleijnen and Françoise Cousin for their recollections of family discussions concerning this period.

52. Lagrou, *Mémoire*, 212–215.

53. A law of 10 March 1954 built on and modified that of 26 February 1947 (see the text on the government website at http://warvictims.fgov.be/fr/rights/laws /1954_10_16.htm). See also Lagrou, *Mémoire*, 212–215; and Rudi van Doorslaer (dir.), Emmanuel Debruyne, Frank Seberechts, and Nico Wouters, *La Belgique docile: les autorités belges et la persécution des Juifs en Belgique durant la Seconde Guerre mondiale*, 2 vols. (Brussels: Éditions Luc Pire, 2007), 1072–1076.

54. Testimony of Nadine Droubaix, Dossier Statut, Marie-José Tinchant, ASVG. An example of an *insigne* made from scraps of different colors can be seen in the museum at the Memorial of Ravensbrück. (Visit to the Memorial of Ravensbrück by Jean M. Hébrard, June 2009.)

55. See the pages compiled during the 6 January 1955 hearing and filed in Dossier Statut, Marie-José Tinchant. On the debate over the *critère de souffrance* see Lagrou, *Mémoire*, 210–214.

56. The phrase is "Attendu dès lors qu'elle ne peut prétendre au titre de Prisonnier Politique." The language in the final portion of the decision is "Elle a été détenue du 18.1.1944 au 28.3.1945. Elle a droit à titre posthume à la qualité de

bénéficiaire du Statut mais non au titre de Prisonnier Politique." See the decision filed 6 January 1955 by the Commission d'agréation pour prisonniers et ayants-droit, copy in TFP-MK, and copy in the Dossier Statut, Marie-José Tinchant, ASVG.

57. See the comprehensive study commissioned by the Belgian Senate and carried out by a team based at CEGES: Van Doorslaer et al., *La Belgique docile,* esp. vol. 2, 1055–1115, on "La reconnaissance d'après-guerre," by Nico Wouters. We thank Emmanuel Debruyne for several discussions of patterns of arrests in Belgium, including those of Latin Americans.

58. On the arrest and deportation of Jews in Belgium see Van Doorslaer et al., *La Belgique docile.*

59. Quoted in Van Doorslaer et al., *La Belgique docile,* 2:1074.

60. On the "Transportliste," dated at St. Gilles, 15 June 1944, her name appears on a list with the designation IV 3. (See the copy held in file TR 6719/497, in ASVG). Emmanuel Debruyne, a specialist on wartime intelligence networks, has pointed out that this IV 3 could conceivably have caused the commission to infer that she was arrested by the Judenabteilung, designated during these months as IV B 3, hence for a "racial reason." Emmanuel Debruyne, personal communications, 29–30 June, 1 July 2009.

61. On the postwar attributions of status see the work of Pieter Lagrou, Rudi van Doorslaer, and Emmanuel Debruyne cited above. We also thank Gert De Prins of the ASVG for his careful explication of the process by which the various SRA, and ASVG files were generated. He points out that the particular copy of the transport list that we obtained from the Memorial at Ravensbrück, which includes the inscription "polit.," was not in the hands of the commission at the time.

62. This document, dated 31 July 1956, at Forest in Belgium, is in the possession of Michèle Kleijnen.

63. Surviving family correspondence suggests that Édouard Tinchant, who as late as 1899 was still very conscious of his parents' Haitian ancestry, had somewhat strained relations with the more prosperous and well-traveled children of his brother José Tinchant y Gonzales. A letter from Marie Tinchant to Vincent Tinchant, 25 November 1889, TFP-FC, discusses uncle Édouard. Édouard's daughter Septima was present at the time of Édouard's death in exile at Oak Hill, Shadwell, Leeds, on 9 June 1915. A "Certified Copy of an Entry of Death" gives his age as seventy-three and the cause of death as "abscess of lung" and "exhaustion." See the 22 May 1928 copy of the original, now in the family papers held by Marie-Louise Van Velsen.

64. For a discussion of the destruction and survival of records concerning the Nazi camps see Tillion, *Ravensbrück,* particularly the introductory material in the 1988 edition; and her earlier study, "Le Système Concentrationnaire Allemand (1940–1944)," *Revue de la Deuxième Guerre Mondiale* 4 (July–September 1954): 3–38, esp. 4, note 1.

65. Copies of this letter and of the identity card were provided to us by Michèle Kleijnen.

66. We thank Michèle Kleijnen for conveying news of our research to her mother Liliane and for sharing with us a newspaper interview carried out in Liliane's garden.

All works of history are collaborative, but this volume is more collaborative than most. Across the past seven years the two of us have co-taught, read documents side by side, and debated interpretation. Coming from opposite sides of the Atlantic, and with very different linguistic backgrounds and historiographical training, we have tried together to figure out this story. Throughout the process of composition we have exchanged ideas and prose back and forth, sharing evidence and argument at each step. We are now conveying our findings in two languages and in somewhat different modes: here in English, and in a forthcoming book in French.

The project is collaborative in another sense as well. At crucial moments generous colleagues have reviewed their own notes and recollections, or gone with us to the archives, to help locate the materials that have moved the inquiry forward. The project was born in the National Archives of Cuba, where Rebecca Scott and Marial Iglesias Utset were working their way through the correspondence of General Máximo Gómez, and Marial called to Rebecca's attention a peculiar letter to Gómez that contained multiple allusions to Haiti and to Louisiana. The letter—a commercial request typed in purple ink on Belgian letterhead, and signed Édouard Tinchant—seemed uncanny in the way that its author's account of his family's history linked together three of the most dramatic struggles for civil rights and racial equality in the nineteenth-century Atlantic world.

After returning to Michigan, Rebecca tracked down Édouard Tinchant's speeches in the Louisiana Constitutional Convention and checked out his claims to fleeting fame. With relatively little to go on, she began telling the story in interpretive outline in various venues. The Tinchant surname was an odd one, and several listeners remembered having seen

243

it in unlikely places. Diana Williams recalled another letter from Édouard Tinchant, written in 1864 to the editor of the New Orleans *Tribune*. Dawn Logsdon, co-producer of the film *Faubourg Tremé: The Untold Story of Black New Orleans,* had seen a reference to an "Édouard Tinchaut" as a schoolteacher in the city in 1867. Upon further inquiry, Irene Wainwright and Greg Osborn located relevant court files in the New Orleans Public Library.

The breakthrough came when the volumes of the New Orleans Notarial Archives yielded a copy of a 1799 baptismal record from colonial Saint-Domingue containing the names of Édouard's maternal grandparents: Michel Vincent and Marie Françoise *dite* Rosalie. Édouard Tinchant's assertion of Haitian ancestry was evidently correct, though not quite in the way he had suggested. Ada Ferrer, who knew that Saint-Domingue refugees in New Orleans had generally spent some years in Cuba first, suggested a look at the records of the French officials who operated as consuls in Cuba. Paul Lachance dug out an old note card of his own confirming that one Michel Vincent had registered a copy of his last will and testament with French officials in Cuba in 1804.

Barbara Snow retrieved Family History Library microfilm of the consular register in which the certification of Vincent's will had been recorded. Hoping that the adjacent reference to a document indexed as "Enregistrement de liberté de Marie Françoise" might yield more, Rebecca proceeded to the Archives nationales d'outre-mer in Aix-en-Provence to consult the originals. Michel Vincent's will was not there (it may have gone to the bottom of the ocean when a French colonel carrying those records departed Cuba), but the *enregistrement de liberté* was indeed an 1803 manumission letter for Édouard Tinchant's maternal grandmother Marie Françoise, *dite* Rosalie. In that carefully crafted freedom paper, drafted in the midst of the turmoil occasioned by Napoléon Bonaparte's effort to crush the Haitian Revolution, Rosalie is referred to as "of the Poulard nation," signaling her birth in Senegambia.

As it became clear that the project would require painstaking interpretation of French colonial materials, as well as archival records from nineteenth-century Pau and Antwerp, Jean Hébrard moved from the role of consultant to that of collaborator. The most challenging part of the research now began, with several returns to the Cuban archives, trips to Belgium and France, and a first journey to Senegal. In early 2007, Mamadou Diouf oriented the two of us in Dakar and in the National Archives of Senegal as we explored what the phrase "of the Poulard nation" implied. Ibrahima Thioub of the Université Cheikh Anta Diop picked up the thread and later joined us for a month in Michigan as we wrote a first draft of the chapter on West Africa. Rudolph T. Ware helped us grapple with the challenge of incorporating material on the revolution of Fuuta Tooro that could not be associated precisely with Rosalie, but which was essential for understanding what identification as Poulard might have meant in the 1790s.

In the spring of 2007, the surname Tinchant on a conference program announcing one of our early lectures emerged in a Google search carried out by a young businessman in Brussels, who showed it to his father, Philippe Struyf, a great-grandson of José Tinchant, who then contacted us by e-mail. We soon traveled to Belgium to meet Philippe and his wife, Josine van Damme. For the next four years they generously welcomed us to Brussels each summer, providing hospitality, information, and suggestions. Philippe introduced us to additional Belgian and French descendants of Édouard and José Tinchant. He has, moreover, accompanied the project right through to the end, scanning documents and photographs, sharing his collection of lithographs and family correspondence, and supervising our rendering of the details of family genealogy. His cousin the indomitable Marie-Louise (Loulou) Van Velsen, great-granddaughter of Édouard Tinchant, welcomed us to Antwerp and allowed us to consult the contents of the suitcase that she refers to with a smile as her *valise diplomatique*. It yielded photographs and letters, which she complemented with many recollections of her mother Marie-Louise and stories about her great-aunt Septima (known as Bébé), Édouard Tinchant's daughter. Michèle Badaroux and Françoise Cousin, from slightly different branches of the family, joined in the discussions, sharing ideas and information on different phases of the Tinchant adventure.

By January 2009 we thought we were almost finished with our research. There was one more surprise in store, however. As a gesture of scholarly solidarity, our colleague Martha S. Jones generally types the word "Tinchant" into any relevant search box before she logs off from online historical inquiries of her own, just in case. She now found and relayed to us an improbable hit in the *Pittsburgh Courier* for 1937. It was a reference to the contested marriage in London of one Marie-José Tinchant, and we thought it might offer the possibility of a story that could serve as an epilogue. We anticipated that we would talk to the family to verify the details of the almost-thwarted marriage, then place it in the context of London in that year of anticolonial agitation, and wrap the book up with an evocation of another moment of antiracist mobilization.

Once we located Marie-José Tinchant in the family genealogy, however, the path plunged suddenly downward, as we realized the magnitude of the catastrophe into which she had tumbled as a result of the German occupation of Belgium in 1940. Susanne Baer, of the Humboldt University in Berlin and now of the German Federal Constitutional Court, put us in touch with the staff of the Memorial of the Ravensbrück concentration camp. Jean Hébrard and Martha Jones traveled there in the summer of 2009. The last stage of our research then followed the painstaking and painful effort of Marie-José's daughter Liliane and her granddaughter Michèle Kleijnen to reconstruct the final years of the life of Marie-José Tinchant. We wish to express our very great thanks to them both. They have shared with us family memories and documents, and they graciously authorized us to consult the dossier generated by the 1954 request for the posthumous attribution of the status of political prisoner, along with the earlier files created by the Service de Documents et Recherche, both held at the Service archives et documentation of the Direction générale Victimes de la guerre (Brussels).

From Belgium, Isabelle Ivens also made contact with us in the summer of 2009. She and her mother, Michèle Tinchant Ivens, daughter of José Pierre Tinchant, the twin brother of Marie-José, shared photographs, selections from letters written by José Pierre after he had retired to Holland, and a copy of an article that José Pierre wrote on his own service in the British army, operating behind German lines in 1944. We thank them warmly for their generosity.

From the beginning of our research in Belgium, Sophie de Schaepdrijver offered advice and guidance and provided many articles, connections, and introductions. Through her we also met Belgian colleagues specializing in the period of the Second World War, including the director, researchers, and staff of the Centre d'études et de documentation Guerre et sociétés contemporaines (CEGES-SOMA) in Brussels. Rudi van Doorslaer, Chantal Kesteloot, and Fabrice Maertens were generous with their time and suggestions, and Emmanuel Debruyne provided material from his own research, along with valuable insight into the development of Resistance networks. Gert De Prins and the other archivists and staff of the Direction générale Victimes de la guerre clarified the structure of the various dossiers and surviving official records. Consultation of several personal dossiers of the Services de renseignement et d'action (SRA) by Rebecca Scott in July 2009 was made possible by the permission granted by David Sommer of the Sureté d'État. Permission to consult military records at the Quartier Reine Élisabeth was given by Adjutant Xavier Van Tilborg.

In addition to these collaborations with fellow researchers and with descendants of the family, we are grateful to the archivists and historians in eight different countries who have welcomed us to their repositories and provided advice and assistance. In Cuba, we owe particular thanks to Laura Cruz Ríos, Barbara Danzie, Reinaldo Funes, Orlando García Martínez, Marial Iglesias Utset, Enrique López Mesa, Jorge Macle, Maria de los Ángeles Meriño, Aisnara Pereira, Olga Portuondo Zúñiga, Carlos Venegas, and many others. We also thank Adriana Chira, Ana Teodoro Cleaver, Edgardo Pérez-Morales, and Romy Sánchez, along with other participants in the 2011 seminar "Hacer Hablar a los Documentos," who have continued to keep an eye out for relevant material as they proceed with their own research. The staff of the Archivo Nacional de Cuba have shown great patience with our many requests over the years, and we thank the director, the chiefs of the research room, and those who bring the dust-covered bundles out from the stacks. As always, Fernando Martínez Heredia and Esther Pérez Pérez were essential interlocutors in Havana, and the Instituto Juan Marinello, its director Elena Socarrás, our visa coordinator Liudmila Rodney, and the entire staff were indispensable hosts.

In France, we received good advice and warm welcomes at the École des hautes études en sciences sociales (EHESS) from Marc Olivier Baruch, Roger Chartier, Vincent Duclert, François Hartog, Christophe Prochasson, Jacques Revel, Bernard Vincent, and Jean-Paul Zúñiga of the Centre de recherches historiques; from Jean-Frédéric Schaub of the Centre de recherches sur le Brésil contemporain; from Roger Botte, José Kagabo, and Catarina Madeira Santos of the Centre d'études africaines; from Cécile Vidal and François Weil of the Centre d'études nord-américaines; from Myriam Cottias, Antonio Almeida Mendes, and Dominique Rogers of the Centre international de recherches sur les esclavages; and from Christian Topalov of the Centre Maurice Halbwachs. We also thank Patrick Weil at the Université de Paris I; Marie-Jeanne Rossignol and Catherine Coquery-Vidrovich at Paris VII; Claudia Moatti and Philippe Minard at Paris VIII; Jacques de Cauna at the Université de Pau; Anne-Marie Pathé of the Institut d'histoire du temps présent; and Françoise Grard, whose love of writing is an inspiration.

We were ably assisted by the staffs at the Archives nationales de France in Paris, the Archives nationales d'outre-mer in Aix-en-Provence, the Service historique de la Défense in Vincennes, the Centre des archives diplomatiques in Nantes, and the Archives départementales of the Pyrénées-Atlantiques, of Sarthe, of the Vosges, and of the Gironde. We also thank the staffs of the musée du Château des ducs de Bretagne in Nantes, the musée du Nouveau Monde in La Rochelle, and the musée d'Aquitaine in Bordeaux, as well as the Bibliothèque nationale de France in Paris, the médiathèque du square Paul Lafond in Pau, and the médiathèque Louis Aragon in Le Mans.

In England, we were dazzled by the breadth of the material on Saint-Domingue contained in the National Archives of the United Kingdom, including stacks of captured letters from French soldiers and civilians, records of the administrators of the 1793–1798 British occupation, and receipts issued to slaveholders whose slaves joined the British forces. We thank David Geggus for having oriented us within these materials, and the staff for their efficient provision of documents. From London, Miriam Margolyes generously opened the pathway to our obtaining a copy of the 1937 marriage certificate of Marie-José Tinchant.

In Spain, we were able to consult a small fraction of the Papeles de Cuba in the Archivo General de Indias. We thank José Luis Belmonte, Javier Pérez Royo, and Ignacio Tovar for their warm welcome in Seville. Edgardo Pérez Morales and Ada Ferrer kindly shared photocopies of additional materials from the Archivo General.

In the United States, we have benefited from the assistance of the staffs of the Historic New Orleans Collection; the New Orleans Notarial Archives Research Center; the Louisiana Division of the New Orleans Public Library; the Supreme Court Historical Collection at the Earl K. Long Library of the University of New Orleans; the Archives of the Archdiocese of New Orleans; the Jérémie Papers at the University of Florida George A. Smathers Libraries; the Municipal Archives of Mobile, Alabama; the Archives of the University of South Alabama; the Maryland State Archives; the Philadelphia Archdiocesan Historical Research Center; the United States National Archives; the William L. Clements Library of the University of Michigan; the Baker Library of the Harvard Business School; and the George Arents Collection and the Schomburg Center for Research in Black Culture of the New York Public Library. Mary Gehman generously shared ideas about the Mexican phase of the Tinchant itinerary, and Keith Manuel assisted with research in the Jérémie Papers.

In Brussels, in addition to our work at the CEGES-SOMA and the ASVG, we were assisted by the staffs of the Archives générales du Royaume and of the Bibliothèque royale. In Antwerp, we benefited from the skills of the staff of the Rijksarchief in de Provincien Antwerpen, as well as those of the Provinciearchief-Provincie Antwerpen, and of the magnificent FelixArchief. Erik Houtman of the Rijksarchief went out of his way to help us find hard-to-locate notarial materials, and Anne Winter shared ideas about Antwerp in the 1800s.

From Germany, Dr. Insa Eschebach, director of the Mahn- und Gedenkstätte Ravensbrück, and her assistant Alyn Bessmann provided much useful information, including a scanned copy of the page of the crucial transport list designating Marie-José as a political prisoner. Michael Zeuske assisted us both with German-language documents, and with understanding the Nazi terminology concerning prisoners. We are gratified to report that we were able to put Marie-José's descendants in touch with the staff of the Ravensbrück Memorial, with whom they have now shared materials for a possible future display at the site.

Our explorations in Senegal and our readings in West African history were guided by Boubacar Barry, Charles Becker, Roger Botte, Mamadou Diouf, Martin Klein, Paul Lovejoy, Kristin Mann, Derek Peterson, David Robinson, Catarina Madeira Santos, Mamadou Sy, Ibrahima Thioub, and Rudolph Ware, all of whom are nonetheless exempt from blame for the idiosyncrasies of our interpretations. The staff of the National Archives of Senegal were patient with our requests. We are also grateful to Ousman Sene, director of the West Africa Research Center, and to the students and faculty at the Université Cheikh Anta Diop in whose seminars we were first able to develop our interpretations of the Senegalese context for Rosalie Vincent's early life.

Finally, Linda Winham joined Rebecca in what turned out to be a wild goose chase through the Public Archives of Nova Scotia. We may never know why in his 1822 marriage contract someone recorded Jacques Tinchant as having been born in "Halifax, Amérique Septentrionale." If he was indeed born in Halifax, Nova Scotia, his mother must have departed rather quickly, for she left no trace that we can find. Moreover, although there were some French prisoners in Halifax in those years, it is difficult to imagine how Marie Françoise Bayot might have gotten there from Saint-Domingue at all. Later in his life, Jacques simply gave his birthplace as Baltimore, and after examination of records in Maryland we find that a more credible attribution.

Although we carried out research in most of the places where a Tinchant or a Vincent put down roots, there are two stopping points for which we relied on sources located outside the country in question: Haiti and Mexico. Jean Casimir, Laurent Dubois, Carolyn Fick, Malick Ghachem, John Garrigus, David Geggus, Graham Nessler, Richard Rabinowitz, and Dominique Rogers provided valuable assistance on the history of Haiti, complementing what we found in French and British archives and in the Haitian records now held at the University of Florida and at the Schomburg Center in New York City. Andrée-Luce Fourcand shared generously of her knowledge of the genealogy of Jérémie and the Grand'Anse. Our key manuscript source for the Mexican sojourn of Joseph Tinchant is the massive bundle of records assembled in conjunction with the lawsuit brought by his brother Jules, a file now located in the FelixArchief in Antwerp. Jean-François Campario, Sarah Cornell, Emilio Kourí, Dalia Antonia Muller, Erika Pani, Cynthia Radding, and John Womack provided expert advice and clues to additional sources on the family's time in Veracruz, and Bruno Renero-Hannan generously made a special trip to Papantla in January of 2011 to consult a key document in the property registry there.

The staff at the University of Michigan Law Library, particularly Seth Quidachay Swan, were very helpful in locating books, articles, and countless texts of statutes and regulations. Barbara Snow, a genealogist as well as a librarian, has provided assistance from beginning to end, particularly with microfilms from the Family History Library.

As we drafted the manuscript, many additional colleagues and family members generously read chapters, answered last-minute queries, and listened to us tell the tale. We thus owe special thanks to Felicitas Becker, Philippe Bernard, Alejandra Bronfman, Kathryn Burns, Marcus Carvalho, Sueann Caulfield, Sidney Chalhoub, Joshua Cole, Natalie Zemon Davis, Catherine Desbarats, Seymour Drescher, Laurent Dubois, Geoffrey Eley, Sam Erman, Ada Ferrer, David Geggus, Ariela Gross, Malick Ghachem, Thavolia Glymph, Alejandro Gómez, Allan Greer, Barbara Hahn, Jennifer Heuer, Sarah Hirschman, Marial Iglesias, Silvia Hunold Lara, Sidney Mintz, Graham Nessler, Vernon Palmer, Lawrence Powell, João José Reis, Anne Firor Scott, David Scott, Will Scott, John Scott-Railton, Thomas Scott-Railton, Sophie de Schaepdrijver, Sarah Shields, Robert W. Slenes, Carroll Smith-Rosenberg, and the late Fernando Coronil. Early on, Robert Forster, Orest Ranum, and Julius S. Scott conveyed important encouragement. Our editor at Harvard University Press, Joyce Seltzer, provided crucial and incisive advice on the penultimate draft, as well as guidance throughout, and her assistant Brian Distelberg accompanied us through the last steps of preparation of the manuscript. Our respective spouses, Peter A. Railton and Martha S. Jones, have offered limitless support and very valuable critical advice.

Any project of this kind requires financial resources, and we have been blessed with such support in both the United States and France. The University of Michigan Law School, History Department, Rackham Graduate School, Provost's Office, and the College of Literature, Science and the Arts, have provided research funding to Rebecca Scott, along with the National Endowment for the Humanities and the Guggenheim Foundation. The University of Michigan Institute for the Humanities hosted Jean Hébrard as the Norman Freehling Visiting Professor in 2010–2011. We are very grateful to the director of the Institute, Daniel Herwitz, for his continuing enthusiastic support for the larger Law in Slavery and Freedom Project that the two of us codirect with Martha Jones.

In France, we have benefited from the support of President François Weil of the EHESS, and his colleagues in the Unité de recherche Mondes Américains, Sociétés, Circulations, Pouvoirs (XVe–XXIe siècle) and the Centre international de recherches sur les esclavages of the CNRS. Funding was also provided from the Ministère de la Recherche through the grant Prosodie 2004, "Histoires croisées des espaces atlantiques." Jean Hébrard also received financial support through the European Research Program EURESCL (7th PCRD), and from the Centre de recherches sur le Brésil contemporain at the EHESS.

In the early stages of our research, Jean benefited from an exchange professorship at Duke University, where he discussed the project with colleagues in Romance Studies, particularly Laurent Dubois and Deborah Jenson. Final drafting of the manuscript was completed while Rebecca held a Fellows' Fellowship at the National Humanities Center in North Carolina, and she expresses her thanks to the Institute's president and director, Geoffrey Harpham, and its vice president and deputy director, Kent Mullikin. The librarians of the NHC were tireless in locating materials, and the entire staff provided moral and practical support in the enterprise.

Additional documentation on the Tinchant family may yet rest in archives that we have not visited, and no story of this kind is ever quite finished. But for now, we have decided to let it rest, hoping that as others read our text they will see things that we did not, and perhaps look for further sources in places that did not occur to us. We might close by quoting the cautionary advice of Arlette Farge:

> One does not bring back to life those whom we find cast up in the archive. But that is no reason to make them suffer a second death. The space is narrow within which to develop a story that will neither cancel out nor dissolve these lives, that will leave them available so that one day, and elsewhere, another narrative may be built from their enigmatic presence.[1]

---

1. Arlette Farge, *Le Goût de l'archive* (Paris: Éditions du Seuil, 1989), 145. An English-language translation of the Farge volume is scheduled for publication in 2012 by Yale University Press.